Norton Desktop™ 2 for Windows®

SELF-TEACHING GUIDE

Wiley SELF-TEACHING GUIDES (STGs) are designed for first-time users of computer applications and programming languages. They feature concept-reinforcing drills, exercises, and illustrations that enable you to measure your progress and learn at your own pace. Other Wiley Self-Teaching Guides:

DOS 5 STG, Ruth Ashley and Judi N. Fernandez
INTRODUCTION TO PERSONAL COMPUTERS STG, Peter Stephenson
OBJECTVISION 2 STG, Arnold and Edith Shulman, and Robert Marion
QUATTRO PRO 3 STG, Jennifer Meyer
LOTUS 1-2-3 FOR WINDOWS STG, Douglas J. Wolf
PARADOX 3.5 STG, Gloria Wheeler
Q&A 4 STG, Corey Sandler and Tom Badgett
FOXPRO 2 STG, Ellen Sander
ALDUS PERSUASION FOR IBM PC'S AND COMPATIBLES STG, Karen Brown and Diane Stielstra
PFS: PUBLISHER FOR WINDOWS STG, Sean Cavanaugh and Deanna Bebb
PERFORM STG, Peter Stephenson
NOVELL NETWARE 2.2 STG, Peter Stephenson and Glenn Hartwig
MICROSOFT WORD 5.5 FOR THE PC STG, Ruth Ashley and Judi N. Fernandez
MICROSOFT WORD FOR WINDOWS 2 STG, Pamela S. Beason and Stephen Guild
WORDPERFECT 5.0/5.1 STG, Neil J. Salkind
WORDPERFECT FOR WINDOWS STG, Neil J. Salkind
SIGNATURE STG, Christine Rivera
MICROSOFT WINDOWS 3.0 STG, Keith Weiskamp and Saul Aguiar
WINDOWS 3.1 STG, Keith Weiskamp
PC DOS 4 STG, Ruth Ashley and Judi N. Fernandez
PC DOS 3.3 STG, Ruth Ashley and Judi N. Fernandez
MASTERING MICROSOFT WORKS STG, David Sachs, Babette Kronstadt, Judith Van Wormer, and Barbara Farrell
QUICKPASCAL STG, Keith Weiskamp and Saul Aguiar
GW BASIC STG, Ruth Ashley and Judi N. Fernandez
TURBO C++ STG, Brian Flamig
SQL STG, Peter Stephenson and Glenn Hartwig
QUICKEN STG, Peter Aitken
CORELDRAW 2 STG, Robert Bixby
HARVARD GRAPHICS 3 STG, David Harrison and John W. Yu
AMI PRO 2 FOR WINDOWS STG, Pamela S. Beason and Stephen Guild
EXCEL 4 FOR WINDOWS STG, Ruth Witken

To order our STGs, you can call Wiley directly at (201)469-4400, or check your local bookstores.

"Mastering computers was never this easy, rewarding, and fun!"

Norton Desktop™ 2
for Windows®

SELF-TEACHING GUIDE

Gerry Litton
Jenna Christen

John Wiley & Sons, Inc.
New York ▲ Chichester ▲ Brisbane ▲ Toronto ▲ Singapore

In recognition of the importance of preserving what has been written, it is a policy of John Wiley & Sons, Inc,. to have books of enduring value published in the United States printed on acid-free paper, and we exert our best efforts to that end.

This publication is designed to provide accurate and authoritive information in regard to the subject matter covered. It is sold with the understanding that the publisher is not engaged in rendering legal, accounting, or other professional service. If legal advice or other expert assistance is required, the services of a competent professional person should be sought. FROM A DECLARATION OF PRINCIPLES JOINTLY ADOPTED BY A COMMITTEE OF THE AMERICAN BAR ASSOCIATION AND A COMMITTEE OF PUBLISHERS.

Library of Congress Cataloging-In-Publishing Data

Litton, Gerry M.
    Norton Desktop 2 for Windows : self-teaching guide / Gerry Litton,
  Jenna Christen.
      p. cm. -- (Wiley's self-teaching guides)
    Includes index.
    ISBN 0-471-57835-5
    1. Utilities (Computer programs) 2. Norton Desktop. 3. Microsoft
Windows (Computer program) I. Christen, Jenna. II. Title.
III. Series.
QA76.76.U84L57   1992
005.4'3--dc20   92-24012
                                                   CIP

Printed in the United States of America

10 9 8 7 6 5 4 3 2 1

To the only man in my life, who is altogether lovely.
—J. C.

Contents

Appendix

Introduction

Norton Desktop satisfies the needs of the serious—as well as not so serious—computer user. If you're time-conscious, you'll appreciate Norton's Backup feature, which will *automatically* back up all or some of your files on a daily basis (you don't even need to be there in some cases!). Your prudent side will like the SmartErase feature, which keeps your most recently deleted files in a special directory so that you can recover any of them if you need to. Your playful side will revel in Norton Desktop's enormous selection of creative icons, which you can assign to whatever desktop or group items you wish, and you'll love it when Sleeper sends leering eyes, fireworks, fish, or a spotlight across your screen whenever you start dozing off.

Norton Desktop also allows you to schedule programs or messages to run at times you specify, shred files you never want recovered for security reasons, and insert special characters (such as the trademark and copyright symbols) into your documents. Norton AntiVirus automatically scans for viruses when you turn your computer on, and it also allows you to scan drives, directories, and files whenever you wish. In short, Norton Desktop brings to Windows all of the functions needed to make working on your computer system smoother and more enjoyable.

How This Book Is Organized

This book is divided into four parts: the basics of Norton Desktop for Windows, techniques for managing your files, other desktop features, and Norton Backup—a complex but important feature.

Basics

Chapter 1, *Using the Basic Features*, familiarizes you with your new desktop, showing you how to manipulate desktop objects. Chapter 2, *Customizing Groups*, tells you all about Quick Access—the main group in which all other groups reside, and shows you how to create new groups and group items. Chapter 3, *Using Drive Windows*, teaches you how to display the files you want in drive windows and how to sort and update the file display, among other things.

Managing Your Programs and Data

Chapter 4, *Managing Your Files*, discusses how to move, copy, delete, print, and shred files. Chapter 5, *Running Programs*, shows you how to launch programs and open documents using drive windows and desktop and group icons; it also teaches you how to have programs run automatically each time you start Windows. Chapter 6, *Recovering Deleted Files*, familiarizes you with the SmartErase feature, which allows you to recover erased files. Chapter 7, *Using the Viewer*, describes how to use Norton Desktop to quickly and conveniently view the contents of your files. Chapter 8, *Using SuperFind to Locate Files*, teaches you how to search for a file or group of files, based either on file names or file contents.

Other Desktop Features

Chapter 9, *Using the Scheduler*, shows you how to schedule programs and messages to run at designated times. Chapter 10, *Protecting Your Monitor*, discusses Norton Desktop's Screen Saver in detail. Chapter 11, *Using Special Symbols*, gives you all the information you'll need to insert special characters into your documents. Chapter 12, *Norton AntiVirus*, shows you how to scan files, directories, and entire drives for viruses, as well as how to repair or delete any infected files. Chapter 13, *Customizing Norton Desktop*, teaches you different ways to configure various Norton Desktop features to more precisely meet your needs.

Backing Up Your Data

Chapter 14, *Backing Up a Group of Files*, shows you how to use Norton Backup on selected files on your hard disk(s). Chapter 15, *Verifying Your Backups*, describes Norton Backup's Compare feature, which allows you to check backups against the original files to make sure they are identical. Chapter 16, *Restoring Files from Your Backups*, tells you how to recover your files from backups. Appendix A is provided to help you through the install process.

How to Use This Book

This book is organized so that you will learn Norton Desktop for Windows quickly and thoroughly. Each chapter contains various features that reinforce the skills you learn, provides helpful suggestions, and summarizes the commands covered in the chapter. These features include the following:

▲ A list of the topics to be covered in the chapter

▲ **Check Yourself** sections, which let you practice the concepts and procedures discussed in the previous section of the chapter. First you are presented with a task, then you are shown the correct way to accomplish it. Try to carry out the task on your own first, but if you have trouble, read the procedural steps for help.

▲ **Practice What You've Learned** sections near the end of each chapter are similar to Check Yourself sections except that they test you on skills covered throughout the chapter.

▲ Helpful **Tips** are found in each chapter. These tips provide you with warnings, helpful strategies or suggestions, and shortcuts.

▲ a **Quick Summary** at the end of each chapter lists each menu command you learned during the chapter, followed by a short summary of the command's function.

Conventions

Throughout this book, the following conventions are used to help you understand the material being discussed:

Menu commands Whenever we refer to a menu command, we write the command in the order you would select it to execute the command. For instance, to save your screen configuration, you would be instructed to select Configure Save Configuration.

In other words, you would first click on Configure to display the Configure menu, then you would choose Save Configuration from the pull-down menu that appears.

Terms Each time a new term is introduced, it appears in italics. A definition for the term immediately follows the italicized term.

User input If you are instructed during an exercise to enter something from your keyboard or to press a specific key, the text you are to enter or the key you are to press appears in boldface type. For example, if you are told to type the file specification **BUD*.WK?**, then press **Enter**, you will notice that the text you are to type and the key you are to press are bolded. This helps you to quickly determine exactly what you are supposed to enter on your keyboard.

Option check boxes Similar to menu commands, all option check boxes appearing in dialog boxes or windows are written in this book exactly as they appear on your screen. Therefore, when we refer to the check box that allows you to enable SmartErase protection, we write: Enable the SmartErase Protection check box. You can use the Alt key plus the underlined letter to turn an option on or off. For example, if SmartErase protection is currently not running, you can press **Alt+E** while you are in the SmartErase window to turn SmartErase protection on. This works as a toggle; if you press **Alt+E** again, you will turn the option back off.

Acknowledgments

Our efforts in writing this book were aided by the support of family and friends. In addition, our appreciation to:

▲ Laura Lewin of John Wiley & Sons, for her helpful suggestions and patience.

▲ The staff at Symantec Corporation—particularly Nancy Stevenson, George Lawrence, and Robert Kerwin, who shared information and kept us up to date on program changes.

▲ Keith Weiskamp for his superior guidance on design.

Using the Basic Features

If you are a seasoned Windows user, the new screen configuration that appears after you have installed Norton Desktop may shock you. You may wonder, *What are all these new icons? What happened to the menu bar I was so familiar with? Where's the File Manager icon?*

Don't panic! This chapter describes the basics of operating Norton Desktop for Windows. After a quick overview of Norton Desktop's basic features, you'll feel at ease once again in the Windows environment.

In this chapter, you will learn to:

▲ **Identify different parts of the desktop**

▲ **Manipulate desktop objects**

▲ **Run programs**

▲ **Use a DOS window**

▲ **Exit Norton Desktop**

The Desktop

After installing Norton Desktop (refer to the appendix toward the back of this book), you'll see the standard type of Windows desktop elements, including title and menu bars, the Control button, the Minimize button, windows, and icons. However, as Figure 1.1 illustrates, there are differences in the appearance of Norton Desktop when compared to the Windows desktop. For example, instead of *Program Manager* appearing in the title bar, *Norton Desktop* appears. Some of the menu bar items have changed as well. The items *Disk*, *View*, *Configure*, and *Tools* now appear in the menu bar, while *Options* does not. Notice that there still remains a lot of empty space in the background. This space represents the desktop surface, on which you can move icons and windows and display pull-down menus.

TIP

In Figure 1.1, and in certain subsequent figures, various items—such as icons, drive windows, group and program names, printer data—may differ from what is displayed on your screen, since many of these items represent specific computer hardware and software configurations. For example, if your computer is running on a network system, you will see a network drive icon(s) (see Figure 1.2) underneath the regular drive icons in Figure 1.1. On the other hand, if your screen shows only two drive icons, A: and C:, this is because your computer has only one floppy and one hard drive.

Drive Icons

On the left side of your screen, a *drive icon* appears for each of your disk drives. A drive icon is a tiny representation of a disk drive, including the drive's identifying letter. There are many types of drive icons, including those for hard drives, 5-1/4-inch and 3-1/2-inch disk drives, RAM drives, and network drives, as illustrated in Figure 1.2. Network drive icons do not appear on your screen unless your computer is connected to a network.

▼ *Figure 1.1. Comparing the Windows Desktop and the Norton Desktop*

The Desktop

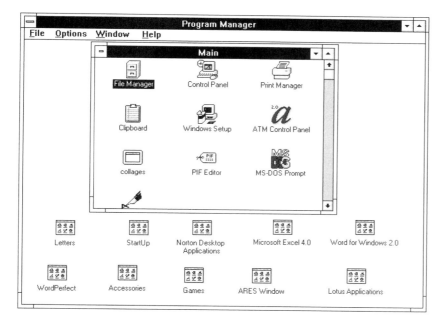

drive icon

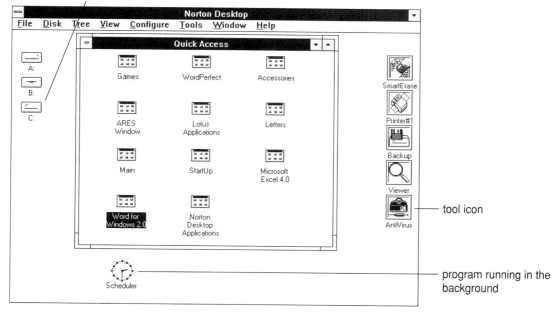

tool icon

program running in the background

▼ *Figure 1.2. 5-1/4-inch, 3-1/2-inch, Hard, RAM, and Network Drive Icons*

By double-clicking on a drive icon, you can display its corresponding *drive window*. Figure 1.3 shows the drive window for the C (hard) drive. (Drive windows are discussed in detail in Chapter 3.) You can then manipulate the files on that drive. For instance, to copy files between disk drives with a simple drag of the mouse, open the drive window containing the files to be copied, select the files, and then drag them to the appropriate drive icon. See Chapter 4, *Managing Your Files*, for complete details.

Tool Icons

On the right side of your screen are four large *tool icons* representing various Desktop features. A tool icon is a graphic representation of a tool feature, including the name of that feature. For instance, the Viewer icon contains a picture of a magnifying glass with the word Viewer below it. When you double-click on a tool icon, you bring up that feature's dialog box. For example, double-clicking on the Printer icon brings up the Print dialog box, as shown in Figure 1.4.

The Printer icon includes a number that identifies the printer currently selected in the Windows Printers dialog box. This number will only be significant to you if you have multiple printers

---

▼ *Figure 1.3. Drive Window for the C Drive*

C:\NDW*.*

| C: | ares | | C: 5,026K free | 8,336,828 bytes in 154 files |

| dos |
| drivers |
| graphics |
| ndw |
| ndwold |
| pclfonts |
| psfonts |
| nfm |

📄	schedule.bak	240	3/20/92	2:00 AM
📄	ndw.bin	8,389	3/26/92	9:05 AM
📄	frame.dat	1,810	3/25/92	11:26 PM
📄	icocache.dat	45,534	3/26/92	11:26 PM
📄	ndw.dat	1,403	3/25/92	11:26 PM
📄	nlaunch.dat	4,050	3/20/92	2:00 AM
📄	nss.dat	812	3/20/92	1:11 PM

| Move | Copy | Delete | View | Refresh | Select | Filter | Edit | NameSrt |

▼ *Figure 1.4. Print Dialog Box, Accessed Through the Printer Icon*

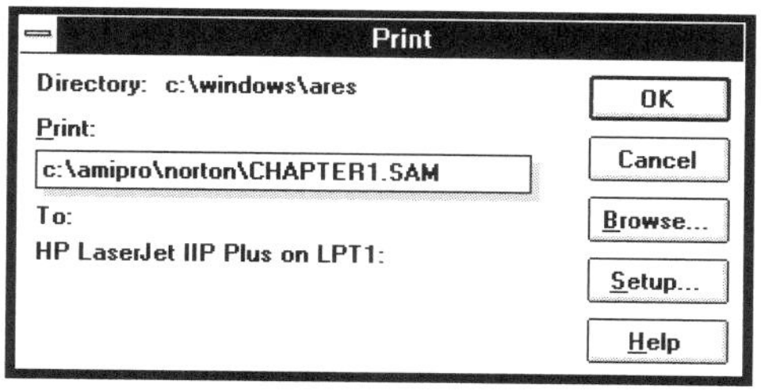

installed, or if you have defined more than one printer configuration in Windows' Control Panel Printers dialog box.

Although only five tool icons are showing, there are actually six available (Table 1.1 displays all of Norton's tool icons). To economize on screen space, the Shredder icon is not displayed. If you wish to display this icon on your desktop, turn to Chapter 13, *Customizing Norton Desktop,* for complete instructions.

Tool icons are not ordinary icons; they do more than just display a feature's dialog box. When you drag a file or group of

▼ *Table 1.1. The Norton Tool Icons*

Icon	Menu Command	Dragging Results
 SmartErase	Tools UnErase	Deletes a single file or a group of files
 Backup	Tools Norton Backup	Backs up directories and subdirectories (but not a single file)
 Viewer	File View	Displays the contents of a single file
 Printer#1	File Print	Prints a single file
 Shredder	Tools Shredder	Permanently obliterates (erases) a single file or a group of files
 AntiVirus	Tools Norton AntiVirus	Checks a single file, a group of files, or an entire drive for viruses

files over to a tool icon, you bypass having to double-click on the tool icon and enter the file name(s) to be treated. By simply dragging a file name from an open drive window and dropping it on a tool icon, the tool's function is performed instantly on that file. For example, instead of double-clicking on the Printer icon and entering the name of the file to be printed in the print dialog box, you can simply drag the file from an open drive window and drop it on the Printer icon. Instantly, the software program used to create the file is launched and the print commands are implemented behind the scenes (that is, you won't see the opened file on screen).

All tool icons operate in a similar manner. For instance, to view the contents of a file, drag the file name from the drive window to the Viewer icon, and immediately you will see the file contents. The Backup icon will not back up a single file for you, but you can back up a directory or subdirectory by dragging it to the Backup icon. Table 1.1 lists each tool icon and the menu commands that will also run the tool feature, and describes the results you will achieve by dragging a file or group of files to the tool icon.

Windows

You will be working with different types of windows on the desktop, such as group windows, application windows, and drive windows. A *group window* contains various icons representing files and groups of files. Figure 1.5 shows a group window called Fiction. Inside the Fiction group window are different group and item icons, such as the item icon representing Ami Pro software and the subgroup icon labeled Short Stories.

▲ To open a group window, double-click the group icon.

▲ To reduce a group window to an icon, click the Minimize button.

Refer to Chapter 2, *Customizing Groups*, for more on group windows.

Whenever you run a Windows program, you open an *application window*. An application window is the window in which

▼ *Figure 1.5. The Fiction Group Window*

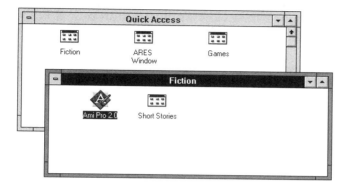

you perform all of your program functions. For example, if you play a game of Windows Reversi, an application window remains displayed throughout the game. Also, when you run a word-processing program, such as Ami Pro, an application window serves as the foundation for all of your file work. Figure 1.6 shows an Ami Pro application window.

Drive windows are an integral part of Norton Desktop, and you'll probably work with them on a regular basis. Similar to

▼ *Figure 1.6. Ami Pro Application Window*

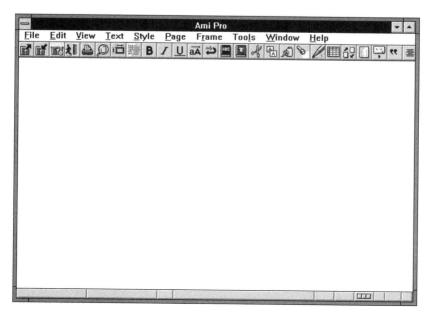

the Windows File Manager, a drive window displays icons and names for all directories, subdirectories, and files on a drive. Refer to Figure 1.3 to review an illustration of a drive window and its contents. You can use a drive window to open a file and manage disks and directories. Unlike the File Manager, however, drive windows allow you to drag any item within them to one of the tool icons for instant results. You can also create a group item icon instantly by dragging a file name from a drive window to a group window, or a desktop item icon by dragging a file name from a drive window to the desktop.

▲ To open a drive window, double-click the drive icon. Figure 1.3 shows a drive window for the C drive.

▲ To exit from a drive window, double-click on the Control menu box in the upper-left corner.

To learn more about the use of drive windows, read Chapter 3, *Using Drive Windows*.

Menus

Menus contain commands for virtually every function you'll perform in Norton Desktop. One of Norton's valuable features is its ability to display short versions of most of its menus so that you can move quickly through the items. Figure 1.7 shows the Tools menu in its full and short forms. You can also choose the items to be placed on menus, and the order in which the items will appear. Thus, you can place frequently used menu items at the top of the menu.

You can switch between the full and short menus quite easily. Short menus are displayed by default, but you'll want to display the full menus while reading this book.

To switch to full menus:

▲ Choose Configure Load Menu. The Load Menu dialog box appears, as shown in Figure 1.8.

▲ Select FULL in the Menu box and click the OK button. Full menus will now be displayed on your screen.

▼ *Figure 1.7. Short and Full Versions of the Tools Menu*

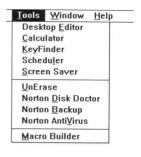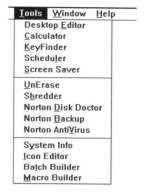

The Desktop

CHECK YOURSELF

Open the drive window for your hard drive that contains word-processing documents, then view and print a file using the tool icons. Then, open a group window and reduce it to an icon.

1. Double-click on the hard drive icon.

2. Drag a text file name from the drive window and drop it on top of the Viewer icon. The file contents displays in the Viewer window. Close the window.

3. Drag a text file name from the drive window and drop it on top of the Printer icon.

4. Double-click on a group icon. Click on the Minimize button in the group window.

▼ *Figure 1.8. The Load Menu Dialog Box*

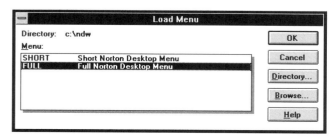

Manipulating Objects on the Desktop

You have a lot of freedom in designing the arrangement of your desktop. For example, to relocate an icon or window, simply drag it to a different location on the desktop. You can have several windows open at the same time, such as group, drive, and tool windows. Norton Desktop saves you from having to spend a lot of time trying to arrange icons on the desktop. You can use the Window menu to rearrange your desktop objects instantly, or use the Snap-to-Grid feature to rearrange items automatically.

Drive Icons

You can remove one or all of the drive icons from the desktop, or move them to a different location on the desktop.

To remove drive icons from the desktop:

▲ Choose Configure Drive Icons. The Configure Drive Icons dialog box appears, as shown in Figure 1.9.

▼ *Figure 1.9. The Configure Drive Icons Dialog Box*

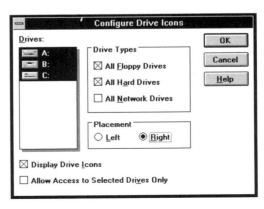

▲ To remove *all* the drive icons from the screen, deselect the Display Drive Icons box. To remove all floppy, hard, or network drive icons, deselect the appropriate check boxes in the Drive Types region.

▲ Click the OK button. The drive icons will no longer appear on the desktop.

To redisplay the drive icons, follow the above procedures but select the appropriate check boxes.

To place drive icons on the right side of the desktop:

▲ Choose Configure Drive Icons.

▲ Select Right in the Placement region of the dialog box.

▲ Click the OK button. The drive icons will now appear on the right side of the screen.

You can also move one or more of the drive icons anywhere on the desktop by dragging the icon(s) to the desired location.

Tool Icons

You can remove any of the tool icons from the desktop. For example, you might not use the Norton Backup icon because you've configured Norton to automatically backup your files at a particular time each week. In this case, there is really no point in having the Backup icon sitting on the desktop.

To remove one or more tool icons from the desktop:

▲ Choose Configure Preferences. The Configure Preferences dialog box appears, as shown in Figure 1.10.

▲ Deselect the check box for each tool icon you wish to remove.

▲ Click the OK button. The icon(s) will no longer appear on the desktop.

▼ *Figure 1.10. The Configure Preferences Dialog Box*

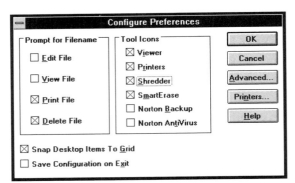

As with drive icons, you can change the placement of one or more tool icons by dragging them to a new location on the desktop.

Desktop Item Icons

One feature of Norton Desktop that you are sure to enjoy is its ability to represent a document file or program as a *desktop item icon*. This type of icon is created when you drag any item from a drive or group window to the desktop. For example, suppose you are going to work on a data file called PROJECT.ABC everyday for the next few months. To simplify your work, you can drag that file from the drive window to anywhere on the desktop and the file will be transformed into a desktop item icon. This item icon will now be sitting on your desktop each morning, just waiting for you. Whenever you double-click on that icon, Windows will launch (that is, run) the corresponding program, and then load that data file.

Similarly, if you plan to use a Windows software program regularly, you can drag the file name of that program (the executable file, which has the extension .EXE) from the drive window, or the group item icon for that program from the group window, to the desktop. Then, to run that program, double-click on the icon.

After a while, your desktop may become cluttered with icons. To keep them in order, you can turn on Norton's Snap-to-Grid feature, which automatically rearranges desktop items whenever you move or add a new item to the desktop. Alternatively, you can use the Window Arrange Desktop menu commands whenever you feel your icons are getting too unorganized.

To configure Norton Desktop to automatically rearrange desktop icons:

▲ Choose Configure Preferences.

▲ Select the Snap Desktop Items to Grid check box.

▲ Click the OK button.

To immediately rearrange desktop icons:

▲ Choose Window Arrange Desktop.

CHECK YOURSELF

Remove the Printer icon from the desktop. Then, create two desktop item icons: one for a data file, using a drive window; the other for a program, using a group window.

1. Choose Configure Preferences. Deselect the Printer check box in the Drive Types box. Click the OK button.

2. Open a drive window. Drag a text file name from the drive window to anywhere on the desktop.

3. Open a group window. Drag a program item icon from the group window to anywhere on the desktop.

Running a Program

Running a Windows program can be as simple as double-clicking on an icon representing that program. You can also launch a program by selecting it from the Launch Manager. Conveniently, several programs can run at the same time in Windows Standard or Enhanced modes. So if you want to work on an Ami Pro for Windows document as well as a Lotus 1-2-3 for Windows spreadsheet, you don't have to close one application to work on the other.

TIP

To switch from one program to another when you have more than one running at the same time, press Ctrl+Esc to bring up the Windows Task List, choose the appropriate program, and click on Switch To. The application window for that program will now appear on your screen.

To run a program:

▲ Create an item icon for the program by dragging the program's group item icon from a group window or the executable (.EXE) file from a drive window to the desktop. Then, double-click on the item icon to launch the program.

or:

▲ Open the group window containing the program, then double-click on the group item icon that represents the program you wish to run.

To learn more about launching programs, refer to Chapter 5, *Running Programs.*

Using DOS Commands

There may come a time when you need to issue a DOS command while you are working in Norton Desktop. By opening a DOS window, you can do this without leaving Norton Desktop.

To open a DOS window:

▲ Choose File Run DOS. After a short pause, the DOS prompt will appear in place of the desktop.

▲ Enter the desired DOS command.

▲ To return to Norton Desktop from DOS, type **exit** at the DOS command prompt and press **Enter**.

Exiting Norton Desktop

Before you exit Norton Desktop, you need to decide whether you want the changes you made during your current session to be saved. By default, all changes will be remembered when you exit Norton Desktop, because the Save Configuration on Exit check box is selected in the Configure Preferences dialog box (see Figure 1.10). This means that if you open a drive window or a new group window and then exit, the next time you start Windows, those windows will automatically be opened.

If you do wish to have your desktop appear the same way each time you start Windows, make sure to choose the Configure Preferences commands and *deselect* the Save Configuration on Exit box in the Configure Preferences dialog box.

Note that saving changes in Norton Desktop does not apply to any application (software) work you have done within Windows, but only to the desktop configuration. Actions such as creating groups, moving icons, switching menu versions, and opening windows are all part of your desktop configuration, and can be saved if you wish.

TIP

To save a desktop configuration immediately after rearranging it, first make your changes—such as moving icons and opening drive, group, or tool windows—then choose the Configure Save Configuration commands.

To exit Norton Desktop:

▲ Choose File Exit, then click the OK button when the Exit Norton Desktop message box prompts you to confirm your exit.

or:

▲ Double-click on the Norton Desktop Control menu box (you will still be asked to confirm your exit).

QUICK SUMMARY

Command	To Do This
Tools UnErase, or SmartErase icon	Delete a single file and groups of files.
Tools Norton Backup, or Backup icon	Back up directories and subdirectories.
File Print, or Printer icon	Print a single file.
Tools Shredder, or Shredder icon	Obliterate (erase) a single file or groups of files.
Tools Norton AntiVirus, or AntiVirus icon	Check a single file or groups of files for viruses.
Configure Load Menu	Display short or full menus.
Configure Drive Icons	Display or remove types of drive icons from the desktop. To place drive icons at the left or right side of the desktop.
Window Arrange Desktop	Immediately rearrange desktop icons.
File Run DOS	Open a DOS window.
Configure Preferences	Configure Norton Desktop to automatically rearrange desktop icons and select or deselect Save Configuration on Exit.
Configure Save Configuration	Immediately save the current desktop arrangement.
File Exit	Exit Norton Desktop.

PRACTICE WHAT YOU'VE LEARNED

Place your hard drive icon(s) on the right side of the desktop. Remove the Norton Backup tool icon from the desktop. Create a desktop item icon using a group window. Open and exit from a DOS window. Exit from Norton Desktop, either saving your desktop changes before exiting or without saving your desktop changes.

1. Choose Configure Drive Icons. Mark the All Hard Drives box. Select Right in the Placement box. Click the OK button.

2. Choose Configure Preferences. In the Configure Preferences dialog box, deselect the Norton Backup check box in the Drive Types box. Click the OK button.

3. Open a group window. Drag an object from the group window to anywhere on the desktop.

4. Choose File Run DOS. The DOS command prompt appears. Type **exit**, then press **Enter**.

5. To exit without saving your changes, choose Configure Preferences and deselect the Save Configuration on Exit box in the Configure Preferences dialog box.

6. To save your changes when exiting, choose File Exit or double-click on the Norton Desktop Control menu box.

2

Customizing
Groups

Norton Desktop helps you manage all of your program and data files by organizing them within groups. In the same way you use file folders to organize your papers within a file cabinet, you can place your computer files in groups within Quick Access. By dragging a file name from a drive window into a group window, you can create a group item icon. Double-clicking on a group item icon will then open the file. What's more, you can configure the Quick Access AutoStart group to automatically run programs and open designated files each time you start Windows. In this chapter, you will:

▲ **Use the Quick Access feature**

▲ **Rearrange, create, delete, move, and copy groups and group items**

▲ **Assign password protection to your groups**

▲ **Use AutoStart**

An Overview of Quick Access

Quick Access, the foundation of your entire file organization, is a container that holds various groups. Usually, Norton Desktop is set up so that all your groups are contained within the Quick Access window. Figure 2.1 shows the Quick Access window and the groups it contains (the group names displayed in the figure will differ from those in your Quick Access window). Inside Quick Access groups are subgroups that separate your files into more specific categories. Inside these subgroups are group items that represent specific data files and software programs.

If the Quick Access window is not currently displayed on your screen, follow these steps to display it:

▲ Choose Window to display the Window menu.

▲ If Quick Access is listed on the menu, select it and the Quick Access window will appear, similar to Figure 2.1.

▲ If Quick Access is not listed on the Window menu, select More (located at the bottom of the Window menu).

▼ *Figure 2.1. The Quick Access Window and Groups*

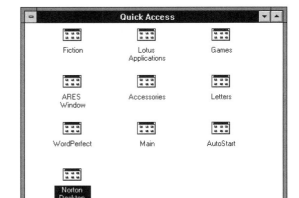

▲ In the dialog box that appears, click on Quick Access and then click the OK button.

TIP

If the Quick Access icon is displayed on your screen, double-click on it to open the Quick Access Window.

For you to use the Quick Access system effectively, you must configure your desktop so that the Quick Access window is automatically displayed each time you start Windows. This way you can simply scroll through the Quick Access window to locate the group or subgroup that contains the icon for the file you wish to run, open that group or subgroup window, then double-click on the appropriate item icon to start your session.

To display the Quick Access window at startup:

1. Choose Configure Preferences. The Configure Preferences dialog box appears.

2. Click on the Advanced button. The Advanced dialog box displays, as shown in Figure 2.2.

3. Select the check box next to Load Quick Access, then double-click the OK button.

4. Open the Quick Access Window and adjust its size and location on the desktop so it appears as you wish each time you start Windows.

5. Choose Configure Save Configuration.

▼ *Figure 2.2. The Advanced Dialog Box*

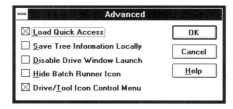

Think of Quick Access as a file cabinet. Just as file drawers rest inside a file cabinet, groups rest inside Quick Access. Carrying the analogy a step further, a single document that exists in a folder in a file drawer is like a disk file that exists as a *group item* within a Quick Access group.

At times you will want to create groups within groups to arrange your files more precisely. Whenever you include a group within another group, the first group becomes a *subgroup* of the second group. Thus, all of the groups that rest directly in the Quick Access window are ordinary groups, while any groups placed inside the Quick Access groups are subgroups.

The example given in Table 2.1 will help you conceptualize the hierarchical ordering of the Quick Access system, as well as demonstrate how similar Quick Access is to a file cabinet. Figure 2.3 further illustrates the similarities between Quick Access and a file cabinet. Refer to this figure as you follow along with the example in Table 2.1.

You have a file named CHAPTER1.SAM on your hard drive, for which you make a printout. Now follow the paths of the disk file and printout in Table 2.1, noting the similarities.

To see what the sample groups and group item icon in Table 2.1 would look like on your screen, review Figure 2.4. Notice that the *group item icon* for Chapter 1 appears in the Gone With

---

▼ *Table 2.1. Printouts vs. Disk File Paths*

Printout	**Disk File**
1. You make a *printout* of CHAPTER1.SAM	1. You create a *group item icon* for Chapter 1.
2. You put the printout into a *folder* labeled GONE WITH THE WINDOWS.	2. You place the item icon in a *subgroup* called Gone With The Windows.
3. The folder is in a *file drawer* which contains folders for your other fictional work, such as poetry, short stories, and novellas.	3. The Gone With The Windows subgroup is in a *group* called Fiction, which contains other subgroups for poetry, short stories, and novellas.
4. The file drawer is located at the top of your *file cabinet*.	4. The Fiction group is the first group in *Quick Access*.

▼ *Figure 2.3. Similarities Between Quick Access and File Cabinet*

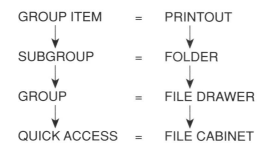

The Windows subgroup window. Also, the *subgroup icon* for Gone With The Windows appears in the Fiction group window, and the *group icon* for the Fiction group appears in the Quick Access window.

Now keep in mind, you will not always use subgroups within groups. Just as you might place a single document directly into a file drawer, you may place an individual disk file or program into a group rather than a subgroup. Later in this chapter, you'll have a chance to create a group and a group item, so if your understanding of group organization is still a bit foggy, be patient. After you've had some practice managing groups, you'll feel more confident about using them.

So then, what are group windows and icons? *Group window* and *group icon* refer to essentially the same thing (a group). The

▼ *Figure 2.4. The Group Windows and Icons in Table 2.1*

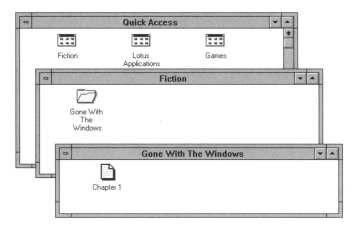

window is an opened group, the icon is an object that represents a closed group. Whenever you double-click on a group icon, you open the group window. Whenever you minimize a group window, the group icon appears at the bottom of your desktop.

To open a group window:

▲ Double-click on the group icon.

or:

▲ Choose Window, then the name of the group. If the group name does not appear on the window menu, choose Window More, then click on the name of the group.

To close a group window:

▲ Double-click on the window's Control menu box.

or:

▲ Choose Close from the window's Control menu.

To change a group window to a group icon (located at the bottom of the desktop):

▲ Click on the Minimize button in the group window.

There are group icons and then there are group item icons. The difference between the two is that, as mentioned earlier, *group icons* represent groups (and subgroups), while *group item icons* represent either single data files or software programs located within a group or subgroup. The functions of the group icon and the group item icon are quite different. If you double-click on a group icon, you'll open a group window. But if you double-click on a group item icon, you'll run the corresponding program.

Looking again at the Gone With The Windows example, if you double-click on the Chapter 1 item icon, Norton Desktop will automatically launch the software program used to created the document—such as Ami Pro or WordPerfect—and then open the document file. But if you double-click on the Gone With The Windows group icon, you'll only bring up the group window containing all of the other chapter icons (no software will be launched).

An Overview of Quick Access

CHECK YOURSELF

Open the Quick Access window and then convert it into an icon located at the bottom of your desktop. Next, restore the Quick Access window and then close it.

1. Choose Window Quick Access (or Window More Quick Access). Or double-click on the Quick Access icon.

2. Click on the Minimize button in the Quick Access window.

3. Double-click on the Quick Access icon located at the bottom of your desktop. Choose Close from the Control menu, or double-click on the Control menu box.

Working with Groups

By using groups, you can put all interrelated programs and documents into one handy container. For example, you might create an Accounts Receivable group that includes the Calculator, subgroups of spreadsheet files, Ami Pro for Windows, invoice files, and pertinent form letters. Double-clicking on one of the group's item icons will run the application. Or, if you assign this group to the AutoStart group, all of the group items will be opened automatically when Windows is started. You can also customize some of the Quick Access features, which is discussed in detail in Chapter 13, *Customizing Norton Desktop.*

Enough about concepts. Let's get down to the procedures. You'll feel comfortable working with groups after you learn how to arrange, create, move, copy, and delete them.

Rearranging Groups

A good place to start is with the groups you already have. When you installed Norton Desktop, it assigned group icons to the program groups that already existed in your copy of Windows. Notice that we said *program* groups; there is a big difference between Norton Desktop groups and the original Windows groups: the only items you could place in a Windows group were software programs, such as Excel, Ami Pro, Solitaire, and so on. You cannot place data files in Windows groups as you can in Norton Desktop groups.

See if you can locate the Accessories and Games group icons that appear in the Quick Access window, as shown in Figure 2.5. If not, you'll need to open the Quick Access window (see *An Overview of Quick Access*, at the beginning of this chapter).

Rearranging groups is as simple as dragging a group icon to another location. To see how simple it is, drag the Accessories icon to the bottom of the Quick Access window. That was easy, but there's a problem. There is now a big gap in your window where the Accessories icon once rested. Rather than fidget over trying to line up the icons evenly once again, you can have Norton Desktop do that for you.

To change the location of a group icon and arrange the icons evenly again:

▲   Drag the icon to the desired location. (It may partially cover another icon for the time being.)

▼ *Figure 2.5. The Accessories and Games Group Icons in the Quick Access Window*

▲ Choose Window Arrange Group Icons. All of the icons are now evenly lined up again.

Notice that the Accessories icon is now the last group icon in Quick Access because you placed it at the bottom of the window.

You can also configure Norton Desktop to rearrange your group icons automatically each time you change the size of a group window or add a new item to it.

To automatically arrange icons after sizing or adding new items to a group window:

▲ Choose Configure Quick Access. The Configure Quick Access dialog box appears, as shown in Figure 2.6.

▲ In the Settings box, select the check box next to Auto Arrange Icons.

▲ Click the OK button.

To see the Auto Arrange feature in action, drag the right bottom corner of the Quick Access window in toward the top left corner. The icons are rearranged to fit inside the smaller window, yet they remain in the original order.

There are three ways to display group icons in a group window: The default display, *icon view,* shows the group's name below its icons, as shown in Figure 2.7.

▼ *Figure 2.6. The Configure Quick Access Dialog Box*

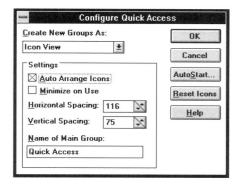

▼ *Figure 2.7. The Icon View*

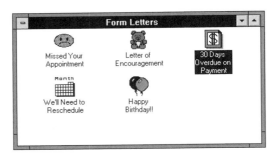

The *list view* displays group names to the right of icons, and each icon is placed on a separate line, as shown in Figure 2.8. One advantage to displaying icons in list view is that if you enter a description about the icon in the New or Properties dialog boxes, the description will appear below the icon's title; descriptions do not appear next to icons when groups are set in icon view.

The third view type is *toolbox view,* which displays icons as a palette of tools, as shown in Figure 2.9. Choose this view only if you can easily recognize your groups by their icons, because group names are *not* displayed in toolbox view.

To change the view type of a group window:

▲ Open the group window.

▲ Choose Window View Group As. The View As dialog box appears.

▼ *Figure 2.8. The List View*

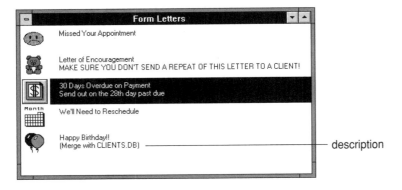

description

▼ *Figure 2.9. The Toolbox View*

▲ Click on the View Group scroll button to display the view types.

▲ Select the desired view type, then click the OK button.

TIP

**If you wish to change the view display for all of your Quick Access groups,
select the Change All Groups check box in the View As dialog box.**

CHECK YOURSELF

Make the Accessories group icon the first icon in Quick Access and
move the Games Group icon to the right of a different group icon.
Then, line up all icons evenly.

1. Drag the Accessories icon to the upper-left corner of the Quick
    Access window.

2. Drag the Games icon to the right of any group icon.

3. Either turn on the Auto Arrange feature if necessary or Choose
    Window Arrange Group Icons.

Creating New Groups and Group Items

Now that we've gone over the why of group management and
you've had some practice manipulating your existing groups,
it's time to move on to the how of creating new ones. An essen-

tial part of creating new groups and group items is first deciding which groups will go where and what items will go in which groups. Remember, a group inside another group is called a subgroup. The groups inside the Quick Access window should be your top-level, broadest-based groups. Then you can create subgroups to put inside each of your Quick Access groups. To these subgroups you can add more subgroups or group items, or both. But the important thing to do before creating any new groups or group items is to map out the hierarchical logistics of how you want them to be arranged.

Creating Groups and Subgroups

To create a new group or subgroup:

1. Open the Quick Access window if you are creating a top-level group. Otherwise, open the group window of the group into which you want the new subgroup placed.

TIP

It is essential that the correct group window be open and active before creating a new group or subgroup.

2. Choose File New. The New dialog box appears, as shown in Figure 2.10.

3. In the Type region, click on Group.

4. In the Title text box, type the name of the new group. The Group File Name box can be left blank.

5. Click the OK button. The new group window appears at the top of your screen.

Note the importance of being in the correct group window when you select the File New commands. A new group is always placed into the group whose window is active at the time of creation. Remembering this makes it easier for you to develop your subgroups and group items.

▼ *Figure 2.10. The New Dialog Box*

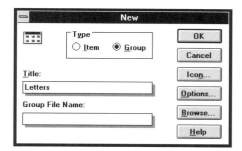

CHECK YOURSELF

Create a new top-level group, then close it.

1. With the Quick Access window open and active, choose File New.

2. In the Type region in the New dialog box, click on Group.

3. In the Title text box, type the name of the new group.

4. Click the OK button. The new group window appears at the top of your screen.

5. Choose Close from the Control menu or double-click on the window's Control menu box.

Creating a Group Item

Remember, a group item will be one of two things:

▲ A data file (a document and its software application).

▲ A program (software application only).

You can create a group item much the same way you create a new group, but there is also a shorter way to do it. Regardless of which method you use (the File New commands or the short-cut using the mouse), you must select the group in which the item icon will be placed *before* you create the item icon.

To create a group item using the File menu:

1. Open the group window of the group into which you wish to place the group item (if it's already open, make sure it is the active window).

2. Choose File New. The New dialog box appears.

3. In the Type region, click on Item.

4. In the Title text box, type a name for the group item. (Try to keep the name under 15 characters.)

TIP

If you don't enter a title, the item icon will be labeled with the name of the file or software program.

5. In the Program Document Script text box, do one of two things:

   ▲ To create a data file item icon, type the full name of the data file, including its path, such as **C:\AMIPRO\NOVELS \CHAPTER1**. (If the file extension is not associated with the software, type the full name of the software, including its path, followed by a space and the full data file name. To find out more about file extension associations, read Chapter 5, *Running Programs.*)

   ▲ To create a program item icon, either type the program and its path name, such as **C:\AMIPRO\AMIPRO.EXE**, or click on Browse, click on the executable file for the program (ending in .EXE), then click the OK button (for example, you would click on AMIPRO.EXE).

6. Click on Icon if you wish to assign a special icon for the file or program, then follow the steps under *Assigning an Icon*, below. (If you do not select an icon, the icon associated with the software program will be assigned.)

Now the shortcut, using the mouse.

To create a group item using the mouse:

▲ Open the group window of the group into which you want to place the group item icon.

▲ Open the drive window for the drive that contains the desired program or document.

▲ Choose Window Tile (so that both the drive and group windows are completely visible).

▲ Scroll through the drive window to locate the program or document. (For more information, see Chapter 3, *Using Drive Windows.*)

▲ Drag the program or document file name from the drive window over to the group window. An icon for that program or document will now appear in the group window.

Creating New Groups and Group Items

Assigning Icons

Norton Desktop is loaded with creative, eye-catching icons. You should scroll though the vast selection of available icons in the Choose Icon dialog box (Figure 2.11) before assigning your first icon. Since many of the icons are descriptive of certain document types or functions, a thoughtful icon assignment could quickly remind you of a subgroup's contents.

If you create a new group without specifying an icon, Norton Desktop will assign the following icon to the group:

You should consider reserving this icon for all of your top-level groups, so that your Quick Access group icons will remain consistent. If you do so, you won't need to specify an icon in the New dialog box when creating a top-level group. However, when creating all lower level subgroups, you must specify an icon in the New dialog box, so that the default group icon will not be assigned to the subgroup.

TIP

You can assign a special icon to an object while you are creating it (in the New dialog box) or after you have created it (in the Properties dialog box).

To assign a special icon to a group:

▲ If you are currently creating the group, click on Icon in the New dialog box. If you are changing the icon for an existing group, select the icon, choose File Properties, then click on Icon in the Properties dialog box. (The New and Properties dialog boxes are the same dialog boxes with different names.)

▲ Click on Icon in the New or Properties dialog box.

▲ The Choose Icon dialog box appears, as shown in Figure 2.11.

▲ Scroll through the icons. When the icon you want is displayed, select it and then click the OK button.

▲ You are returned to the New or Properties dialog box, where the new icon is displayed. Click the OK button.

TIP

You can type a note (up to 64 characters) for any group or group item icon by choosing Options and entering the note in the Description text box. The description will be displayed to the right of the icon only if you display your icons in list view.

▼ *Figure 2.11. The Choose Icon Dialog Box*

Changing Other Group or Group Item Properties

Changing Other Group or Group Item Properties

If you ever wish to change the properties of an existing group or group item, you can do so easily using the Properties dialog box.

To change a group or group item's properties:

▲ Select the group icon or the group item icon to be changed.

▲ Choose File Properties. The Properties dialog box appears. This dialog box is exactly the same as the New dialog box, except that the Title Bar name is different.

▲ Make the desired changes to any of the properties, such as the title, description, shortcut key, and so on.

CHECK YOURSELF

Using the shortcut (mouse) method, create a group item that will be placed in the ACCESSORIES group.

1. Open the Accessories group window.

2. Open a drive window.

3. Choose Window Tile.

4. Drag a program or document file name from the drive window over to the Accessories group window. An icon for that program or document now appears in the group window.

Protecting Your Documents

You can assign a password to any group or group item icon, so that only you can access the associated program or document by that icon. Keep in mind, however, that a document or program can still be accessed through other means (such as a drive window or the Program Manager). The password only prevents the opening of an application from the icon.

An important aspect of the password protection feature is that you cannot delete a password-protected icon without first entering the password. This feature is important because when you delete a group icon, all of its subgroups and items are deleted along with it. Because deleting a group is as simple as pressing the Delete key, password protection can prevent a large group from being easily deleted.

To assign a password to a group or group item icon:

1. Select the group icon or the group item icon to be protected.

2. Choose File Properties. The Properties dialog box appears.

3. Click on Options Password. The Set Password dialog box appears, as shown in Figure 2.12.

4. Enter the password (up to 20 characters) in the New Password box and click the OK button.

5. Confirm the password in the Confirm Password box and click the OK button.

TIP

You can also assign a Password from the New dialog box when you first create a group or group item. Click on Options Password.

▼ *Figure 2.12. The Set Password Dialog Box*

If you decide to change or remove a password, you can do so easily.

To change a password:

1. Follow Steps 1 through 3 above for assigning a password.
2. In the Old Password box, type the current password and then click the OK button.
3. Enter and confirm the new password.

To disable a password:

▲ Follow Steps 1 through 3 for assigning a password.

▲ In the Old Password box, type the current password, then click the OK button. A message appears asking if it is okay to delete your password.

▲ Click on Yes in the message box.

Moving and Copying from One Group to Another

After months of organizing, creating, configuring, deleting, using (and sometimes cursing) groups, subgroups, and group items, you might want to do some cleaning up. Perhaps you'll need to copy a subgroup to another area or move a group item, and so on. Chances are you already understand the difference between moving and copying objects, but we'll touch on it here anyway.

When you move a group, it is removed from its current location and placed in a new location. On the other hand, when you copy a group, it is left in its current position *and* added to the new position. Note that you can have more than one group icon or item icon for the same object.

Moving a Group or Group Item

Perhaps after organizing your groups you realize that one or more objects really shouldn't be located where they are. Don't fret; just move the items out of one group into another. What's especially nice about the Move feature is that when you move an entire group, all of its subgroups and group items are moved as well. Thus, if you have a subgroup containing fifty item icons, you don't have to move each item icon separately. However, this also means that if you want to move only certain objects into another group, you'll have to move those objects individually, because moving the group itself will transfer *all* of its items.

As with most other Desktop features, you can move an object in two ways: with the File menu or by dragging objects with the mouse.

To move a group or group item with the File menu:

▲ Choose File Move. The Move dialog box appears, as displayed in Figure 2.13.

▲ In the From list box, select the object to be moved.

▲ In the To list box, select the group into which you want the object moved.

To move a group or group item with the mouse:

▲ Open the group window containing the object to be moved.

▲ Open the group window into which the object will be added.

▼ *Figure 2.13. The Move Dialog Box*

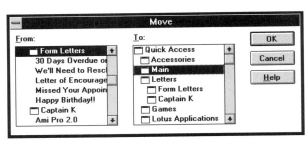

▲ Choose Window Tile so that both windows are fully displayed.

▲ Drag the group or group item icon from its current window to the new window.

Moving and Copying from One Group to Another

TIP

If you drag a group or group item to the AutoStart group, that group or item will be copied, not moved. This is the only situation in which an item will be copied rather than moved.

Copying a Group or Group Item

Why copy a group? Why have more than one version of a group or group item? You might want to be able to access one document or group of documents from two different places. For instance, if you regularly send invoices to a certain company, you might want to place an Invoice group within the group window for that company and also within a top-level group labeled Accounts Receivable. Contrary to what you might imagine, copying groups or group items does not take up a lot of disk space because the programs and documents themselves are not copied, just the information about how to access them.

As with moving an object, when you copy a group, all of its subgroups and group items are copied with it. You can copy an object by using the File menu or the mouse.

To copy a group or group item with the File menu:

▲ Close all Quick Access groups.

▲ Choose File Copy. The Copy dialog box appears. This box is exactly the same as the Move dialog box, except that Copy appears on the title bar.

▲ In the From list box, select the object to be copied.

▲ In the To list box, select the group into which you want the object added.

To copy a group or group item with the mouse:

▲ Follow the steps for moving an object (above), except press **Ctrl** as you drag the object to be copied.

TIP

You don't need to hold down the Ctrl key when you copy an object to the AutoStart group.

Deleting Unwanted Groups or Group Items

Part of your general cleanup will include deleting groups or group items that you no longer use or wish to be included in a particular group. Don't be too afraid of deleting objects; only the icon is deleted, not any programs or documents associated with it. However, do remember that when you delete a group, *all of its subgroups and item icons are deleted* along with it.

To delete a group or group item:

▲ Open the group window of the object to be deleted.

▲ Choose File Delete. A dialog box appears asking you to confirm the deletion of the object. (If you assigned a password to the object, you must enter that password now for the icon to be deleted.)

▲ Click the OK button to delete the object.

TIP

You can also delete a group or group item by selecting it and then pressing the Delete key.

Using AutoStart

Using AutoStart

Good-bye to the File Manager's directory tree scroll buttons. Good-bye to endless double-clicking and scrolling through your software's Open File dialog box. And hello to Quick Access AutoStart.

TIP

If you're running Windows 3.1, the AutoStart group is called the StartUp group instead.

AutoStart automatically opens whatever programs and documents you wish each time you start Windows. Suppose you want to open the Calculator, Lotus 1-2-3 for Windows, an invoice spreadsheet, and the Calendar each time you start Windows. To accomplish this, copy those items to the AutoStart group and make sure Quick Access is configured to load at startup.

Quick Access automatically opens application windows for each object in AutoStart. For example, if you place four items in the AutoStart group, four application Windows will be opened; you can then switch between windows to work on whichever application you desire.

To launch AutoStart applications each time you start Windows:

▲ Make sure Quick Access has been configured to load at startup (for instructions, see *An Overview of Quick Access* at the beginning of this chapter).

▲ Copy all desired items to the AutoStart (or StartUp) group window (see *Copying a Group or Group Item* above).

▲ Choose Configure Save Configuration.

Saving Your Changes

Wouldn't you hate it if you spent several hours:

▲ creating new group and group items

▲ making changes to the group hierarchy and group properties

▲ opening group windows and moving icons around to configure the desktop just the way you wanted it

▲ configuring Quick Access

only to find out the next time you started Windows that all of those changes were lost? Well, unless you use one of the configuration-saving methods described below after working with Quick Access, that's exactly what will happen. All of the actions listed above will be lost after your current Quick Access session unless you save your changes.

To make your actions permanent, either:

▲ Choose Configuration Save Configuration

or:

▲ Choose Configure Preferences and select the check box next to Save Configuration on Exit in the Configure Preferences dialog box.

If you're the type of person who likes to have everything just right each time you start a session, do *not* select the Save Configuration on Exit check box, because if you do, any changes you make will become permanent if this box is checked, meaning that each time you start Windows, the desktop will appear just as you left it the session before. So leave the option *unchecked*. Set your screen up the way you want it once and for all, then choose Configure Save Configuration. After this, regardless of any fooling around you do on your desktop, your screen will always appear just as it did when you chose the Save Configuration command.

QUICK SUMMARY

Command	To Do This
Window More	Open a group that does not appear on the Window menu.
Configure Preferences Advanced Load Quick Access at Startup	Load Quick Access at startup.
Window Arrange Group Icons	Instantly rearrange group icons.
Configure Quick Access Auto Arrange Icons	Automatically rearrange icons after sizing or adding new items to a group window.
Window View Group As	Change the view display for the current group window or for all group windows.
File New Group	Create a new group.
File New Item	Create a new group item.
Window Tile	Fully display multiple windows.
File New Icon	Assign a specific icon to a group or group item.
File Properties Icon	Change the existing icon of a group or group item.
File Properties Options Description	Assign a description to a group or group item icon, which will be displayed in list view.
File New Options Password	Assign a password to a group or group item or to disable or change an existing password.
File Move	Move a group or group item to a different group.
File Copy	Copy a group or group item to another group.
File Delete	Delete a group or group item.

PRACTICE WHAT YOU'VE LEARNED

You've just become a novelist and your first book is *Gone With The Windows*. As part of your file management system, you will create a top-level group that will hold all of your fictional writing. Then, you will tighten your file organization by creating a subgroup.

Re-create the group configuration depicted in Figure 2.4 (using the same icons).

1. Open the Quick Access window and make sure it is the active window.

2. Choose File New.

3. In the Type region, click on Group.

4. In the Title text box, type Fiction and click the OK button. A new group window appears, called Fiction.

5. Choose File New.

6. In the Title text box, type Gone With The Windows.

7. Click on Icon.

8. Click on the Icon(s) scroll button.

9. Scroll through the icons until you see the open folder icon that appears above the name Gone With The Windows in the Fiction group window, as shown in Figure 2.4.

10. Click on the open folder icon, then double-click the OK button.

11. Close each window in turn by double-clicking on each window's Control menu box.

12. You should now be in the Quick Access window. Double-click on the Fiction icon. The Fiction group window appears and the Gone With The Windows icon sits inside it.

13. Double-click on the Gone With The Windows icon. The Gone With The Windows group window appears. Your screen should now match Figure 2.4.

3 ▶

Using Drive Windows

Drive windows help you manage disks, directories, and files. You can launch a file from a drive window (as discussed in Chapter 5, *Running Programs*), view a file's contents in a drive window, and check the status of your disks from the drive window status bar. You can have as many drive windows open as your computer memory will support—multiple windows for different drives, or multiple windows for one drive. And as you'll learn in Chapter 4, *Managing Your Files*, using drive windows to move and copy files between disks makes an otherwise laborious chore more enjoyable. In this chapter, you will learn the basics of using drive windows, including:

- ▲ **Opening and closing a drive window**
- ▲ **Iconizing a drive window**
- ▲ **Configuring the file display**
- ▲ **Sorting and updating the file display**
- ▲ **Using multiple drive windows**

Opening and Closing a Drive Window

In the same way you open a car window by rolling it down or pressing a button, you can open a drive window by pulling down the Window menu or by double-clicking on a drive icon.

To open a drive window using the Window menu:

▲ Choose Window Open Drive Window. The Open Drive dialog box appears, similiar to Figure 3.1.

▲ Click on the Drive scroll button to display a list of available drives (see Figure 3.1).

▲ Select the drive you want and click the OK button. The drive window will appear at the top of your screen, as shown in Figure 3.2.

To open a drive window using the mouse:

▲ Double-click on the appropriate drive icon.

To close a drive window:

▲ Click on the drive window's Control menu, then choose Close

or:

▲ Double-click on the drive window's Control menu box.

▼ *Figure 3.1. Open Drive Dialog Box*

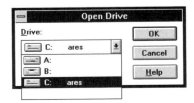

▼ *Figure 3.2. Default Drive Window*

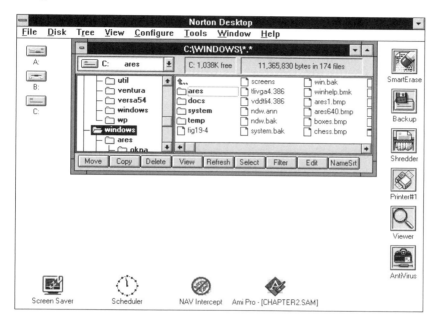

Iconizing a Drive Window

Perhaps you wish to work on something else besides your drive window for the moment, but you don't want to close the drive window because you'll be returning to it later. You can iconize (that is, reduce to an icon) the drive window for the time being, and then restore the drive window when you are ready to use it again.

Do not confuse an iconized drive window with a regular drive icon. A drive icon creates a new drive window when you double-click on the icon, whereas double-clicking on an iconized drive window will only redisplay a drive window that was already open. Notice the different appearance of the icons here:

A Drive Icon

An Iconized Drive Window

To iconize a drive window:

▲ Choose Minimize from the drive window's Control menu.

or:

▲ Click on the drive window's Minimize button.

To restore an iconized drive window:

▲ Click on the icon representing the iconized drive window, then choose Restore.

or:

▲ Double-click on the icon representing the iconized drive window.

CHECK YOURSELF

Open a floppy drive window, then reduce it to an icon. Next, restore the drive window, then close it.

1. Make sure a disk is inserted in the floppy drive, then double-click on the appropriate floppy drive icon.

2. Click on the drive window's Minimize button.

3. Double-click on the icon representing the iconized drive window.

4. Double-click on the Control menu box.

Understanding Drive Windows

There are five basic components in a drive window. Figure 3.3 will give you an idea of what these components look like, and Table 3.1 will help you understand their functions.

▼ *Figure 3.3. The Five Components of a Drive Window*

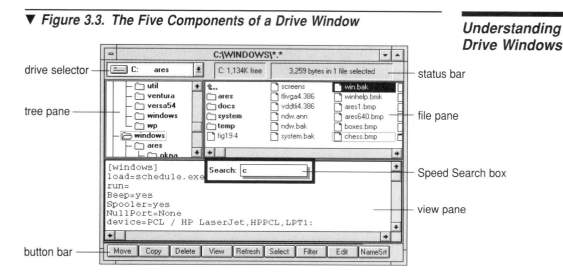

▼ *Table 3.1. Functions of the Drive Window Components*

Component	Description
drive selector	Lets you switch drive windows quickly. Selecting a different drive in this box does not open a second drive window; rather, it replaces the current drive display with data for the new drive.
status bar	Displays important information about the current drive.
panes	There are three panes altogether: the tree pane, which lists disk directories; the file pane, which shows directory files; and the view pane, which displays the contents of a file.
button bar	Provides shortcut operations for mouse users for such functions as moving, sorting, and filtering files.
Speed Search box	This box doesn't appear until you type a letter in the tree or file panes. Using this box moves you quickly to a file and will spare you a lot of scrolling around.

Paneless Viewing

It's truly painless to work in a drive window, thanks to the different types of window panes that are available. Each of the three panes displays a different component of a disk: the *tree pane* lists all of the directories on the disk; the *file pane* lists all of the files belonging to one or more directories that you specify in the tree pane; and the *view pane* displays the contents of a single file that is specified in the file pane. To see a drive window displaying all three panes, refer to Figure 3.3.

By default, only the tree and file panes are displayed when you open a drive window (see Figure 3.2). If you wish to display the view pane as well, you can easily do so.

To display the view pane in a default drive window:

▲ Choose View View Pane. The view pane will now appear at the bottom of the drive window.

TIP

Mouse users can click on the View button on the drive window button bar to instantly display the view pane.

You can also configure the drive window to display only one of the panes, as shown in Figure 3.4. However, it is more likely you'll display at least two of the panes at a time.

▼ *Figure 3.4. A Drive Window with Only the Tree Pane Showing*

When you are searching for a file whose name you know, leave the tree and file panes displayed just as they are by default. However, if you have forgotten the name of a file you want to open but know which directory it is in, you should display the file and view panes together. This way, as you move quickly through each file in the file pane, you can view the contents of each file in the view pane. Figure 3.5 shows a drive window in which only the file and view panes are displayed.

Paneless Viewing

To display only one pane in the drive window:

▲ Choose View and select the pane you wish to view, if it is not already selected.

▲ Choose View and deselect the pane you don't wish to see in the drive window. Repeat this step if there are still two panes left in the drive window.

Modify the steps above if you wish to display the file and view panes together, as shown in Figure 3.5.

A convenient way of finding out how much disk space you have left on your hard disk(s) or on a floppy disk is to refer to

▼ *Figure 3.5. A Drive Window with the File and View Panes*

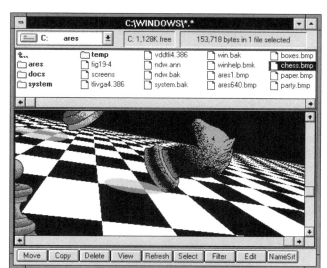

the drive window status bar. When you select one or more directories in the tree pane, the left side of the status bar displays the amount of disk space that is available on the current drive, and on the right side it shows the amount of bytes that exist in the files contained in those directories. Look at the status bar in Figure 3.3 to see an example of such a display.

On the other hand, when you select one or more files in the file pane, the status bar information changes. Now it displays the number of bytes that are taken up in the specified number of files.

TIP

To find out a directory's total byte size and number of files, select that directory in the tree pane of the appropriate drive window, then refer to the data on the status bar. To find out the total byte size of one or more files, select the file(s) in the file pane of the appropriate drive window, then refer to the status bar readings.

CHECK YOURSELF

Open a drive window and display the view pane. How much disk space is left on the drive? How many files are on the drive? Now display only the tree pane in the drive window.

1. Double-click on a drive icon. Choose View View Pane.

2. Look at the left side of the status bar to determine the amount of remaining disk space.

3. Look at the right side of the status bar to determine the total number of files on the drive.

4. Choose View View Pane. Choose View File Pane.

Choosing the Files You Want Displayed

*Choosing the
Files You
Want Displayed*

Good "window-dressing" skills are essential to working efficiently and expediently in drive windows. Do you want to display only programs in your drive window? Just archived files? What about hidden files? The View Filter menu option lets you decide which type of files you want displayed in the drive window. And if you decide you want to see *all* of your drive files, there's a menu option for that as well.

Filtering Your Files

Imagine having to sort through all of your hard disk directories in search of read-only files. Or having to sift through your many document files in search of a few system files. The View Filter menu option lets you forgo such time-burning searches. By using options in the Filter dialog box, as shown in Figure 3.6, you can configure your drive window to display only program or document files, or files containing certain file extensions. You can narrow the selection even further by displaying only those files with certain attributes, such as hidden, read-only, or archive file attributes.

▼ *Figure 3.6. Filter Dialog Box*

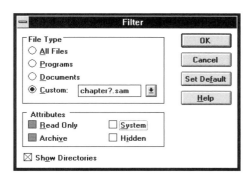

TIP

When the Show Directories box is checked, subdirectories are shown in the file pane along with files. When unchecked, only files are shown in the file pane.

Filter Types

There are many options to choose from in the Filter dialog box. Table 3.2 outlines the File Type options for you.

The Custom option is especially helpful in finding files that have been created with a program that does not assign a file extension for you. For example, unlike Word for Windows, which assigns a .DOC extension to all of its document files, WordPerfect lets you assign your own extension. Thus, if you have designed a system for labeling files, such as assigning the extension .MEM to all of your memo files, you can enter that extension in the Custom box to display all of your memo files at once.

You can enter *wildcard* symbols in the Custom box to display particular types of files. A wildcard symbol represents groups of characters. For instance, an asterisk (*) wildcard represents any combination (up to eight characters) of letters, numbers, or other characters. A question mark (?) wildcard represents any one character.

For example, suppose you're a writer and you want to display your files for Chapters 1 through 9 in the file pane. You've named your files CHAPTER1.SAM, CHAPTER2.SAM, and so

▼ Table 3.2. Filter Dialog Box File Type Options

File Type Option	Description
All Files	All file names in a selected directory are displayed.
Programs	Only files having extensions .EXE, .BAT, .PIF, or .COM are displayed.
Documents	All text and graphics files that are associated with an application are displayed. (For example, Ami Pro files have the extension .SAM.)
Custom	Only files matching a particular wildcard file specification are displayed. Use this option to display files with unique extensions, such as .MEM for all memo files.

▼ *Figure 3.7. Results of Entering CHAPTER?.SAM in the Custom Box*

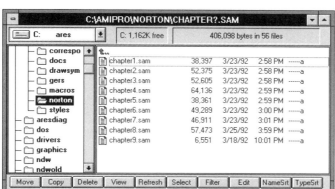

on. To display these files, you would enter CHAPTER?.SAM in the Custom box and click the OK button. The current drive window would now display all files for Chapters 1 through 9, as shown in Figure 3.7.

Carrying the illustration a step further, your files for Chapters 10 and above have been named CHAPTR10.SAM, CHAPTR11.SAM, and so on. To display these chapters, you would enter CHAPTR*.SAM in the Custom box.

Notice that a scroll button appears next to the Custom box. Norton Desktop remembers the last ten file combinations you entered in the Custom box, so that if you wish to display a certain type of file whose extension you have previously entered, you can select the file combination from the pull-down menu that appears when you click on the scroll button.

Attributes

A file can have any combination of these four attributes: read-only, archive, hidden, and system. Although a file does not need to have any attributes, many of your files will. Table 3.3 defines each attribute and explains how to use an attribute check box to display or not display (*filter out*) files with or without the attribute.

The attribute check boxes are *three-state check boxes,* meaning they can be configured in three ways: they can be left clear, grayed, or checked. You might get somewhat confused trying to

▼ Table 3.3. Filter Dialog Box Attributes

Attribute	Description	Check box settings will produce these results:
Read Only	Can't be deleted or modified	By default (gray box), read-only files are displayed along with all other files (that is, the attribute is *ignored*). Clear the box to display all files that are *not* read-only. Check the box to display *only* read-only files.
Archive	Needs to be backed up	By default (gray box), archived files are displayed along with all other files (that is, the attribute is *ignored*). Clear the box to display *only* files that have been backed up. Check the box to display *only* files that need to be backed up.
System	DOS or system-related files	By default (clear box), these files are *not* displayed. Make the box gray if you want system files displayed along with all other files (i.e., the attribute is *ignored*). Check the box to display *only* system files.
Hidden	Crucial files that are hard to access	By default (clear box), these files are *not* displayed. Gray the box if you want hidden files displayed along with all other files (that is, the attribute is *ignored*). Check the box to display *only* hidden files.

figure out whether a box should be clear, gray, or checked to display or not display files based on their attributes. Use Table 3.3 for configuring the check boxes for every possible situation. The following information will help you to understand further the differences among three available check box settings. Each state on the left tells the Filter to:

▲ **Gray**   Ignore the attribute (files *with* or *without* the attribute will be displayed).

▲ **Checked** Display only those files that have the attribute.

▲ **Cleared** Display only those files that do not have the attribute.

Changing between check box states is simple. Try it. Click on the Read Only check box. What happens? It turns from gray to clear. Click on it again. This time it becomes checked. Click on it one last time. It turns back to gray again.

To switch between Attribute check box states:

▲ Click on the check box until it displays the state you wish.

To make your selections in the Filter dialog box:

▲ While working in a drive window, choose View Filter. The Filter dialog box appears, as displayed in Figure 3.6. (Mouse users can click the Filter button on the drive window button bar.)

▲ Click on the appropriate option in the File Type box. Enter file specifications in the Custom box if you choose this option.

▲ Click on the appropriate check boxes in the Attributes box (following the instructions above) so that they accurately reflect the files you wish to display.

▲ Click on Show Directories if you wish to include subdirectories in the file display.

▲ Click the OK button. The new settings will now be in effect.

TIP

Click on the Set Default button only if you wish the current Filter dialog box settings to be in effect for all subsequently opened drive windows in this and future Norton Desktop sessions.

Only One for Me, Please

If you are looking for a specific file, you can use the Speed Search feature to find it. Whether you know the complete file name or can only remember how the name begins, the Speed Search box will move you quickly to the file's location.

You might be wondering, *Where is the Speed Search box? I don't see it in the drive window.* The Speed Search box only appears when you type a letter in the file pane. Try it. It's also displayed in Figure 3.3.

When you type a letter in the file pane, Speed Search appears and your letter becomes the first letter in the box. At the same time, the file pane setting moves to the files that begin with the letter you specified. When you type the next letter, you are moved even closer to the file. However, if no file in the file pane begins with the two letters you specified, the file pane setting doesn't move and the second letter you entered does not get displayed in the Speed Search box. In other words, Speed Search is telling you that there's no such file in the file pane.

Here's an example of how Speed Search works. Imagine you are searching for a file called SEARCH.ME. The file pane is currently showing files that begin with A through D. When you type "S" in the file pane, you are immediately brought to files that begin with "SA." When you type "E," you are brought to files that begin with "SEA," and so on. Now suppose you are in the wrong subdirectory and there is no such file called SEARCH.ME in the current file pane, nor even a file that begins with "SA." When you type in "A" after the "S," nothing happens. Speed Search is telling you that the file you're looking for is not in the current subdirectory. You'll have to look elsewhere.

If you enter a file's entire name in the Speed Search box, then press **Enter**, you are not only moved to that file but the file becomes selected (or highlighted) as well. But in this chapter, we're only concerned about locating files. For complete details on selecting files, read *Selecting the Files You Want* in Chapter 4.

To locate a file using the Speed Search box:

▲ Type the first letter of the file you're looking for in the file pane of a drive window. The Speed Search appears below the file pane, as shown in Figure 3.3.

▲ Type as many other letters as you know.

▲ Look for your file; if it resides in the current directory, it should now appear somewhere in the file pane.

TIP

You can also use the Speed Search box to help you find a directory. The Speed Search box works exactly the same way in a tree pane for directories as it does in a file pane for files.

Showing All Files on a Drive

You can instantly show all of the files on one of your drives.

To display all of the files on a drive:

▲ Choose View Show Entire Drive. All files for the selected drive will be displayed in the drive window.

Use the Show Entire Drive option with the Speed Search feature to find a file instantly, without having to sort through directories and subdirectories.

CHECK YOURSELF

In a hard drive window, display all system files beginning with an "S" with the extension .EXE.

1. Double-click on a hard drive icon.

2. Click on the Filter button or choose View Filter.

3. In the Custom box of the Filter Type box, enter: S*.EXE.

4. In the Attributes box, select the System check box.

5. Click the OK button. The files (if there are any) will now appear in the drive window.

Tell Me All the Details

Now that you've learned the details on how to pick the files you want, you are going to learn about the different ways you can display those files. If you want to see as many files as possible in the file pane, you can configure the pane to show only file names. Or to get all the details on files, you can configure the file pane to show subdirectory names; file sizes, attributes, and icons; and the date and time you created or last modified each file, as displayed in Figure 3.8. Different options in the File Details dialog box allow you to design your file pane just the way you want it.

To specify how files should appear in the file pane:

▲ While working in a drive window, choose View File Details. The File Details dialog box appears, as displayed in Figure 3.9.

▲ Select the check boxes of the items you wish to display.

▲ Deselect the check boxes of the items you do not wish to display.

TIP

Look in the Sample box to see an example of how your files will be displayed under the current settings. Experiment by selecting and deselecting check boxes in turn until the sample reflects what you want to see in the file pane.

▼ *Figure 3.8. File Pane Displaying All Six File Details and the Four Icon Types*

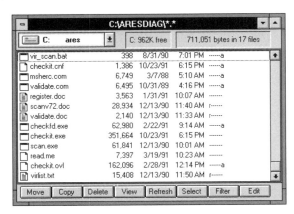

▼ *Figure 3.9. File Details Dialog Box*

Icons

Different icons are displayed in the file pane for different file types. Four specific icons are reserved to represent the following categories of files: executable program or batch files, text or word processor documents, generic data files, and directories. You can see samples of all four icon types in the file pane displayed in Figure 3.8.

Attributes

If you have marked the Attributes check box in the File Details dialog box, the following letters will be displayed in the file pane to represent these file attributes:

Letter	Attribute
R	Read Only
A	Archive
S	System
H	Hidden

The file pane in Figure 3.8 displays some of the above letters for various files. For specific information on the file attributes, refer to Table 3.3 on page 56.

Saving the Detail Settings

The selections you make in the File Details dialog box will be in effect for the current drive window and for all subsequently opened drive windows during your current Windows session. However, if you wish to make the settings permanent, you must choose Configure Save Configuration (if you haven't marked the Save Configuration on Exit box) For more on saving changes, see the last section in Chapter 2, *Customizing Groups.*

CHECK YOURSELF

Configure the file pane of an open drive window to show only file sizes and attributes, and date and time information.

1. Open a drive window if necessary.

2. Choose View File Details.

3. Deselect the Icon and Directory check boxes.

4. Select the Size, Date, Time, and Attributes check boxes.

5. Click the OK button.

Sorting Options

If you have chosen to display file details in the file pane, you can sort your files by some of those details, such as size and date. You can also sort your files in ascending or descending order. By default, files are listed alphanumerically by name, in ascending order (from A to Z). You can change this default sort order using the View Sort By commands.

When you select the View Sort By commands, a new menu appears listing sort options, as shown in Figure 3.10.

▼ *Figure 3.10. The View Sort By Menu*

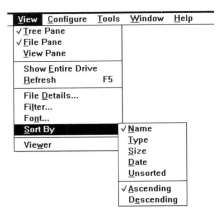

Table 3.4 describes each of the seven sort options listed on the Sort By menu.

In alphanumerical sorts, numbers and letters are sorted together, with numbers appearing first. In this type of sort, numbers are sorted just like regular characters (that is, from left to right). For example, the numbers 1, 2, 3, 10, 11, and 21 would be sorted alphanumerically as: 1, 10, 11, 2, 21, 3.

Norton Desktop will sort by the View Sort By menu item you have selected, as a primary sort. If there is a "tie" between files (they share the same property), Norton Desktop will then sort by name. For example, if you are sorting by file size and three of your files are the same size, those files will then be sorted alphanumerically by name.

To sort your files in a specified order:

▲ Choose View Sort By.

▲ Choose the sort criterion. A check mark appears next to the sort criterion, and your files are sorted.

▲ If you wish to switch the sort order, choose View Sort By, and then either Ascending or Descending.

TIP

Mouse users can sort by name or file type instantly by clicking the NameSrt button or the TypeSrt button on the drive window button bar.

▼ Table 3.4. View Sort By Menu Options

Sort Option	Default Functions
Name	Sorts file names in alphanumeric order.
Type	Sorts file extensions in alphanumeric order, then sorts alphanumerically by name.
Size	Sorts by size in ascending order (from smallest to largest).
Date	Sorts by time and date in ascending order (the most recently created or modified file appears on the bottom of the list).
Unsorted	Lists files in the same order that a DOS directory listing would.
Ascending	Letters sorted from A to Z, numbers from smallest to largest.
Descending	Letters sorted from Z to A, numbers from largest to smallest.

Sorting Options

CHECK YOURSELF

In an open drive window, sort your files first by size in ascending order, then by size in descending order, and finally by date, showing the most recently created or modified file *first*.

1. Open a drive window if necessary.

2. Choose View Sort By Size.

3. Choose View Sort By Descending.

4. Choose View Sort By Date.

Updating the Display

There are times when you should update your file display. For example, if you are working in a floppy drive window and you change diskettes, you'll need to refresh the drive window to display the information for the new disk. Also, whenever you create a new directory, subdirectory, or file using another software program or from the DOS prompt, you should update the drive window afterward.

To update the current drive window:

▲ Choose View Refresh. The Refresh dialog box appears, showing you Norton Desktop's progress as it scans the drive.

Using Multiple Drive Windows

There are sure to be times when using one drive window isn't enough. Perhaps you want to compare original hard disk files with their corresponding backups on a floppy disk. Or you might want to open two drive windows for the same drive because you want to view files in different directories at the same time. Also, you might want to compare the file pane data listed under different sort orders. Whatever your reason, working with multiple drive windows is easy to do in Norton Desktop.

Using Multiple Drive Windows

If you have two or more drive windows open at the same time, you may end up doing the drive window shuffle in an attempt to organize the windows. Following the guidelines below might help you make that drive window shuffle something to be admired.

To move a drive window:

▲ Drag the drive window's title bar to a new location.

To work with drive windows side-by-side (rather than in a cascaded format):

▲ Choose Window Tile. Note that choosing this will place *all* open windows (including open group windows) in a tiled format.

To move quickly from one drive window to another when windows are cascaded (do one of the following):

▲ Click on the appropriate drive window.

▲ Choose Window, then the name of the desired drive window.

TIP

If you wish to change to a different drive without opening another drive window, use the drive selector (see Table 3.1 and Figure 3.3) instead of clicking on a new drive icon or using the Open Drive Window menu command. Click on the drive selector's scroll button to display a pull-down list of available drives, then select the appropriate drive. Drive window data will change instantly to reflect the new drive.

QUICK SUMMARY

Command	To Do This
Window Open Drive Window	Open a drive window.
View View Pane	Display or remove the view pane from a drive window.
View Tree Pane	Display or remove the tree pane from a drive window.
View File Pane	Display or remove the file pane from a drive window.
View Filter	Choose *which* files are displayed in a drive window.
View Show Entire Drive	Display *all* of the files on a drive.
View File Details	Choose *how* files are displayed in a file pane.
View Sort By	Sort the files in a file pane (see Table 3.4 for specific commands).
View Refresh	Update a drive window display.

PRACTICE WHAT YOU'VE LEARNED

In a drive window with all three panes showing, display only your document files that need to be backed up, showing only the date and size for each file in the file pane. Next, sort the files by type in descending order, then reduce the drive window to an icon.

1. Open a drive window and choose View View Pane.

2. Choose View Filter. In the File Type box, select Documents. In the Attributes box, double-click on the Archive box so that the box is checked. Click the OK button.

3. Choose View File Details. Deselect the Icon, Time, Attributes, and Directory check boxes. Select the Size and Date check boxes. Click the OK button.

4. Choose View Sort By Type or click the TypeSrt button.

5. Choose View Sort By Descending.

6. Click the Minimize button.

Managing
Your Files

Managing files is much more enjoyable than managing people. These submissive clusters of code won't get upset when you try to move them, sue you when you try to copy them, or fight back when you try to delete them. What's more, you can quickly print and rename files, or even change their properties with no questions asked.

In the previous chapter, you learned how to choose *which* files you wanted displayed and *how* to display them in a drive window. You will now learn how to manipulate those files. In this chapter, you will learn how to:

▲ **Select and deselect files**

▲ **Move, copy, delete, and obliterate files**

▲ **Rename a file**

▲ **Print a file**

▲ **Assign file attributes**

▲ **Make a new directory**

Selecting the Files You Want

Before you can use Norton Desktop to perform any type of operation with one or more files, you must first select those files (that is, indicate which files you want to manipulate). You can select just a single file or a group of files.

TIP

The procedures below describe how to select and deselect files in the file pane. You can use these same procedures to select and deselect directories in the tree pane as well.

Selecting a Single File

Selecting a single file is as easy as clicking on that file. When you select a file, it appears highlighted on the screen, as shown in Figure 4.1.

To select a file in the file pane:

▲　Click on the desired file.

▼ *Figure 4.1. A Selected File*

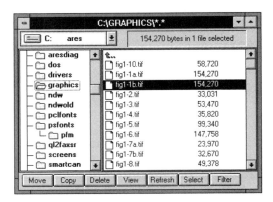

Selecting a Block of Files

At times you will want to select two or more files in a row. Try clicking on one file and then clicking on the one below it, to highlight both. What happened? When you clicked on the second file name, the first became deselected. There is a trick to selecting a block of files, as you will see below.

To select two or more files in a row:

▲ Press the right mouse button and drag the mouse cursor over the files you want to select.

or:

▲ Click on the first file to select it.

▲ Point to the last file name in the row to be selected.

▲ Press **Shift** while you click on the last file. The group of files are selected, as shown in Figure 4.2.

Selecting a Group of Noncontiguous Files

But how do you select two or more files that are not adjacent to each other? If you want to select a file along with another file located, say, six lines below it, the files in between the two will

▼ *Figure 4.2. Selected Block of Files*

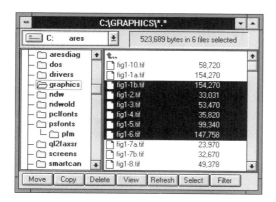

end up being selected if you try to use the Shift key. Instead, you use the Control key.

To select two or more non-adjacent files:

▲ Use the right mouse button to click on each file you want to select.

or:

▲ Press **Ctrl** while you click the left mouse button to make your selections. Several noncontiguous files are selected, as shown in Figure 4.3.

Selecting All Files

When you want to select every file displayed in the file pane, use the Select command (accessed from the File menu). When you choose File Select, an extended menu displays that lists the All, Some, and Invert options. Choosing All will select all objects in a pane.

It is very important that you be in the correct pane when you choose Select All. For instance, if you wish to select all files in a different directory, be sure you make the file pane active again (by clicking in it) after selecting the new directory in the tree pane. Otherwise, you will select all tree pane directories

▼ *Figure 4.3. Noncontiguous File Selection*

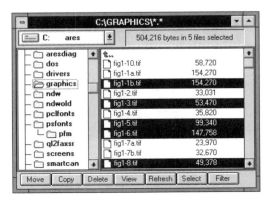

instead of all file pane files, which could be disastrous if you were deleting files.

To select all files in the file pane:

▲ Choose File Select All.

Be careful when selecting all files, especially if you are planning to delete them. A mistake could cause you to erase valuable data. Use the Select All and Delete commands together with care.

Using File Select

You can also use the Select command to select files that share some of the same file name characters. Using Select can be much faster than selecting noncontiguous files individually using the mouse, as described earlier.

But what's the difference between using the Custom option in the Filter dialog box (discussed in Chapter 3) and Select Some to select the files you want? The difference lies in the word *select*: The Filter's Custom option only lets you *display* files inside the file pane, while Select Some actually lets you select files that already appear in the file pane.

When using Select Some, you must enter a file specification in the Select Some dialog box, as shown in Figure 4.4. For example, if you want to select all files that have the extension .WK? (where *?* represents a number) and that begin with the characters BUDG, you would type **BUDG*.WK?** in the Select Some File box. Conveniently, your last five entries in the File box will be remembered by Norton Desktop. Thus, you won't have to reenter a file specification over and over again each time you wish to select the same group of files.

TIP

Be sure to scroll through the entire file pane after using Select Some, because selected files will usually be scattered throughout the pane.

▼ *Figure 4.4. The Select Some Dialog Box*

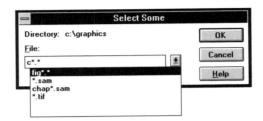

To select a particular group of files:

▲ Choose File Select Some. The Select Some dialog box appears, as displayed in Figure 4.4.

▲ Enter the file specification in the File box, or click on the File box scroll button and choose an item from the pull-down list of previously entered specifications.

▲ Click the OK button. The specified files will be selected in the file pane.

TIP

Mouse users can click on the Select button on the drive window button bar to display the Select Some dialog box (Figure 4.4).

Inverting the Selection

After you have selected files in any manner—with the mouse, the keyboard, or Select Some—you can *invert* your selection so that unselected files become selected and selected files become deselected.

To invert your current selection of files:

▲ Choose File Select Invert.

CHECK YOURSELF

Select a file in the file pane of a drive window. Then, switch to a new directory, select all files in the file pane that begin with the letter C (using Select Some), and invert the selection.

1. Click on a file in the file pane of a drive window.

2. Click on a new directory in the tree pane, then make the file pane active again by clicking in it.

3. Choose File Select Some.

4. In the File Select Some box, type **C*.***.

5. Choose File Select Invert.

Deselecting Files

Fortunately, deselecting in Norton Desktop is as easy as selecting. You can deselect a single file, specified files, or all files using the mouse, keyboard, or the Deselect command (accessed from the File menu).

Using the Mouse and Keyboard to Deselect Files

To deselect a single file:
▲ Using the *right* mouse button, click on the selected file.

or:

▲ Press **Ctrl** while you click on the selected file (using the *left* mouse button).

To deselect a group of files:

▲ Press the *right* mouse button and scroll through the files you wish to deselect.

or:

▲ Press **Ctrl** and the *left* mouse button while you scroll through the files you wish to deselect.

Using the Menu to Deselect Files

As you might expect, you use File Deselect in the same way as File Select, though obviously with different results. The same extended menu (containing the All, Some, and Invert options) that appears when you choose File Select appears when you choose File Deselect.

To deselect every file in the file pane:

▲ Choose File Deselect All.

To deselect only some of the selected files:

▲ Choose File Deselect Some. The Deselect Some dialog box appears. (This dialog box is identical to the Select Some dialog box.)

▲ Enter the file specification in the File text box, or click on the File box scroll button and choose an item from the pull-down list of previously entered specifications (for details, see *Using File Select*, above).

▲ Click the OK button. The specified files will now be deselected.

TIP

You can also invert a file selection after deselecting it by choosing File Deselect Invert, which works the same way as Select Invert.

CHECK YOURSELF

What happens if you select File Deselect Invert when only one file has been selected?

▲ The selected file becomes unselected and every other item in the file pane becomes selected.

Moving and Copying Files

Have you ever labored over moving or copying a directory or file using DOS? If so, you're sure to appreciate moving and copying within Norton Desktop. You can move or copy directories, subdirectories, groups of nonadjacent files, and single files simply by dragging the selection from one drive window to another. And if you're moving or copying from a hard disk to a floppy disk, you can drag the selection directly to a floppy drive icon—you don't even have to open a floppy drive window. Sound too easy to be true? Read on.

When you are moving or copying files from one directory to another within the same drive, instead of trying to move or copy from within the same drive window, make your operation easier by opening two drive windows for that drive. By opening two drive windows, you can display the *source* directory (the directory containing the files to be moved or copied) in one drive window and the *destination* directory (the directory to be added to) in the second. On the other hand, if you don't need to move or copy a file into a specific directory on a disk, don't bother opening a second drive window. Instead, simply drag and drop the file name directly onto the appropriate drive icon. The file will be placed into the root directory on the drive.

Using File Move

You can move directories and files with the mouse or by using the Move command (accessed from the File menu). If you have a mouse, get into the habit of using it to move files instantly. However, if you're a loyal menu user, you can also use File Move.

If you move a directory from the tree pane using the mouse, all of the directory's subdirectories and files will be moved or copied along with it. To move or copy only certain subdirectories, drag them from the file pane.

When you move a directory to another directory, the directory you move becomes a subdirectory of the one you moved it to. For example, if you move C:\LETTERS to D:\CORRESPO, a new subdirectory called D:\CORRESPO\LETTERS will result. On the other hand, when you move a file, it will go directly into whichever directory or subdirectory you specify.

Using the Mouse to Move Files

To move directories or files with the mouse:

1. Select the directories or files you want to move, following the selection procedures discussed in *Selecting the Files You Want,* at the beginning of this chapter.

2. Press **Alt** while you drag the selection to its destination. Notice that the icon changes as you move the selection.

3. Release the mouse button and Alt key. A confirmation box appears, asking you to confirm or cancel your mouse operation.

4. Click the OK button. The selection now resides in the new location.

TIP

You can bypass Step 4 by configuring Norton Desktop so that confirmation boxes will not appear when you move or copy items using the mouse. To do this, choose Configure Confirmation. In the Configure Confirmation dialog box, deselect the Mouse Operation check box and click the OK button. Keep in mind, though, that confirming before moving or copying with the mouse is a good way for you to prevent mistakes from occurring.

It is essential that you keep the Alt key depressed while you are dragging a selection; if you don't, the selected files will be *copied,* not moved. The mouse procedures for moving and copying groups from one group window to another is almost the

▼ Table 4.1. Using the Mouse to Move and Copy Groups and Files

Moving and Copying Files

	Move	Copy
Group Item	Drag the item	Press **Ctrl** while you drag the item
Drive Window Item	Press **Alt** while you drag the item	Drag the item

exact reverse of what you must do to move and copy files from one drive window to another using the mouse. Just dragging a group item will move it; but you must press **Ctrl** to copy it. Table 4.1 shows you when to use mouse and key combinations for moving and copying group items and files.

CHECK YOURSELF

Move a file from a hard drive window to another directory on the same drive.

1. Open two drive windows for your hard drive and reposition them so that both are fully displayed.

2. Click on the file to be moved in the first drive window to select that file.

3. Adjust the file pane in the second drive window so that the directory into which you will place the selected file is showing.

4. Press **Alt** while dragging the selected file to the destination directory.

Using the Menu to Move Files

Instead of using the mouse, you can use the Move command to relocate files. You might remember that you used File Move in Chapter 2 to move groups. However, Move is not a typical menu item; it changes functions depending on the circumstances in which you choose it. The dialog box that appears when you choose File Move from a drive window differs from the dialog box that will appear when you choose File Move from a group window. For example, if a group window is active when you

▼ *Figure 4.5. The Move Dialog Box Accessed from a Group Window*

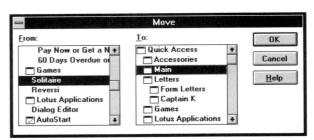

choose File Move, the dialog box shown in Figure 4.5 will display. But if you choose File Move while a drive window is active, the dialog box shown in Figure 4.6 will display. So when you're planning to move files and both group and drive windows are open, make sure the drive window is active.

TIP

The same is true for the Copy menu item; choosing File Copy from a group window will display a different dialog box than choosing File Copy from a drive window.

To move directories and files with the Move menu command:

1. Choose File Move, or click the Move button on the drive window button bar. The Move dialog box appears, as displayed in Figure 4.6.

▼ *Figure 4.6. The Move Dialog Box Accessed from a Drive Window*

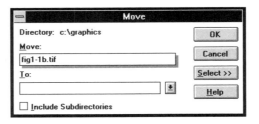

2. In the Move box, enter the name of the item you want to move.

TIP

If you select a file before choosing the Move command, the file will already be displayed in the Move box. If you select multiple files or directories, the Move dialog box will change in appearance, identifying the number of selected items, as shown in Figure 4.7.

3. In the To box, do one of the following:

   ▲ Enter the full path name of the destination directory (such as C:\AMIPRO\DOCS\LETTERS).

   ▲ Click the To scroll button to display a pull-down list of previously entered destinations (refer to Figure 4.6), and choose the appropriate destination. Norton Desktop will remember the last ten destinations you entered in this box.

   ▲ Click on the Select button. The Move dialog box appears as shown in Figure 4.8. Highlight the destination directory in the Destination scroll box.

4. Select the Include subdirectories check box if you are moving a directory and want to also move its subdirectories.

5. Click the OK button. The items are moved to the new directory.

▼ *Figure 4.7. The Move Dialog Box when Multiple Files Have Been Previously Selected*

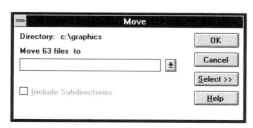

▼ *Figure 4.8. The Move Dialog Box, after Pressing Select*

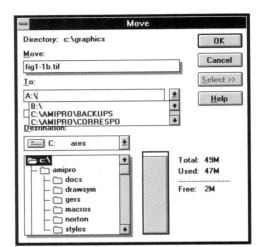

Using File Copy

Copying is identical to what you previously learned about moving files, groups of files, directories, subdirectories, and so on, with the following exceptions:

▲ When copying using the mouse, don't press Alt. (See Table 4.1.)

▲ When copying using the menu, choose File Copy. The Copy dialog box that appears is exactly the same as the Move dialog box (Figure 4.6), except the title bar displays *Copy*.

Remember, unlike moving an item, when you copy an item it remains in its present location *and* is added to the new location.

CHECK YOURSELF

Use the Copy command to copy a directory only (that is, without its subdirectories) from a hard drive window to a floppy drive.

1. Open a hard drive window.

2. Select the directory to be moved by clicking on it in the tree pane.

3. Choose File Copy.

4. Make sure the Include subdirectories check box is deselected.

5. In the To box, enter the letter of the floppy drive followed by a colon (for example, A:).

6. Click the OK button.

Moving and Copying Files

Deleting and Obliterating Files

When you delete a file in Norton, in most cases you can still recover it at a later time (assuming you are running SmartErase—see Chapter 6, *Recovering Deleted Files*). But when you *obliterate* a file, it can never be restored, even with a data recovery program. The only way to obliterate a file in Norton Desktop is to shred it. So think twice before placing the Shredder tool icon on your desktop, and be very cautious when using it.

Deleting Files

You can delete a file either by dragging the file from a drive window to the SmartErase tool icon or by using the File Delete command.

To delete directories and files from a drive window with the mouse:

▲ Select the file or files to be deleted in the drive window.

▲ Drag the selection to the SmartErase tool icon, then release the mouse button. A warning box appears.

▲ Click on Yes to delete one file at a time, and Yes to All if you want to delete all files within a subdirectory at once.

For more about the SmartErase feature, read Chapter 6, *Recovering Deleted Files*.

To delete directories or files with the Delete command:

▲ Choose File Delete, or click the Delete button on the drive window button bar. The Delete dialog box appears, as shown in Figure 4.9.

▲ In the Delete box, type the name of the item you want to delete. You can use wildcard characters if you wish to delete multiple files. (If you select a file *before* choosing the Delete command, the file will already be displayed in the Delete box.)

▲ Click the OK button to delete the items.

TIP

You can also display the Delete dialog box by pressing Delete on the keyboard after you have selected a file.

Shredding Your Files

The Shredder will *permanently destroy* your directories and files. However, it does give you *two* opportunities to change your mind before it writes graffiti all over your files so that they are no longer recognizable.

To shred directories and files with the mouse:

▲ Select the file or files to be shredded.

▲ Drag the selection to the Shredder tool icon, then release the mouse button. A warning box appears.

▼ *Figure 4.9. The Delete Dialog Box*

▲ Click on Yes. A second and final warning box appears.

▲ Click on Yes again. If you dragged a directory, you will need to click on Yes twice for *each* file in the directory.

To shred directories or files with the Shredder menu command:

▲ Choose Tools Shredder. The Shred dialog box appears, as shown in Figure 4.10.

▲ In the Shred text box, enter the name of the item you want to shred.

Deleting and Obliterating Files

TIP

It's easier if you select a file before choosing **Tools Shredder** because the file will already be displayed in the Shred text box. If you select multiple files or directories, the Shred dialog box will identify the number of items that are to be shredded.

▲ Select the Include subdirectories check box if you are shredding a directory and want to shred its subdirectories as well.

▲ Click on Yes twice for each file. The files will now be impossible to recover.

Renaming Files

Unlike with DOS, you can rename directories as well as files in Norton Desktop, which can come in very handy. Suppose, as a

▼ *Figure 4.10. The Shred Dialog Box*

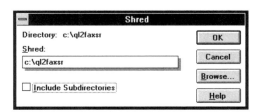

writer, you've set up all of your chapter files for your book, *Gone with the Rain,* in a subdirectory of the same name. Later, when your novel is accepted for publication, the publisher wants to rename it *Away with the Rain.* Naturally, you would want to rename your subdirectory to reflect the new title.

To rename directories and files:

▲ Choose File Rename. The Rename dialog box appears, as shown in Figure 4.11.

▲ Enter the full path name of the directory or file in the Rename box. If you selected the item before choosing File Rename, the name of the directory or file will already appear in the Rename box.

▲ Enter the full path of the new name in the To text box.

▲ Click the OK button. The directory or file will now be labeled with the new name.

TIP

If the subdirectory or file you are renaming will remain in its current directory or subdirectory, you don't have to enter the path name in the To text box—just the new name.

CHECK YOURSELF

Rename a file that will remain in the current directory.

1. Open a drive window.

2. Select the file to be renamed.

3. Choose File Rename.

4. Enter the new name (do not include its path).

5. Click the OK button.

▼ *Figure 4.11. Rename Dialog Box*

Printing Files

One of the great features of Norton Desktop is its ability to print a file without you first having to open the original program that created the file. This feature is very handy because you may frequently print and reprint certain files regularly, and if you don't need to make any changes to a document, it becomes very tedious having to open it just to print it.

When you print a file, Norton Desktop launches the program used to create the file, opens the file, then executes that program's print command. But you never see it doing this; all the work is done behind the scenes. All you'll notice are two icons that appear at the bottom of your desktop: one representing your software program, and the other the Windows Print Manager icon. A nice thing about having the Print Manager on your desktop while your file is printing is that you can quickly and easily cancel the print job if necessary by restoring the Print Manager icon and deleting the job in progress.

Just as you've seen in the Norton Desktop file management features, you can either use the mouse or the menu to activate the Print feature. By dragging a file to a Printer tool icon or by choosing the Print command from the File menu, you can print almost any file you wish. And like the SmartErase icon, you can also drag a group or desktop item icon to a Printer tool icon to print a particular file.

Using the Mouse to Print a File

It is possible for you to have more than one Printer icon on the desktop. If you have access to multiple printers or if you specified more than one printer configuration using the Windows Control Panel, you can display a Printer tool icon for each of the installed printers. For example, if you have three printer configurations installed on Windows, you can display all three Printer icons on the desktop, as shown in Figure 4.12. This way you can print a file to whichever printer you want by dragging the file or its item icon to the appropriate Printer icon. By default, the Printer icons are numbered according to the port they are assigned to, such as Printer #1 for LPT1, Printer #2 for LPT2, and so on.

TIP

If you want to make a Printer icon label more descriptive, click on the icon and choose Label. In the Edit Label dialog box, enter the new name (for example, HP LaserJet II, Dot Matrix, or The Old Clinker). Figure 4.12 shows a desktop with three customized Printer icons.

To print a file from a drive window using the mouse:

▲ Drag the file name from the drive window to the appropriate Printer icon.

To print a file using its group or desktop item icon:

▲ Drag an Item icon to the appropriate Printer icon.

TIP

If you want to disable the confirmation dialog box that appears when you drag an icon to a Printer icon, choose Configure Preferences and deselect the Print File check box.

▼ *Figure 4.12. Personalizing Your Printer Icons*

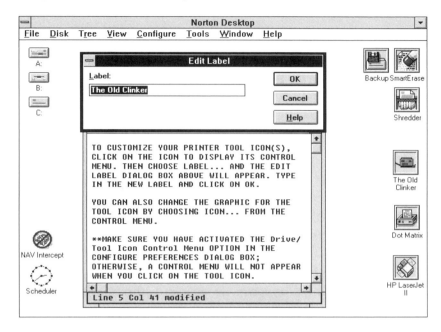

Using the Menu to Print a File

To print a file using the menu:

▲ Choose File Print. The Print dialog box appears, as shown in Figure 4.13.

▲ Enter the file name in the Print box, including its path, unless the file is in your current directory. If you selected a

▼ *Figure 4.13. Print Dialog Box*

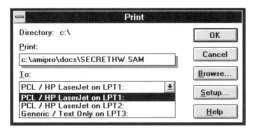

file *before* choosing the Print command, its name will already appear in the Print box.

TIP

You can also click on the Browse button and scroll through the Files and Tree boxes to select the file you want. Then, click the OK button and the file name will appear in the Print box.

▲ Click on the To scroll box to display a pull-down list of available printers, then select the desired printer. (If you only have one printer installed, its name will already appear in the To box.)

▲ Click the OK button to print the file.

If you want to configure another printer or change the current printer settings, you can do so using the Setup button in the Print dialog box. Clicking on this button brings up the Windows Setup Printer dialog box. Refer to the *Microsoft Windows User's Guide* for details on how to configure this dialog box.

Stopping a Print Job

As mentioned earlier, when you print a file in Norton Desktop, both an icon for the program being used and the Print Manager icon appear at the bottom of the desktop. After the printing has been completed, both icons will disappear. If you want to cancel or pause a print job while printing is still in progress, you can do so using the Print Manager icon.

To terminate or pause a print job while printing is still in progress:

▲ Double-click on the Print Manager icon (or click on it once and choose Restore). The Print Manager window now appears.

▲ *To cancel a print job:* When the name of your print job appears in the Print Manager window, click on it and then click on the Delete button. (You can only click on this button *after* you've highlighted a print job.) Click the OK button when you are prompted to confirm the termination of the print job. It will take a few seconds for all printing to stop.

Printing Files

▲ *To pause a print job:* Click on the Pause button. After a few seconds, printing will stop. To resume printing, click on the Resume button.

▲ Close the Print Manager window by double-clicking on its Control menu box or by choosing Close from the Print Manager Control menu.

CHECK YOURSELF

Print a file using its group item icon.

1. Open the group window in which the group item is located.

2. Drag the icon from the group window to a Printer icon.

Assigning File Attributes

You're familiar with attributes in people: a sense of humor, a positive outlook on life, a foul mouth. All of these attributes help to distinguish one person from another. In the same way, a file possesses certain *attributes,* or properties, that distinguish it from other files.

A file can have as many as four attributes: read only, archive, system, and hidden. Table 4.2 gives a brief description of each attribute.

TIP

With few exceptions, you'll assign only the read only attribute to files, since the archive attribute is automatically assigned to applicable files, and the other two attributes relate to files you won't be working with.

▼ Table 4.2. File Attributes

Attribute	When assigned to a file, it means that:
Read Only	The file cannot be changed or deleted. Assign this attribute to files you want to protect from accidental erasure or from modification.
Archive	The file needs to be backed up. Check this attribute in the Filter dialog box to display all of your files that need to be backed up.
System	The file is an internal DOS or system-related file and is usually hidden. This is not a commonly used attribute.
Hidden	The file is crucial to the operation of your computer system. Most hidden files cannot be deleted or executed. You will rarely, if ever, assign this to a file.

The Properties command (accessed from the File menu) allows you to assign attributes to a single file or a group of files. After choosing this command, the Properties dialog box displays. This dialog box will appear differently, depending on the circumstances. If no files are selected before you choose the Properties command, the Properties dialog box will appear as it does in Figure 4.14. However, if you select a single file before choosing the Properties command, the appearance of the Properties dialog box changes: data on the selected file is displayed, including the file's size, as well as the date and time it was last modified. Additionally, if the file has any attributes, all corresponding attribute boxes will be checked. Finally, if you are assigning attributes to a group of files and you select those files in a file pane before choosing the Properties command, the Properties dialog box will appear differently again, this time indicating how many files you have selected.

To assign attributes to a file:

▲ Choose File Properties. The Properties dialog box appears, as displayed in Figure 4.14.

▲ Enter the file name or use the Browse command to select the file.

▲ Click on the check boxes for the attributes you wish to assign.

▲ Click the OK button.

▼ *Figure 4.14. Properties Dialog Box in Its Original State*

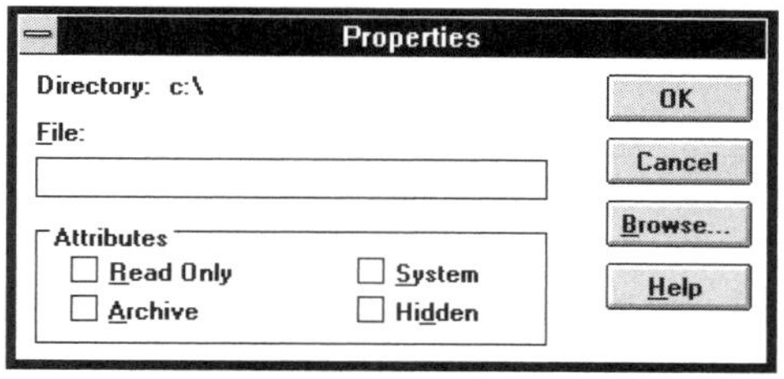

Assigning File Attributes

```
┌─────────────────────────────────────────┐
│ ═         Properties                      │
├───────────────────────────────────────────┤
│ Directory:  c:\              ┌──────────┐ │
│ File:                        │    OK    │ │
│ ┌─────────────────────────┐  └──────────┘ │
│ │                         │  ┌──────────┐ │
│ └─────────────────────────┘  │  Cancel  │ │
│ ┌─Attributes──────────────┐  └──────────┘ │
│ │ □ Read Only  □ System   │  ┌──────────┐ │
│ │ □ Archive    □ Hidden   │  │ Browse...│ │
│ └─────────────────────────┘  └──────────┘ │
│                              ┌──────────┐ │
│                              │   Help   │ │
│                              └──────────┘ │
└───────────────────────────────────────────┘
```

CHECK YOURSELF

Make a selected file read only.

1. Open a drive window and select the file.

2. Choose File Properties.

3. Click on the Read Only check box so that it is marked.

4. Click the OK button.

Making a New Directory

You can create a new directory quickly using the Make Directory command (accessed from the File menu). When you use this command, Norton Desktop places the new directory within the current directory listed at the top of the Make Directory dialog box (the new directory is called a subdirectory).

Your directory names can range from one to eight characters, and can include any combination of letters, numbers, and symbols, with the following exceptions:

. , ; : < > = + " * ? \ | [ ]

Also, you cannot use blanks and spaces within a directory name.

▼ *Figure 4.15. Make Directory Dialog Box*

```
┌─────────────────────────────────────────────┐
│ ─              Make Directory                 │
│ Directory:  c:\               ┌──────────┐   │
│ New Directory:                │    OK    │   │
│ ┌─────────────────────────┐   └──────────┘   │
│ │INVOICE$                 │   ┌──────────┐   │
│ └─────────────────────────┘   │  Cancel  │   │
│                               └──────────┘   │
│                               ┌──────────┐   │
│                               │ Select >>│   │
│                               └──────────┘   │
│                               ┌──────────┐   │
│                               │   Help   │   │
│                               └──────────┘   │
└─────────────────────────────────────────────┘
```

To make a new directory:

▲ Choose File Make Directory. The Make Directory dialog box appears, as shown in Figure 4.15.

▲ If you wish to change the current directory, which is displayed at the top of the dialog box (this is the directory your new subdirectory will be placed in), click on Select. Select the desired directory from the directory tree that now appears, then click the OK button.

▲ Enter the name of the new directory in the New Directory box.

▲ Click the OK button.

QUICK SUMMARY

Command	To Do This
File Select All	Select all items in a drive window pane.
File Select Some, or Select button	Select certain files in a file pane.
File Select Invert	Reverse the current selection in a pane.
File Deselect Invert	Reverse the current selection in a pane.
File Deselect All	Deselect all items in a drive window pane.
File Deselect Some	Deselect certain selected files in a file pane.
File Move	Move a directory or file to a new location.
File Copy	Copy a directory or file to a new location.
File Delete, Delete button, or Delete key	Delete a directory or file.

Command	*To Do This*
Tools Shredder, or Shredder icon	*Permanently* destroy a directory or file.
File Rename	Rename a directory or file.
File Print, or Printer icon	Print a file.
Configure Preferences Print File	Turn off prompt boxes so you do not have to confirm a print job when you drag a file from a drive window to a Printer icon.
File Properties	Assign one to four properties to a file.
File Make Directory	Create a new directory.

PRACTICE WHAT YOU'VE LEARNED

Select the first five files in a file pane, then every third file after that. *Attempt* to delete these selected files. Then, make a new directory on a floppy disk and copy a file from your hard drive to that new floppy drive directory.

1. Click on the first file in the file pane. Then, press **Shift** as you click on the fifth file name. Skip two files, press **Ctrl** as you click on the third file. Repeat this last step as needed.

2. Click anywhere in the shaded selection and drag the selection over to the SmartErase icon. Choose Cancel to discontinue the delete operation.

3. Open a floppy drive window. Choose File Make Directory. Enter the name of the new directory in the New Directory box, then click the OK button.

4. Open a drive window for each drive and reposition or tile the windows (Window Tile). Locate the file to be copied in the hard drive window file pane. Drag that file name to the subdirectory in the floppy drive window tree or file pane. Click the OK button in the Warning box that appears.

5

Running Programs

Running a program might mean more than you think it does. If you think it refers just to starting a software application on its own, you're only half right. In addition to starting an application, "running a program" can also mean opening a document in that application. In this chapter, you'll learn how to:

▲ **Start an application from a group, the desktop, a drive window, and the File menu**

▲ **Start an application by dragging one item to another**

▲ **Start applications automatically at startup**

▲ **Create a file association**

Getting to Know the Terminology

Before getting into procedures, we will review some of the vo-cabulary that you will frequently use when running programs. Our purpose is not to give you a dictionary definition for each term used in this chapter, but rather to help you see how the terms are connected and how they can differ in meaning when used in different situations. Also, once you realize that many of the terms are used interchangeably and refer to the same thing, you'll have an easier time understanding them in the future. For example, knowing that *launch, run,* and *start* all refer to the same action, and that *application, program,* and *software* all refer to the same item, you'll understand that *launch an application, run a program,* and *start a piece of software* all refer to the same function. Here are some other terms you will use in this chapter:

▲ *Program* is used interchangeably with *application* to refer to a piece of software. Though a program consists of many files, the one file you will be concerned with is the *program file.* Each program file (also called an *executable file*) has the ex-tension .EXE or .COM. You'll use program files to run soft-ware from the File menu and to create a program icon—an icon that will launch that software program. (For example, drag the program file AMIPRO.EXE from the drive window to the desktop to create a program icon for Ami Pro soft-ware. Then, click on that icon to start Ami Pro.)

▲ *Document* (sometimes called a *document file*) refers to any type of data file that's created with a software program. This could be a spreadsheet you build with Microsoft Excel, a letter you generate with Ami Pro, or a database you set up with dBASE IV.

▲ *Run, start,* and *launch* a program all refer to running a software program. On the other hand, you *open* a document. A pro-gram already has to be running before you can open a docu-ment in it. (For example, launch WordPerfect for Windows, then open the document you created with it yesterday.)

▲ *Launch a program* refers to starting only the software.

▲ *Launch a document* refers to starting the software, then opening a document.

▲ A *program icon* is an icon that will launch a software program *only*. For example, if you double-click on a program icon representing Lotus 1-2-3 for Windows, you start *only* Lotus 1-2-3 for Windows. A *document icon*, on the other hand, will launch the software, then open a particular document. For example, if you have a document icon called EXPENSES, which represents a Lotus 1-2-3 for Windows spreadsheet called EXPENSES.WK1, when you double-click on the EXPENSES icon, 1-2-3 for Windows will start, and then the EXPENSES.WK1 file will be opened.

▲ *Startup* refers to starting a program from the DOS command.

Remember, there are two types of icons: group icons, which reside in a group; and desktop icons, which reside on the desktop. You can have a program icon in a group or on the desktop. In the same way, you can have a document icon in a group or on the desktop.

Getting to Know the Terminology

Starting Programs

Norton Desktop almost always gives you more than just one way to accomplish a task. You can usually accomplish the same function in at least three different ways. In fact when it comes to running a program, you have *eleven* ways to choose from! While these eleven ways are listed below, don't be too concerned about understanding just what each of them refers to; except for Launch List, each will be covered in this chapter. In Norton Desktop you can launch a program by:

▲ using AutoStart.

▲ using the Launch List.

▲ using File Run.

▲ using File Open.

▲ double-clicking on a group document icon.

▲ double-clicking on a group program icon.

▲ double-clicking on a desktop document icon.

▲ double-clicking on a desktop program icon.

▲ double-clicking on a document file in a drive window.

▲ double-clicking on a program file in a drive window.

▲ dragging one item to another.

It's up to you to decide which of the eleven methods you should use to run your programs. Most likely, you'll use several of them, depending on the situation. However, we'll make some suggestions as to which methods work best under particular circumstances. Look at the categories in the left column of Table 5.1 and decide which one best describes you (or which one appeals to you most if you're a brand-new user). Then try the methods on the right to see if you like them and are comfortable using them.

TIP

One mistake you really want to avoid is running two versions of the same program at once, which can cause major problems on your hard disk. Remember, each time you double-click on an item to run a program or to open a document, the related software application is launched, even if the program is already running in another application window.

CHECK YOURSELF

What different results would be achieved by double-clicking on a group program icon called WORDPERFECT on the one hand, and a group document icon called PROJECT 1 (representing a WordPerfect document called PROJECT.1) on the other?

▲ Double-clicking on the WORDPERFECT icon would launch WordPerfect only, while double-clicking on the PROJECT 1 icon would launch WordPerfect *and* open the PROJECT.1 file.

▼ Table 5.1. Norton Desktop Launching Methods

If you:	Use this method to launch programs
Have set up a Quick Access group system, including top-level groups, subgroups, and group items,	▲ Double-click on a group program icon to create a new document. ▲ Double-click on a group document icon when you want to open that document.
Leave your most important software programs & documents on the desktop (you usually work with the same documents),	▲ Double-click on a desktop program icon to create a new document. ▲ Double-click on a desktop document icon when you want to open that document.
Work with the same program(s) on a daily basis,	▲ Drag the software program(s) to the AutoStart group so that these programs will launch whenever you start Windows.
Don't have a mouse,	▲ Use Launch Manager to assign your most frequently used programs to the Launch List, then select a program from the Launch List whenever you want to run that program.
Use drive windows whenever you work in Norton Desktop,	▲ Double-click on a program file in a drive window when you want to create a new document. ▲ Double-click on the name of a document in a drive window to open that document.

Launching from a Group

As discussed in Chapter 2, you can create a group item icon for either a software program or a document. If you create a group icon for a program, it is called a *group program icon*. Double-clicking on this icon will launch the software program represented by that icon. When you create a group icon for a document, it is called a *group document icon*. Double-clicking on this icon will launch the related software program and open the document represented by that icon.

Suppose you create a group system similar to the one shown in Figure 5.1. One of your top-level groups is called Letters. Inside this group is a subgroup called Form Letters. Using Ami Pro, you create separate files for five different form letters that you send out regularly to clients. Each time you want to work with a particular form letter, you could start Ami Pro, then open the appropriate form letter. However, there's a better way: first, create a group document icon for each of the form letters. Then, to open a particular form letter, simply double-click on the corresponding icon.

Taking the example a step further, there is a second subgroup in the Letters group called Captain K. Inside this subgroup are document icons representing letters that you send out on a regular basis to a particular client called Captain Knight. But you do not use these letters alone to correspond with the Captain; sometimes you create new letters. So in addition to the document icons inside the Captain K group, you will also have a program icon for Ami Pro. This way, if you want to create a new letter, you can double-click on the program icon to run Ami Pro; and when you want to work on a letter that has already been created, you can double-click on the corresponding document icon.

▼ *Figure 5.1. Use Group Program and Document Icons to Run Programs and Open Documents*

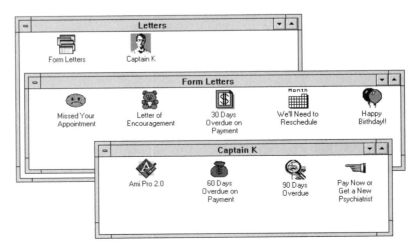

To launch a program or open a document from a group:

1. Open the group window containing the program or document icon.

2. Do one of the following:

   ▲ Double-click on a program icon to launch a program alone.

   or:

   ▲ Double-click on a document icon to launch a program and open the document.

   To learn how to create a program or document icon, read the *Creating a Group Item Icon* section in Chapter 2.

TIP

Remember, you can create as many group program icons as you'd like for one piece of software. For example, you might create 15 program icons representing Lotus 1-2-3 for Windows to place in each of your 15 subgroups so that you can easily run 1-2-3 from any subgroup window.

Launching from the Desktop

Perhaps you generally work on only a few documents over a long period of time. Rather than creating a detailed grouping system, you might choose to place icons representing the documents you work with most frequently directly on your desktop. This way, these document icons will be resting on your desktop each time you start Windows. Opening a document will be as simple as double-clicking on the document icon. And you can also place a program icon on the desktop for the times you want to create a new document.

For example, imagine that you are working on a proposal that is divided into seven sections, and you'll continually have to revise sections throughout the writing process. In this situation, you should place document icons for each of the seven

▼ *Figure 5.2. Use Desktop Document Icons to Open Existing Documents*

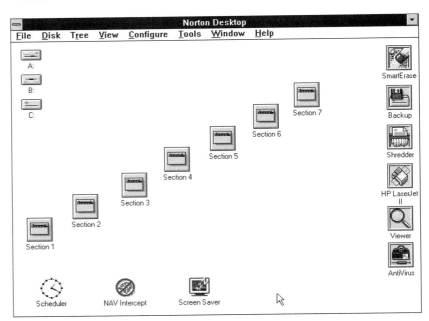

sections right on your desktop, as shown in Figure 5.2. Then, each time you sit down to work, you can double-click on the document icon for the section you want to work on.

On the other hand, perhaps you always start new documents and rarely work on finished projects. In this situation, you can place program icons for each of the applications you work with most frequently directly on your desktop. For example, if you use WordPerfect, Lotus 1-2-3, and dBASE software regularly, you can place program icons on your desktop for each of these applications, then double-click on one of the program icons to launch the desired application. Figure 5.3 shows a desktop containing three program icons.

To launch a program or document from the desktop:

▲ Double-click on the appropriate desktop program or document icon.

▼ *Figure 5.3. Use Desktop Program Icons to Create New Documents*

Launching from the Desktop

```
┌──────────────────────────────────────────────────────────┐
│ ═           Norton Desktop                             ▼  │
│ File  Disk  Tree  View  Configure  Tools  Window  Help    │
│                                                           │
│  ▭                                                  🖥     │
│  A:                                              SmartErase│
│  ▭                                                  📠     │
│  B:                                               Backup  │
│  ▭                                                  🖨     │
│  C:                                              Shredder │
│                                                     ◈     │
│                                               HP LaserJet │
│                                                    II     │
│  🖥                                                 🔍     │
│ Screen Saver                                      Viewer  │
│  🚫                                                 💻     │
│ NAV Intercept                                    AntiVirus│
│  🕐            📄       📊        📇                       │
│ Scheduler   WordPerfect Lotus 1-2-3  dBASE               │
│                                                           │
└──────────────────────────────────────────────────────────┘
```

TIP

Read Desktop Item Icons in Chapter 1 to find out how to create desktop program and document icons.

CHECK YOURSELF

If you rarely work on documents more than once, which type of desktop icons should you create? Why?

▲ Program icons, because double-clicking on this type of icon will launch a program alone, while double-clicking on a document icon will open an existing document, which you don't want to do.

Launching from a Drive Window

If you're the type of person who doesn't like to work with icons, then the drive window is definitely for you. You can launch a program from a drive window much the same way you launch a program from a group or from the desktop—by double-clicking on an item. But instead of double-clicking on a program icon as you would from a group or from the desktop, you double-click directly on a program file name to run that program by itself. Or to open a document you double-click on the name of that document file. To display the desired file(s) in the file pane, you can use any of the methods described in Chapter 3, *Using Drive Windows.*

To launch an application only, you'll need to double-click on the *executable file* for that application in the drive window. An executable file name usually contains an abbreviated version of the name of the program and the extension .EXE or .COM, such as NDW.EXE for Norton Desktop for Windows; PRINTMAN.EXE for Windows Print Manager; and COMMAND.COM to open a DOS window.

TIP

To help you find the executable file name for a software program, you can look in the Launch Manager's browsing list, which displays the executable file names of all the applications installed on your computer. To access this list, choose Launch Manager from the Norton Desktop Control menu, click on Add, then on Browse. In the Tree box, click on the directory likely to contain the executable file (for instance, the Windows directory for Reversi), then look through the Files box to find the executable file name.

To launch a program or document from a drive window:

1. Open a drive window for the appropriate drive.

2. Do one of the following:

   ▲ To open an existing document, double-click on the file name in the file pane.

▲ To launch a program alone, double-click on the executable file for that program in the file pane.

CHECK YOURSELF

Launch the Windows Solitaire game (it has an executable file name of SOL.EXE).

1. Open a hard drive window.

2. Click on the Windows directory in the tree pane.

3. Scroll through the file pane to locate the SOL.EXE file (or use Speed Search, as discussed in Chapter 3.).

4. Double-click on SOL.EXE. A Solitaire application window will be displayed on your screen.

Launching from the File Menu

In addition to using a group, the desktop, or a drive window to launch a program, you can also use the File menu. You can use either the Open command or Run command off the File menu to open an existing document or to run a program alone. Both commands operate in a similar manner; however, you must first select a file before using the Open command, while the Run command lets you enter a file name after you have chosen the command; and with Run, you can use the Browse button to help you find the file name you're looking for.

To launch a program or open a document using the Open command:

▲ Either select the appropriate file name (for a program, its executable file name) in a drive window, or select a group icon representing the program or document.

▲ Choose File Open. The program will now start, and if applicable, the document will be opened.

To launch a program or open a document using the Run command:

1. Choose File Run. The Run dialog box appears, as shown in Figure 5.4.

2. In the Command Line text box, do one of the following:

    ▲ Enter the file name (including its path) of the program you wish to run. (You can also use the Browse button and select the appropriate file name from the Files box.)

    or:

    ▲ Enter the file name (including its path) of the document you wish to launch. In this case, there must be an association between the document's extension and the application (see *Creating File Associations* later in this chapter).

3. In the Run Style box, select one of these options:

    ▲ Normal, to open a standard (intermediate-sized) application window.

    ▲ Minimized, to start the application and immediately minimize it to an icon on the bottom of your desktop. Use this option to preload programs you will be using later.

    ▲ Maximized, to make the application window as large as the screen.

TIP

You should only use the Open and Run commands to launch seldom-used programs or documents. If you use a program or document often, consider creating a group or desktop icon for it.

▼ *Figure 5.4. Run Dialog Box*

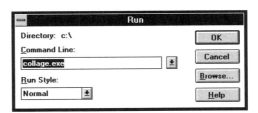

CHECK YOURSELF

Start a game of Solitaire in a maximized application window using the Run command.

1. Choose File Run.

2. While in the Command Line text box, click on Browse.

3. Select the executable file for Solitaire (SOL.EXE), then click the OK button.

4. In the Run Style box, select Maximized.

5. Click the OK button. A Solitaire game will start in a maximized application window.

Launching by Dragging One Item to Another

You can also run a program by dragging and dropping one item onto another. In other words, you can drag the name of a document from a drive window to a group or desktop icon to start that document.

But why not just double-click on the name of the document to start it? One reason why you might choose to drag the file name to a group program icon is because the document presently has no association with a program (discussed later in this chapter), and therefore, the document can't be opened by double-clicking on it. In this situation, dragging the name of the document file to a group or desktop program icon is the simplest way for you to open the document.

For instance, imagine you recently purchased a fax modem. Included in the software for the modem is a README file, which provides valuable information on the software. When you try to open the README.DOC file by double-clicking on it, you get an error message telling you that no association exists for that file. Now, if you have created a desktop or group icon for Norton's

Desktop Editor, you could simply drag the README.DOC file to the Editor icon to open the document. This is just one example of why you might want to drag an item to another icon to open a document.

You can also drag desktop items to group items and vice-versa. And in addition to dragging documents to programs, you can drag programs to documents. Each time you drag an object to another object, a tiny rocket appears, shown in Figure 5.5, telling you that a launch is about to happen. The rocket won't appear until you are directly over the destination object. If you release the mouse button while the rocket is showing, the document will be opened immediately.

To launch a program or document by dragging one item to another:

▲ Drag the appropriate icon or file name to a desktop or group icon, then release the mouse button when the rocket icon appears.

Automatic Launch at Startup

If you work with the same programs and/or documents every day, you might want to consider placing them in the AutoStart group. (If you are running under Windows 3.1, the AutoStart group will be called StartUp.) AutoStart, a subgroup of Quick

▼ *Figure 5.5. Rocket Icon Indicating when a Program Is Going to Launch*

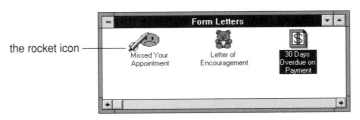

Access, will automatically launch whatever programs or documents you specify each time you start Windows. You must configure Quick Access to run at startup for the items specified in the AutoStart group to be run automatically.

Suppose you want to open the Calculator, Microsoft Excel, Ami Pro, and the Calendar each time you start Windows. To accomplish this, copy those items to the AutoStart group and make sure Quick Access is configured to load at startup. Application windows for each of these items will then be opened whenever you start Windows. This way, you can quickly switch between windows to work on whichever application you desire.

TIP

Be careful not to open two documents that will run the same program! Remember, it's dangerous to have a software program running in two different places at the same time. For example, don't make the mistake of placing a group icon for Ami Pro software together with a group icon for an Ami Pro document in the AUTOSTART group window. If you do, two versions of Ami Pro will be running at the same time—a situation definitely to be avoided.

To launch AutoStart applications each time you start Windows:

▲ Make sure Quick Access has been configured to load at startup (for instructions, see *An Overview of Quick Access* at the beginning of Chapter 2).

▲ Open the Quick Access window.

▲ Open the AutoStart group window by double-clicking on the AutoStart group icon in Quick Access.

▲ Drag all desired items into the AutoStart group window. You can drag a group icon, a desktop icon, or a program or document file name from a drive window to accomplish this.

▲ Choose Configure Save Configuration.

CHECK YOURSELF

Arrange your desktop so that Reversi is launched each time you start Windows.

1. Make sure that Quick Access is set to load at startup.

2. Open the Quick Access window, then the AutoStart group window.

3. Open the Games group window.

4. Drag the Reversi group icon into the AutoStart group window.

5. Choose Configure Save Configuration.

Creating File Associations

With a few exceptions (WordPerfect is one), most software programs automatically assign a file extension to their data files. For example, files with the extension .DOC are associated with Word for Windows, .SAM files with Ami Pro for Windows, .XLS files with Microsoft Excel, and .TXT files with Notepad. Whenever you see these extensions, you can be pretty sure the file belongs to the corresponding software program.

If the extension used by a Windows program is unique (that is, no other Windows programs use the same extension), Windows sets up a *file association* between the program and that extension. This means that Windows will always associate that extension with that program.

A software program can have more than one extension associated with it, but an extension can only be associated with one software program. For instance, you can have the extension .STY be associated with Ami Pro in addition to the extension .SAM. But then .STY and .SAM cannot be associated with any other program.

Sometimes, it might be convenient for you to associate a new file extension with a program (other than the standard one recognized by Windows). For instance, suppose you frequently write letters to Mr. Jones. All of your letters to Mr. Jones have the extension .MJ (notice that your extension can contain less than three letters), which lets you quickly group together these documents. If you created all of your letters to Mr. Jones with Ami Pro, you might want to associate the .MR extension with the Ami Pro software.

Creating File Associations

To create a new file association:

▲ Choose the Associate command from the File menu. The Associate dialog box appears, as shown in Figure 5.6.

▲ In the Extension box, type the extension you wish to associate with the given program. (Do not type a period, just the characters.)

▲ In the Associate With box, click on the executable file name of the program you wish the extension to be associated with. Alternatively, you can type in the executable file name (including its path) or click on the Browse button and search though the subsequently listed files to locate the right executable file.

▲ Click the OK button. The extension will now be associated with the software program.

TIP

Once you have associated a file extension with a software program, you can double-click on any document with that extension in a drive window to automatically run the associated software and open the document.

▼ *Figure 5.6. The Associate Dialog Box*

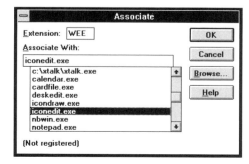

QUICK SUMMARY

Command	*To Do This*
File Open	Open an existing document and run its associated program or run only a program.
File Run	Open an existing document and run its associated program or run only a program.
File Associate	Create a new association between a program and a file extension that you designate.

PRACTICE WHAT YOU'VE LEARNED

Launch the Windows Setup program using the Open command, then open any data file from a drive window. Next, create a file association between the file extension .NEW and the Notepad application.

1. Open the group window that contains the Windows Setup icon, then click on that icon once.

2. Choose File Open.

3. Open a drive window, then double-click on any data file in the file pane.

4. Choose File Associate.

5. In the Extension box in the Associate dialog box, type **NEW**.

6. In the Associate With box, click on notepad.exe. If this file is not showing, click on the Browse button and search through the subsequently displayed files until it appears.

7. Click the OK button.

6

Recovering Deleted Files

If you have had any previous experience with computers, then at some point you've probably deleted a file you shouldn't have. You weren't thinking, you accidentally entered the wrong file name, or you thought you really didn't need that file any longer. If only SmartErase had been running, you probably could have restored that deleted file! In this chapter, you will learn about the SmartErase feature, including how to:

▲ **Restore a deleted file**

▲ **Display older versions of a deleted file**

▲ **Purge files from the Trashcan**

▲ **Customize SmartErase**

An Overview of SmartErase

In Chapter 4, you learned how to use SmartErase to quickly delete files. But SmartErase does much more than just delete files; in fact, you usually can restore a deleted file using SmartErase almost as quickly as you can delete a file. You can restore files that were deleted with another program. For example, if you regularly delete your files from the Ami Pro File Manager rather than from Norton Desktop, SmartErase can still restore those files, just as quickly as it restores files deleted using the SmartErase tool icon.

When you delete a file, it is placed in a directory called SMARTCAN (discussed below) where it can't be touched for the time being. As long as the file remains in this directory, it can be completely recovered. The file will eventually be tossed out of the directory, however, since SmartErase purges its files automatically after a certain number of days, which you specify in the Configure SmartErase dialog box.

You can tell SmartErase which type of files to save and which to ignore. You can also specify which hard drives you want protected, if you have more than one. Finally, you can determine how much disk space you want reserved for deleted files. You'll learn more about how to do all of this in *Configuring SmartErase,* later in this chapter.

If SmartErase is not currently running on your system, you'll get a message to that effect each time you start Norton Desktop. If this is the case, your deleted files are *not* being protected.

So that they won't be overwritten, SmartErase stores all of your deleted files in SMARTCAN, a hidden directory also referred to as the *Trashcan.* So long as you have enough space on your disk for new files to be created without having to tap into the disk space reserved for the files in the SMARTCAN directory, recovery of all of your deleted files is a sure thing. But even if a file was purged from the Trashcan some weeks ago, there still is a good chance it can be retrieved, though some of its data may have been overwritten.

TIP

In this chapter, we'll often refer to the Trashcan, which is actually the SMARTCAN directory. The two terms are used synonymously.

The SmartErase Window

Whenever you want to retrieve deleted files, list older versions of deleted files, or purge old files in the SMARTCAN directory, you must open a SmartErase window. You can quickly display this window on the desktop by double-clicking the SmartErase tool icon or by choosing UnErase from the Tools menu. Figure 6.1 displays a SmartErase window for the Norton Desktop for Windows (NDW) directory. Does this window look familiar to you? It looks rather like a basic drive window, doesn't it? However, there's a basic difference: the files listed in this window are those that have been deleted.

In addition to their similar appearances, many of the menu commands that work in drive windows also work in the SmartErase window. For instance, you can use View menu commands to display a view pane or to sort the files in the file pane the same way you do in a drive window. The Show Entire Drive command is especially useful in the SmartErase window, since it will show you all the files on your drive that have been deleted.

Notice that some of the files listed in the SmartErase file pane in Figure 6.1 have question marks at the beginning of their names. Any file that starts with a question mark has been deleted, but it is not currently protected by SmartErase, which means that the file's data can be overwritten at any time.

To open a SmartErase window:

▲ Double-click the SmartErase tool icon.

or:

▲ Choose Tools UnErase. The SmartErase window will appear, as shown in Figure 6.1.

▼ *Figure 6.1. The SmartErase Window Closely Resembles a Drive
Window*

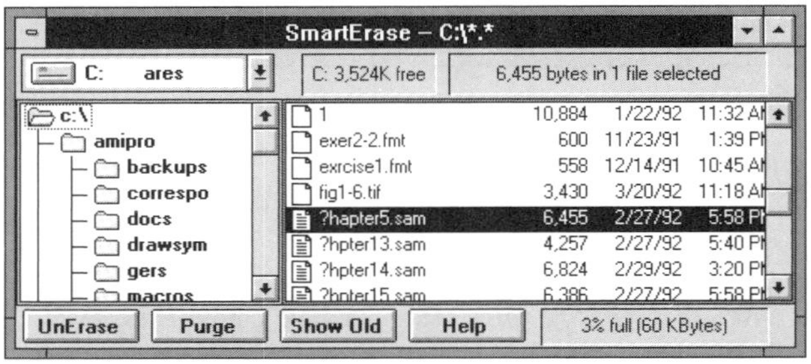

Drive windows and SmartErase windows share many common features. You can have as many SmartErase windows open as you'd like, and the drive selector in a SmartErase window works just as it does in a drive window. Similarly, the tree, file, and view panes can be displayed or removed from a SmartErase window. The view pane is especially helpful in the SmartErase window since you might not remember the contents of files that were deleted a long time ago or recognize files whose names have been altered by a question mark.

As always, the status bar displays current information on a drive's size, or on the size of certain files on that drive. You can use the same techniques to display and select files in the SmartErase window as you do in a drive window, including the Filter and Details commands and Speed Search. (Refer to Chapter 3 for more on displaying files and Chapter 4 for details on selecting files.)

There are also several features unique to the SmartErase window. Notice that a second status bar appears at the bottom right corner of the window. This bar tells you what percentage of the Trashcan is full and, in parentheses, the size of the Trashcan. The SmartErase button bar is quite different from the drive window button bar. Here you have buttons for unerasing, purging, and displaying old files. Table 6.1 outlines the functions of the SmartErase button bar commands.

▼ Table 6.1. SmartErase Window Button Bar Commands

An Overview of SmartErase

Button	Function
UnErase	Recovers the files that are currently highlighted in the drive window. If the file begins with a question mark, the SmartErase dialog box (Figure 6.2) will prompt you for the first letter of the file name. Type in any letter (preferably the original one).
Purge	Frees up disk space by purging all deleted files selected in the current SmartErase drive window.
Show Old	Displays all older (deleted) versions of a file, including entries that were deleted a long time ago.
Hide Old	Appears while you are in the Show Old mode. This command will return you to the default display, which shows only the most recent deleted version of a file.
Help	Brings up the SmartErase help index.

TIP

Remember, a deleted file is not protected if:

▲ **SmartErase is not running**

or:

▲ **the file doesn't match the criteria set up in the Configure SmartErase dialog box (see Configuring SmartErase later in this chapter)**

or:

▲ **SMARTCAN is overloaded (see Emptying the Trashcan later in this chapter)**

or:

▲ **The Shredder was used to delete the file.**

▼ Figure 6.2. SmartErase Dialog Box

CHECK YOURSELF

Open a SmartErase window for your hard drive and display the view pane.

1. Double-click the SmartErase tool icon or choose Tools UnErase.

2. Choose the appropriate drive in the drive selector, if the hard drive is not currently displayed.

3. Choose View View pane.

Restoring a Deleted File

The best time to recover a deleted file is immediately after the deletion takes place. If a file was deleted some weeks ago, some or all of its data may have been overwritten by other files, since that file lost foolproof protection when it was dumped from the Trashcan (remember that SmartErase purges SMARTCAN on a regular basis).

To recover an erased file:

▲ Double-click the SmartErase tool icon or choose UnErase from the Tools menu.

▲ Click on the appropriate directory in the tree pane, then search through the files in the file pane to see if you can locate the deleted file. Remember, the file's first letter may have been changed to a question mark. (Display the file's contents in the view pane if you're still not sure it's the right one.)

▲ Click on the deleted file to select it.

▲ Click the UnErase button to recover the file.

▲ If the first character in the deleted file name has been changed to a question mark, you will be asked to enter a new first letter in the SmartErase dialog box, as shown in Figure 6.2.

▲ Type any letter, then click the OK button. The erased file is now removed from the SmartErase window and restored to the regular drive window.

Restoring a Deleted File

You can now open a drive window to view the restored file; it will appear in its original directory.

TIP

If a drive window was already open, click the Refresh button; otherwise, the restored file will not be displayed.

If you want to open a file you've restored, don't do it by double-clicking on that file name if that file's original software program is already running. Instead, go into that application and Open File to access the restored file. Otherwise, two versions of the same program will be running simultaneously.

Be sure to examine the entire contents of a recovered file after you restore it. In some cases, only a portion of the file may be recovered, especially if you were trying to restore a file that was either deleted some time ago or deleted when SmartErase was not running. If part of the file has been overwritten or is missing, run UNERASE.EXE from the Norton Emergency Disk. This program collects bits and pieces of lost file data and may be able to restore some of the corrupted parts of your file.

CHECK YOURSELF

Delete the SOL.EXE file (the executable file for the Solitaire game), then recover it.

1. Open the appropriate hard drive window, then choose View Show Entire Drive.

2. Type **sol.exe** in the Speed Search box (which will appear when you type the first letter), then press **Enter**.

3. Drag the SOL.EXE file to the SmartErase icon, then click on Yes in the dialog box that appears. SOL.EXE is now deleted.

4. Double-click the SmartErase tool icon or choose UnErase from the Tools menu. A SmartErase window appears.

5. Find the SOL.EXE file, then select it.

6. Click the UnErase button.

7. Click the Refresh button in the original hard drive window. The restored SOL.EXE file will now appear in the file pane.

Looking Through the Trash

Each time you save a file, the previous version of that file, rather than being overwritten, actually becomes a deleted file. For instance, most word processors have an auto-save feature, which can save a file as often as once every minute. Suppose you've been working for six hours on a file called SAVE.ME, which your word processor saves every 10 minutes. That would be a total of 36 deleted files! And if you worked on the same file another six hours the next day, you would have 72 deleted files. What's more, if you have an auto-backup system on your word processor, each time you save SAVE.ME, two deleted files are created: one in the regular directory, and the other in the backup directory. If you reviewed all of the deleted versions of the SAVE.ME file in the Trashcan under these circumstances, you'd see something similar to the SmartErase window configuration seen in Figure 6.3. That's a lot of SAVE.ME files!

The Show Old command button on the SmartErase window allows you to see all older versions of a deleted file, or in some cases, all the deleted versions of a regular file. When you open a SmartErase window, you will see only the most recent version of a deleted file. This display makes sense because normally when you want to restore a deleted file, you want the file restored in its most recent configuration. Therefore, you only need to see the latest version of a file in the SmartErase window. However, there are times when you might want to see older versions of a file. To do so, you can use the Show Old button.

▼ *Figure 6.3. The Show Old Command in Action*

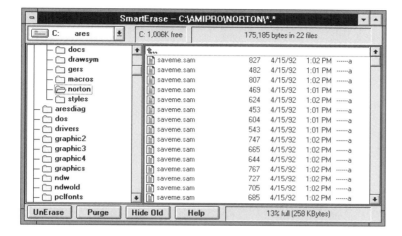

After you click the Show Old command button, the Hide Old command button takes its place. When you want to return to the regular display mode in which only the most recent version of a file is displayed, click the Hide Old button.

To see all older versions of a file:

▲ Open a SmartErase window.

▲ Select the appropriate directory in the tree pane.

▲ Click the Show Old button. Old versions of each file in the current directory will be displayed in the file pane.

TIP

When you use the Show Entire Drive command in the Show Old mode, keep in mind that only the older versions on that drive are displayed. That is, the most recent versions will not be displayed. This can be significant, for example, when you are planning to purge the SMARTCAN directory.

CHECK YOURSELF

First display the older versions of all files on a hard drive and then only the most recent versions.

1. Open a SmartErase window for the hard drive.

2. Choose View Show Entire Drive.

3. Click the Show Old button.

4. Click the Hide Old button.

Emptying the Trashcan

Each time you start Norton Desktop, SmartErase purges files from the Trashcan that have been held longer than the time limit specified in the Configure SmartErase dialog box (see the section below). SmartErase also purges old files when the storage limits you specify have been exceeded. In addition, you can purge files yourself.

To purge files from the SMARTCAN directory:

▲ Open a SmartErase window for the appropriate drive.

▲ In the tree pane, select the directory containing the files to be purged.

▲ In the file pane, select the files to be purged.

▲ Click the Purge button. A dialog box appears asking you to confirm the purge, as shown in Figure 6.4.

▲ Click on Yes to purge the files.

You can also purge entire directories and subdirectories. Just highlight the ones you wish to purge in the SmartErase window tree pane before clicking on Purge.

Earlier, you learned that files can build up fast in the Trashcan. You might want to purge the files from the SMARTCAN directory when you think a multitude of older versions are using up a lot of space. If you do so, use the Show Entire Drive and Select All commands to make the purge simpler. The status bar on the bottom of the SmartErase window will tell you how many bytes will be freed up when you purge all of the old files.

▼ *Figure 6.4. Click Yes to Purge All Files*

CHECK YOURSELF

Purge an old version of a deleted file.

1. Open a SmartErase window for the appropriate drive.

2. Click the Show Old button.

3. Select the file to be purged.

4. Click the Purge button.

Configuring SmartErase

You can instruct the SmartErase Trashcan to purge its contents on a regular basis or when its contents reach a certain level. You can also specify which files and drives SmartErase should protect, and even tell SmartErase to stop running. You can do all of this and more by making the appropriate selections in the Configure SmartErase dialog box, shown in Figure 6.5.

To access the Configure SmartErase dialog box:

▲ Choose Configure SmartErase. The dialog box seen in Figure 6.5 appears.

Disabling SmartErase

If you enabled SmartErase during the Norton Desktop installation process, the Enable SmartErase Protection check box will be selected when the Configure SmartErase dialog box appears.

▼ *Figure 6.5. The Configure SmartErase Dialog Box*

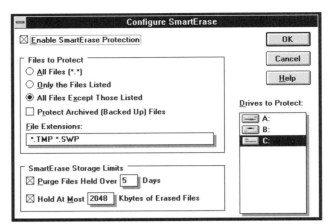

This check box lets you know whether your deleted files are being protected. Though we strongly advise against it, you can disable the SmartErase feature by deselecting the Enable SmartErase Protection check box. This will save disk space, but the potential consequences might not be worth it. When you disable SmartErase, deleted files will no longer be preserved, and protected files are not automatically purged to make room for new data.

Nevertheless, disabling SmartErase doesn't mean that you lose all of the SmartErase features. In fact, a file that has *just* been deleted can be immediately restored without any bad consequence. Additionally, you can still use the SmartErase window to purge files and to attempt to restore files that were deleted within the last few days, though recovery is no longer guaranteed.

To disable SmartErase:

▲ In the Configure SmartErase dialog box, deselect the Enable SmartErase Protection check box.

▲ Click the OK button. Your files will no longer be preserved by SmartErase.

TIP

Once you have disabled SmartErase and exited Norton Desktop, the only way you can reactivate SmartErase is by installing it in your AUTOEXEC.BAT file. The Enable SmartErase Protection check box will be dimmed (that is, inaccessible) if you start Windows without SmartErase running.

Choosing the Files You Want Protected

You can choose which files you want to be protected by SmartErase. First, you can specify which drives are to be protected, then you can specify all files on the drives, only the files that you list, or only the files that you *don't* list to be protected. By default, all files on each hard drive are protected, except those that have been backed up and those with the extensions .TMP and .SWP (which are Windows temporary swap files and need not be protected because you will never need to restore them). If you wish to specify other groups of files *not* to be protected, you can do so easily.

To specify additional groups not to be protected:

▲ Make sure the All Files Except Those Listed option is selected in the Configure SmartErase dialog box. (This option is selected by default.)

▲ After the last extension in the File Extensions box, press the **Spacebar**, type *., then the new file extension, so that it looks something like *.BAK. You can enter up to nine extensions.

▲ Click the OK button. The new group of files will no longer be protected.

TIP

We suggest you add .BIN, .DAT, .QAG, and .GRP files to the .TMP and .SWP file extensions already listed in the File Extensions box. Doing so will speed up your system response time.

If you prefer to list the files you *do* want protected rather than those you do not want protected, you can accomplish this by selecting a different option in the Files To Protect box.

To specify only certain groups of files you want protected:

▲ Click the Only the Files Listed option in the Configure SmartErase dialog box.

▲ Remove existing file extensions from the File Extensions box by highlighting them, then pressing **Delete** (if you don't want those files protected).

▲ In the File Extensions box, type *., the file extension for each group of files you want protected, then press the **Spacebar**. You can enter up to nine extensions.

▲ Click the OK button. Only the group(s) of files specified will be protected.

TIP

If you follow the above steps to specify which files to protect, delete the .TMP and .SWP file extensions when specifying files you want protected. Otherwise, needless disk space will be used to save temporary swap files, and your system response time will lag as well.

At this point you might say: forget all the fuss, just protect *all* of my files! Telling SmartErase to guard all of your files is simple to do but not recommended because it will slow down your system and lessen the number of files you can restore with 100-percent accuracy.

To protect all files on your drive(s):

▲ Click the All Files (*.*) option in the Configure SmartErase dialog box.

▲ Click the OK button. All of the files on your drive(s) will now be protected.

By default, archived files (files that have been backed up) are not protected by SmartErase. SmartErase figures that since you can simply recover a file from its backup, there's no need to protect the file. However, you may disagree; if so, you can tell SmartErase to protect all of your backed up files as well.

Configuring SmartErase

To protect backed-up (archived) files:

▲ In the Configure SmartErase dialog box, select the check box next to Protect Archived (Backed Up) Files.

▲ Click the OK button. Backed-up files will now be protected by SmartErase.

TIP

Remember, choosing to protect all files on your drive, including files that have already been backed up, will cause the Trashcan to fill up much faster than it would under the default settings. Older files will be purged sooner, giving you less time to recover files with 100-percent accuracy, and your system will slow down as it works to save a huge number of erased temporary (.TMP) files.

CHECK YOURSELF

Protect your files that have the extensions .SAM, .WK1, and .DOC, as well as all archived files.

1. Choose Configure SmartErase.

2. Click the Only the Files Listed option in the Configure SmartErase dialog box.

3. Delete the .TMP and .SWP file extensions from the File Extensions box by highlighting them, then pressing **Delete**.

4. In the File Extensions box, type ***.SAM *.WK1 *.DOC**.

5. Select the check box next to Protect Archived (Backed Up) Files.

6. Click the OK button.

Choosing the Drives You Want Protected

By default, files on your hard drives are protected, but files on your floppy drives are not. If you work with floppy diskettes on a regular basis, you should consider customizing SmartErase so that your floppy drive files are also protected.

To make a drive protected by SmartErase:

▲ In the Configure SmartErase dialog box, click on the drive you want protected in the Drives to Protect box. The drive becomes highlighted.

▲ Click the OK button. The selected drive(s) will now be protected.

TIP

You can also configure SmartErase not to guard one of your hard drives, if you have more than one. Deselect the drive(s) you don't want protected in the Drives to Protect box.

Put a Lid on It

SmartErase needs disk space for its SMARTCAN directory, but not an unlimited amount. You need to decide how large a Trashcan you want and how often files should be purged.

By default, SmartErase places a limit of two megabytes on the size of the SMARTCAN directory. In addition, SmartErase purges files from the Trashcan after they have resided there for five days. You can place a different limit on the SMARTCAN directory or alter how often files are purged, if you desire. For instance, if you want to minimize disk usage, make the SMARTCAN directory smaller by having SmartErase purge its files more frequently so that they don't continue to build up.

An alternative way to save disk space is to set aside only a small amount of space for the erased files in SMARTCAN (16 kilobytes is the smallest amount you can reserve). But it is generally a better idea to manipulate the size of the Trashcan by emptying its contents more frequently, rather than by limiting its size. The reason for this is that if you limit the Trashcan's size, when you delete a large file, many of the files currently residing in the Trashcan will be dumped to make room for the big newcomer. If you have the Trashcan emptied every few days as a way of controlling its size, the current files in the Trashcan will not be dumped automatically when a new one is added.

To specify the amount of time deleted files should remain in the SMARTCAN directory:

▲ In the Configure SmartErase dialog box, select the check box next to Purge Files Held Over [5] Days, if necessary.

▲ Place the insertion point before the number 5, then type the number of days you wish files to remain in the SMARTCAN directory.

▲ Press **Delete** to remove the old number (5).

▲ Click the OK button.

Remember, the smaller the number, the smaller amount of used disk space. However, your chances of restoring older files with 100-percent accuracy also decreases.

When the Purge Files Held Over [X] Days check box is deselected, only the Trashcan's size limitations will affect how frequently files are purged. When the SMARTCAN directory reaches its limit (2M by default), SmartErase begins purging the files that have been protected for the longest period. In other words, the earliest files deleted will be the first to be purged.

To set a specific size limit on the SMARTCAN directory:

▲ In the Configure SmartErase dialog box, select the check box next to Hold At Most [2048] Kbytes of Erased Files, if necessary.

▲ Double-click in the Kbytes box so that the number 2048 is highlighted.

▲ Type the desired size in kilobytes for the SMARTCAN directory.

▲ Click the OK button. The SMARTCAN directory will now automatically purge some of its files when the specified number of kilobytes has been exceeded.

Configuring SmartErase

TIP

If you limit the Trashcan size to less than 16 kilobytes, the number you specify will not be accepted. Instead, the number 16 will show in the Kbytes box, since the lowest size acceptable for the Trashcan is 16 kilobytes.

CHECK YOURSELF

Instruct Norton Desktop to purge files after they have been held in the SMARTCAN directory for four days.

1. Make sure the Purge Files Held Over [x] Days check box is selected.

2. Place the insertion point before the number specified in the box.

3. Type **4**.

4. Press **Delete**.

5. Click the OK button.

QUICK SUMMARY

Command	*To Do This*
Tools UnErase, SmartErase icon	Open a SmartErase window.
UnErase button (on SmartErase button bar)	Recover a deleted file.
Purge button (on SmartErase button bar)	Purge files from the Trashcan.
Show Old button (on SmartErase button bar)	Display all older (deleted) versions of a file in the SmartErase window.
Hide Old button (on SmartErase button bar)	Display only the most recent version of a deleted file in the SmartErase window.
Configure SmartErase	Modify SmartErase settings, such as Trashcan size, the purge schedule, and which files and drives are to be protected.

PRACTICE WHAT YOU'VE LEARNED

Do not protect files containing the extensions .BIN, .DAT, .QAG, and .GRP. Purge *all* old versions of every deleted file on a drive.

1. Choose Configure SmartErase.

2. Make sure the All Files Except Those Listed option is selected.

3. After the last extension in the File Extensions Box (probably .SWP), type ***.BIN *.DAT *.QAG *.GRP**.

4. Click the OK button.

5. Choose UnErase from the Tools menu or double-click the SmartErase tool icon to open a SmartErase window. Use the drive selector to switch to the appropriate drive, if necessary.

6. Choose View Show Entire Drive.

7. Click the Show Old button.

8. Choose Select All from the File menu.

9. Click the Purge button. A dialog box appears asking you to confirm the purge.

10. Click on Yes to confirm the purge.

Using the Viewer

Imagine shopping in a department store where all the merchandise is packaged in boxes or wrapped up with ribbons and bows. Each box is labeled with a description of its contents, such as Sweater (Women's) and Jeans (Men's). To find the brand, style, and size you're looking for, you must open box after box until you find the right item. Sound ridiculous? You'll do something similar on your computer if you're sorting through dozens of files to find a particular file whose name you've forgotten, or if you're deleting files from your hard drive and can't remember what data certain files contain. You'd have to open file after file to find what you're looking for. Worse yet, you'd have to run each program associated with each file before you could open that file.

Fortunately, Norton Viewer spares you from such wasted time. You can use the Viewer to take a peek at any file's contents without having to run its associated software program. In this chapter, you will learn about the Norton Viewer, including:

▲ **The types of files you can view**

▲ **How different viewers are used for different file types**

▲ **Selecting a file you want to view**

▲ **Manipulating graphics in the Viewer**

▲ **Changing the default viewer**

▲ **Viewing multiple files**

▲ **Finding text in a file you're viewing**

What Is Norton Viewer?

Norton Viewer allows you to display the contents of just about any file. You might not have realized it, but you were introduced to Norton Viewer in Chapter 3 when you displayed the view pane in a drive window. And in the last chapter, you used the Norton Viewer to view the pane of a SmartErase window. Yet the Viewer is capable of much more than just operating within another window. In fact, there's a good chance you'll use the Viewer most often on its own, as shown in Figure 7.1.

Most software applications do not have file viewing capabilities, which means that if you want to see the contents of a file, you first have to run the application used to create it, then open the file. This can become quite time consuming if you're viewing files created with different programs. For example, imagine trying to find a certain Excel spreadsheet whose data matches the data in an Ami Pro table. Suppose you were also planning to import a Corel Draw graphic into that same Ami Pro document, but you can't remember the name of the Excel file you're searching for, and you aren't sure which graphic you want to use. You'd have to exit Ami Pro, run Excel, open each spreadsheet until you found the right one, then start Ami Pro again to compare the table with the spreadsheet that you *think* is right. Then, you would have to run Corel Draw and search for the image you want.

▼ *Figure 7.1. The Viewer's Own Window*

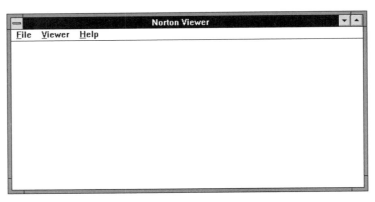

On the other hand, with Norton Viewer you can look inside word-processed, graphics, spreadsheet, and database files *without* having to start the applications they're associated with. What's more, you can open any combination of these file types at one time, because you can open as many document windows in the Viewer as you want, as shown in Figure 7.2. As for the above example, with Norton Viewer you wouldn't have to run *any* of the specified applications, and you could compare the Excel spreadsheet and the Ami Pro table at the same time.

Even if a software application does have file viewing capabilities (such as WordPerfect for Windows), you usually cannot view graphics files, or even tables in some cases. You certainly wouldn't be able to look at the contents of compressed and executable files, as you can in Norton Viewer.

Beyond just viewing a file's contents, Norton Viewer also lets you locate a particular piece of text within a file. This could be helpful if a particular word or phrase is certain to make a file's identity clear to you when its name fails to do so.

What Is Norton Viewer?

▼ *Figure 7.2. You Can Open as Many Files as Your System Memory Will Support*

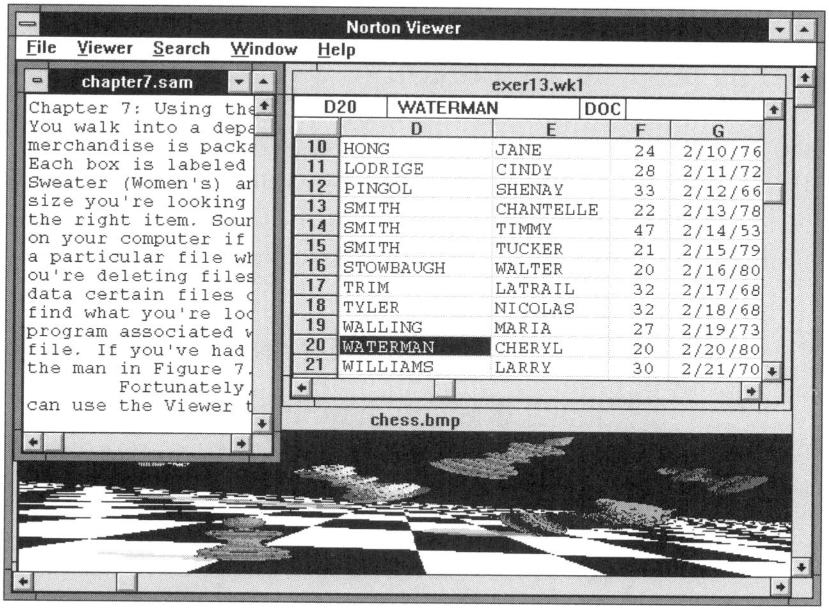

Types of Files You Can View

With Norton Viewer, you can view just about any file you work with, including word-processed, graphics, spreadsheet, database, executable, and *compressed files*. A compressed file is a file whose size has been reduced by code alterations to save disk space. You'll appreciate the ability to view compressed files, since Norton backup files are always compressed. This way, instead of decompressing a backup to reveal its contents, then having to recompress it, you can use the Viewer to view the backup while it's still compressed.

File Viewers

Norton Desktop uses *file viewers* to let you view files from more than 70 software applications. A file viewer filters and interprets codes from a file's application to make them usable by the Viewer. For example, the Lotus 1-2-3 file viewer allows you to view files created in 1-2-3, and the Compressed Archives viewer allows you to look at the contents of compressed files. The file viewers appear in the Set Default Viewer dialog box (shown in Figure 7.3).

File Types and Extensions

When you select a file to be viewed, Norton Viewer determines what type of file is selected, then determines which file viewer to use. Table 7.1 shows the different types of files you can view, along with corresponding software applications for each file type.

▼ *Figure 7.3. File Viewers Listed in the Set Default Dialog Box*

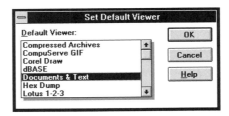

TIP

The following table contains a sample of software applications. Keep in mind that your Set Default Viewer dialog box might show viewers for applications not listed below. Also, the dialog box might not show viewers for some of the applications in the Table unless those applications are installed on your system.

▼ *Table 7.1. File Types and Associated Applications*

File Type	Software Applications
Word Processor	Ami & Ami Pro for Windows
	Word & Word for Windows
	WordPerfect & WordPerfect for Windows
	Windows Write
	ASCII text files
Graphic	CompuServe GIF
	Corel Draw
	Micrografx Designer & Draw
	Paintbrush (PCX)
	TIFF (Grayscale & Color)
	Windows Metafile, Bitmap, & Icon
	WordPerfect Clipart & Image Graphics
Spreadsheet	Lotus 1-2-3
	Microsoft Excel
	Quattro Pro
Database	dBASE
	Paradox
Compressed	PKZIP & PKPAK
	SEA ARC
	ZOO
	LZH
Executable (Program)	DOS & Windows Executables

CHECK YOURSELF

Which types of files can you display in the Viewer, and where can you find which file viewers are installed on your system?

▲ You can display word-processed, graphics, spreadsheet, database, compressed, and executable files in the Viewer. The Set Default Viewer dialog box displays all of your file viewers.

Selecting a File You Want to View

You can select a file either before you start Norton Viewer, or after it is already running. The most expedient method is to select a file first, in which case the file is instantly displayed when the Viewer starts. You can select a file in a drive window and then start the Viewer, or you can drag a file name from the drive window to the Viewer icon. On the other hand, you will often want to display multiple files in the Viewer; under these circumstances, you can use the Viewer's File menu to view each file.

To start Norton Viewer, without first selecting a file:

▲ Double-click on the Viewer tool icon. The Viewer appears. Follow the instructions (later in this section) on how to view a file once the Viewer is already running.

To start Norton Viewer after you have selected a file:

▲ Drag the file from the drive window to the Viewer tool icon.

or:

▲ Select the file in a drive window, then choose File View.

In both cases, the file will appear in a document window within Norton Viewer, as shown in Figure 7.4.

▼ *Figure 7.4. File Displayed in a Document Window Inside Norton Viewer*

Selecting a File You Want to View

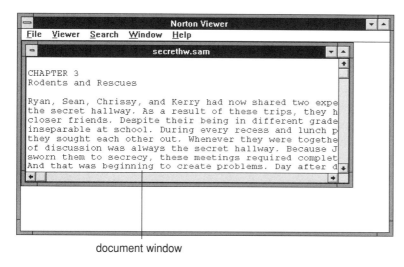

document window

TIP

You can also start Norton Viewer by choosing Run from the File menu, then entering *NVIEWER* in the Command Line box.

To view a file when Norton Viewer is already running:

1. Choose Open from the Viewer File menu. The Open File dialog box appears, as shown in Figure 7.5.

2. Click on the appropriate drive if the file you want to view is on a different drive.

3. Click on the file's directory in the Tree box.

4. Click on the file in the Files box.

5. Click the OK button. The file appears in a document window within Norton Viewer.

If you know the complete path of the file you want to view, you can skip Steps 2 through 4 by entering the file name (including its path) in the File box. To view multiple files, repeat the steps above for each file. Or you can drag each file name from the Files box to the Viewer icon.

To exit (close) the Viewer:

▲ Choose Exit from the Viewer File menu or double-click on the Control menu box.

TIP

If you want to leave the Viewer temporarily, without losing the data displayed in it, click on the Viewer's Minimize button rather than exiting. The Viewer is unique in that when you minimize it, an icon does not appear at the bottom of your desktop. To restore the minimized Viewer, double-click on the Viewer icon.

CHECK YOURSELF

Start the Viewer, view the REVERSI.EXE FILE, then close the Viewer. View the REVERSI.EXE file again, this time by selecting the file first.

1. Double-click on the Viewer tool icon.

2. Choose Open from the Viewer File menu.

3. Type **REVERSI.EXE**, including its path (usually C:\WINDOWS \REVERSI.EXE) in the File box, or select the file name in the Files box.

4. Click the OK button. (Alternatively for Steps 1–3, you can choose File View, then type **C:\WINDOWS\REVERSI.EXE** in the View box.)

5. Choose Exit from the Viewer File menu, or double-click on the Control menu box.

6. Drag the REVERSI.EXE file from a drive window to the Viewer icon.

Viewing and Copying Graphic Images

Norton Viewer handles graphics files differently than other types of files. You can copy the contents of a graphics file to the Clipboard. Also, when you open a graphics file in the Viewer, the image will often appear in only a small portion of the document window, in the upper-left corner, as shown in the top-left window of Figure 7.5. You can then enlarge, reduce, and zoom in on the image. You can also adjust the image to fit the entire window, as shown in the bottom-left window of Figure 7.5, or alter the window to fit the image, as displayed in the bottom-right window of Figure 7.5. Additionally, you can zoom in on the graphic to see a portion of it, as shown in the top-right window of Figure 7.5.

What you'll appreciate even more than the ability to manipulate the display size of the graphic is that you can copy the graphic in any size or shape to the Clipboard, then use it later in other Windows applications. For instance, if you wanted to copy only a portion of the graphic in Figure 7.5, you could modify the document window so that it appears similar to the upper-right window in the figure, then copy it to the Clipboard.

Viewing and Copying Graphic Images

▼ *Figure 7.5. You Can Enlarge, Reduce, or Zoom in on a Graphic*

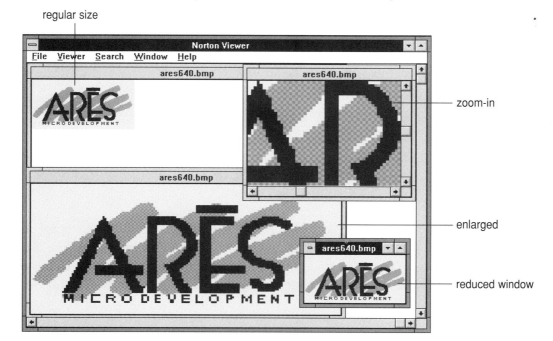

Changing the Size and Shape of the Image

To make the procedures below easier to follow, you should open a graphics file in the Viewer, such as PAPER.BMP, located in the WINDOWS directory. In general, when working with graphics files in the Viewer, you should not maximize the document window in which the graphic appears; otherwise, some of the zooming and sizing procedures below may not work consistently.

To make the graphic fill the entire document window:

▲ Double-click anywhere on the image. It will now fill the entire document window, as shown in the bottom-left window of Figure 7.5.

To zoom in on a particular area:

▲ Press the mouse button (so that a cross appears) in the upper-left corner of the area you want to zoom in on.

▲ Drag the mouse button to the lower-right corner of the target area. A box forms around the area, as shown in Figure 7.6.

▲ Release the mouse button. The portion you specified will now fill the entire window, as shown in Figure 7.6.

To change the shape of an image:

▲ Double-click on the image in its original state so that it fills the whole document window.

▲ Move the sides and/or corners of the document window until the image appears as you prefer. Each time you alter the size of the window, the image will be distorted accordingly, as displayed in Figure 7.7.

Changing the shape of the image is helpful if you want to copy the image into a document in a different form than the original. When you copy an image, it will be imported into the new document looking exactly the way it does in the Viewer.

▼ *Figure 7.6. Zooming In on the Image*

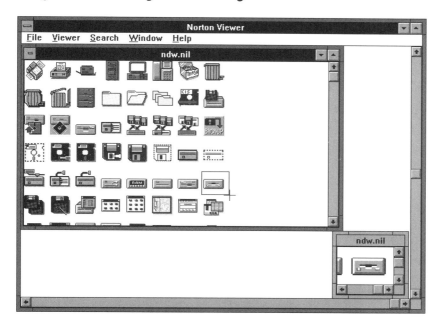

▼ *Figure 7.7. Changing the Shape of the Image*

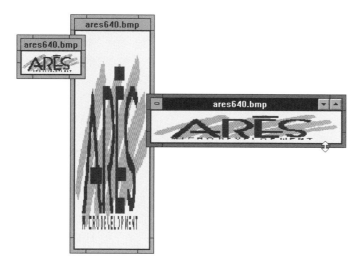

To make the window fit the image size:

▲ Click the *right* mouse button anywhere in the window.

Clicking the right mouse button does more than just make the window fit around the image. If you've altered the shape of an image and later decide that you want the original form back, clicking the right mouse button will restore the image to its original shape. Also, if you change your mind again and want to return to the modified shape, clicking the right mouse button again will restore that shape. Clicking the right mouse button works like a toggle between the two forms.

Copying Graphics to the Clipboard

As we mentioned earlier, you can copy a whole image or a portion of it, in any shape, to the Clipboard. First you have to design the image in the Viewer the way you want it to appear in the document you'll eventually be copying it into, then execute the copy.

TIP

You can copy a graphics image (whole or partial) from the view pane of a drive window to the Clipboard in the same way you copy it from the Viewer—except that you cannot copy an altered shape, because you cannot alter an image's shape in the view pane.

To copy the entire graphics image:

▲ Display the graphics image fully in the document window.

▲ Press **Ctrl+Insert**.

To copy a portion of an image:

▲ Display the portion of the image you want to copy in the window, following the steps specified earlier in this section.

▲ Press **Ctrl+Insert**.

TIP

You can immediately copy a portion of an image to the clipboard by holding down the Ctrl key while you define the area to be copied using the mouse.

When you're ready to insert the copied image into a new file, move the insertion point to where you want to place the image and press **Shift+Insert**. You can also use the Paste command to insert the copied image.

CHECK YOURSELF

Open BOXES.BMP (located in the WINDOWS directory) in the Viewer, then alter its shape to match the three different shapes seen in Figure 7.7.

1. Drag the file from a drive window to the Viewer icon, or choose Open from the Viewer File menu and select the file.

2. Double-click on the image so that it fills the entire document window.

3. Drag the bottom bar of the window up so that the image resembles the right window in Figure 7.7.

4. Drag the bottom bar back down, then drag the right side of the window in toward the left side, so that the image resembles the middle window in the figure.

5. Drag the bottom bar up so that the image resembles the left image in the figure.

Changing Viewers

If Norton Desktop is unfamiliar with a file's extension, it will select the *default viewer* to display the file. The default viewer is usually Documents & Text, which will work fine in most situations. However, suppose you were going to view dozens of Corel Draw drawings to which you gave the extension .AAA to make them easy to identify. Since the extension is not .CDR, the Corel Draw file viewer will not automatically recognize them. Rather, the default viewer (Documents & Text) will be used, and this won't work! Thus, you would need to change the default viewer to Corel Draw to view the graphics files.

To change the default viewer:

▲ Choose Configure Default Viewer. The Set Default Viewer dialog box appears.

▲ Scroll through the Default Viewer box and click on the appropriate viewer.

▲ Click the OK button. The specified viewer will now be the default viewer.

TIP

You can also change the default viewer from within the Viewer by choosing the Set Default Viewer command from the View menu.

CHECK YOURSELF

From within Norton Viewer, change the default viewer to *Compressed Archives*.

1. Double-click the Viewer tool icon to start Norton Viewer.

2. Choose Set Default Viewer from the Viewer's View menu.

3. Scroll through the Default Viewer box, then click on *Compressed Archives*.

4. Click the OK button.

Viewer Mania

One great feature about the Viewer is its ability to open more than one document window, which means that you can compare different sections of the same file at once, as shown in Figure 7.8, or you can compare different files at the same time, as shown in Figure 7.9. Comparing different files can be especially helpful if, for example, you're reviewing a financial report and wish to refer to data in related spreadsheets at the same time.

You can organize multiple windows in different ways using commands from the Viewer's Window menu. Each time you open a new window, it is placed on top of the current one, in a cascaded fashion. However, you'll most likely want to see parts of each file fully on the screen in a tiled format.

▼ *Figure 7.8. Viewing Two Parts of the Same Document in a Tiled Arrangement*

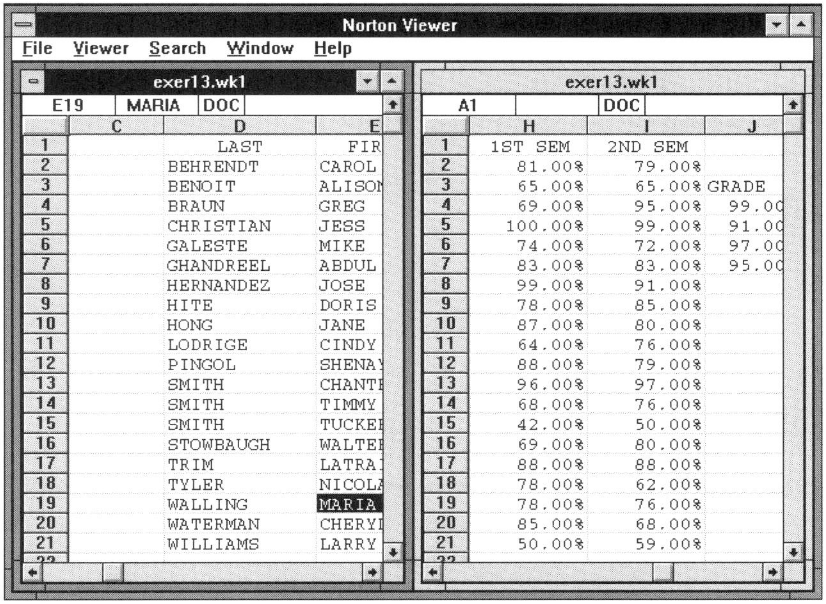

▼ *Figure 7.9. Minimized Windows Are Displayed as Icons at the Bottom of the Viewer*

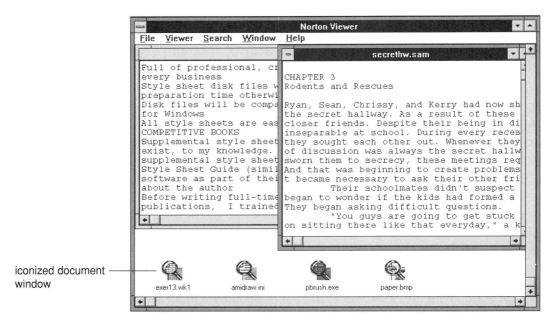

iconized document window

To tile multiple windows:

▲ Choose Tile from the Viewer's Window menu. The Viewer will look something like Figure 7.8.

When you are ready to close a document window, first make sure it is the active window.

To close a window:

▲ Choose Close from the Viewer's File menu.

TIP

If you want to close a window only temporarily to make more room for others, minimize the window rather than close it. The window will be reduced to an icon at the bottom left of the Viewer, as shown in Figure 7.9. Then, when you wish to view it again, double-click on the icon to restore the document window.

CHECK YOURSELF

Open three files in the Viewer, tile them, then close one and minimize another. Next, restore the minimized window.

1. Choose Open from the Viewer File menu.

2. Click on the appropriate file in the Files box, then click the OK button. Repeat Steps 1 and 2 until all three files are open.

3. Choose Tile from the Viewer's Window menu.

4. Choose Close from the Viewer's File menu.

5. Click on the Minimize button of one of the windows.

6. Double-click on the icon to restore the document window.

Finding Text in a File You're Viewing

Perhaps there's one item in a file you're viewing—a name, place, or phrase—that will identify that file for you. For instance, suppose you're viewing letters addressed to I. B. Smart, trying to find a letter that references a particular case number. The problem is that each of the eight letters addressed to Mr. Smart is more than five pages long. You would have to scroll through each file in search of the correct letter, if it weren't for the Viewer's search features.

Using the Search menu, you can instantly locate a particular item of text within a file—saving you a lot of scrolling. In fact, Viewer is so smart that you can search for text in spreadsheet and database files, as well as word processor files.

TIP

You can use similar searching procedures to those discussed below in the view pane of a drive window. Choose the Find, Find Next, Find Previous, and Goto commands from the View Viewer menu instead.

To search a text file:

▲ With the file displayed in an active document window within the Viewer, choose Find from the Viewer's Search menu. The Find dialog box appears, as shown in Figure 7.10.

▲ Type the word, phrase, or number you're searching for in the Find box.

▲ Click on the Match Upper/Lowercase check box to find only those occurrences that match upper- and lowercase letters in the word or phrase in the Find box.

▲ Click the OK button.

The search will begin with the first word showing in the document window. If you want to search the entire document, make sure you choose the Find menu command at the beginning of the document. On the other hand, if you want to start the search on page 2, for example, scroll to either of those pages before choosing the Find menu command.

If you are searching databases and spreadsheets, a different dialog box will appear when you choose the Find command (see Figure 7.11). You can specify the search to begin at a particular cell or field and record if you wish. You can also have the search look through only one column, row, record, or field to find a specified item. This is a valuable feature when you are searching through the records of a database to find a particular name or city.

To search a spreadsheet or database file:

1. With the file displayed in an active document window within the Viewer, choose Find from the Viewer's Search menu. The Find dialog box appears, as shown in Figure 7.11.

▼ *Figure 7.10. Find Dialog Box When You Are Searching Text Files*

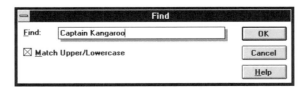

Finding Text In a File You're Viewing

▼ *Figure 7.11. Find Dialog Box When You Are Searching Spreadsheet or Database Files*

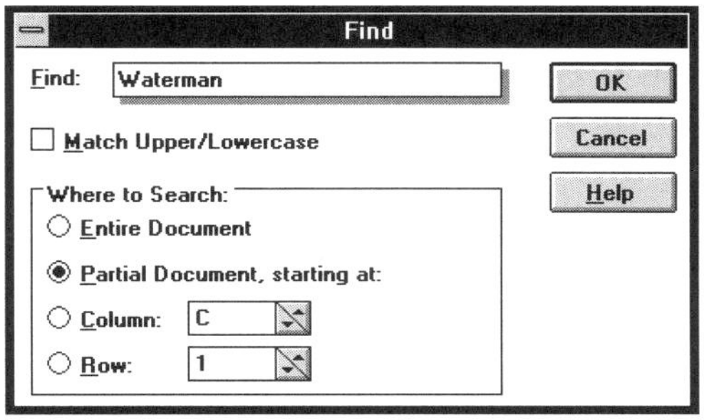

2. Type the word, phrase, or number you're searching for in the Find box.
3. Click on the Match Upper/Lowercase check box to find only those occurrences that match upper- and lowercase letters in the word or phrase in the Find box.
4. In the Where to Search box, indicate where you would like to begin the search. If you want the entire file to be searched, click on Entire Document. If you want to search only a portion of the document, click on one of the following options:

    ▲ Partial Document, starting at: Choose this option if you want use *both* of the items below to specify where the search should begin. It will search to the right and below the coordinate specified.

    ▲ Column: (Field:) Choose this option only if you wish to search one column in a spreadsheet, or one field in a database.

    ▲ Row: (Record:) Choose this option only if you wish to search one row in a spreadsheet, or one record in a database.

5. Click the OK button.

TIP

If you click on the cell in a spreadsheet or database file you wish a partial search to begin with, the coordinates will automatically be entered in the Column and Row boxes for a spreadsheet, or the Record and Field boxes for a database.

When searching through a file, the search pauses whenever a match is found, and the matching item is highlighted. To continue to search forward, choose the Find Next command (accessed from the Search). To search backward through the document, choose the Find Previous command. If there are no matching occurrences, a dialog box is displayed that reads "No occurrences found."

If you already know the coordinates for a particular cell in a spreadsheet you want to go to, you can get there quickly using the Viewer's Goto command. Similarly, you can use the command to go to a specific field and record in a database file.

To go to a particular cell in a spreadsheet or record in a database:

▲ With the file displayed in an active document window within the Viewer, choose Goto from the Viewer's Search menu. The Goto dialog box appears, as shown in Figure 7.12.

▲ Specify the desired column and row for a spreadsheet, or the field and record for a database.

▲ Click the OK button. The specified coordinate will be displayed in the document window.

▼ *Figure 7.12. Goto Dialog Box*

QUICK SUMMARY

Command	To Do This
File View, or Viewer tool icon	Start Norton Viewer.
Viewer: File Open	View a file in the Viewer.
Viewer: File Exit	Close the Viewer.
Viewer: Ctrl+Insert	Copy a graphics image to the Clipboard.
Configure Default Viewer	Change the default file viewer.
Viewer: View Set Default Viewer	Change the default file viewer while you're working in the Viewer.
Viewer: Window Tile	Tile document windows within the Viewer.
Viewer: File Close	Close a document in the Viewer.
View Viewer Find	Find a word, phrase, or number in a file you're viewing in a drive window view pane.
View Viewer Find Next	Go to the next occurrence of the word, phrase, or number in a file you're viewing in a drive window view pane.
View Viewer Find Previous	Go to the previous occurrence of the word, phrase, or number in a file you're viewing in a drive window view pane.
View Viewer Goto	Go to a specific location in a spreadsheet or database file you're viewing in a drive window view pane.
Viewer: Search Find	Find a word, phrase, or number in a file you're viewing in the Viewer.
Viewer: Search Find Next	Go to the next occurrence of the word, phrase, or number in a file you're viewing in the Viewer.
Viewer: Search Find Previous	Go to the previous occurrence of the word, phrase, or number in a file you're viewing in the Viewer.
Viewer: Search Goto	Go to a specific location in a spreadsheet or database file you're viewing in the Viewer.

PRACTICE WHAT YOU'VE LEARNED

Copy the 3-1/2-inch floppy drive icon, seen in Figure 7.6, from the NDW.NIL file into any Windows document that supports bit-mapped graphics.

1. In a hard drive window, locate the NDW.NIL file by clicking on the NDW subdirectory in the tree pane and then typing **ndw.nil** in the file pane (the Speed Search box will appear when you type the first letter).

2. Drag the file over to the Viewer tool icon. The NDW.NIL file appears inside the Viewer.

3. Point to area at the upper-left of the 3-1/2-inch drive icon and drag the mouse so that a box appears around the icon.

4. Release the mouse button. The drive icon should now appear somewhat like the image in the bottom window in Figure 7.6 (except in a larger document window).

5. Press **Ctrl+Insert**.

6. Open a document in any software application that supports the importing of bit-mapped graphics and place the insertion point where you'd like the drive icon to appear. If necessary, perform any other setup steps required for importing graphics.

7. Press **Shift+Insert**. The drive icon is copied from the Clipboard into the new document.

Using SuperFind

Without having SuperFind available, an administrative assistant stares at her computer screen as her boss's recent words reverberate though her mind: *I want to see every file—letter, contract, invoice, spreadsheet— that contains the name Sosume, Inc.* Well, it's only a matter of sorting through some eight hundred filenames to find the ones she needs. With SuperFind available on the other hand, an editor tells her assistant: *Find every chapter file that contains the word "nit-picky" and change it to "petty."* The assistant smiles because she can easily find the files in a few minutes.

SuperFind searches can be as narrow as finding each read-only Quattro Pro file beginning with the letter S that was created before March 20, 1991, at 4:30 p.m on hard drive F, or as broad as looking for all program files on all of your drives. What's more, SuperFind can tell you the names of all files whose contents contain a certain word, phrase, or number. In this chapter, you'll learn how to:

- ▲ **Find files by name**
- ▲ **Find files containing certain text**
- ▲ **Specify file attributes for SuperFind to look for**
- ▲ **Define SuperFind options**
- ▲ **Make SuperFind work in the background**

Finding Files

SuperFind is ideal for finding files you're looking for, based on file name or file content. For example, it can find all files with the characters EXPO in their names, or with the word Expo in their contents. The search can be as broad or as narrow as you wish. For instance, you can limit the search to two drives, to only specific directories on one drive, to a combination of drives and directories, or to myriad other locations.

If you have a particularly long search to perform, you can make SuperFind work in the background while you work on other documents. There are also certain tricks that will speed up the search.

When SuperFind locates all of the files you specified, it places them in a drive window. You can then treat the files as any other group of files that would appear in a drive window. You can move, copy, delete, rename, sort, print, or view the files following the procedures outlined in Chapter 4, *Managing Your Files*.

Opening and Exiting from the SuperFind Dialog Box

You will define your search by making selections and choosing menu commands in the SuperFind dialog box.

To open the SuperFind dialog box:

▲ Choose File Find. The SuperFind dialog box appears, as shown in Figure 8.1.

To exit SuperFind:

▲ Double-click on the SuperFind Control menu box, or choose Close from the Control menu.

▼ *Figure 8.1. SuperFind Dialog Box*

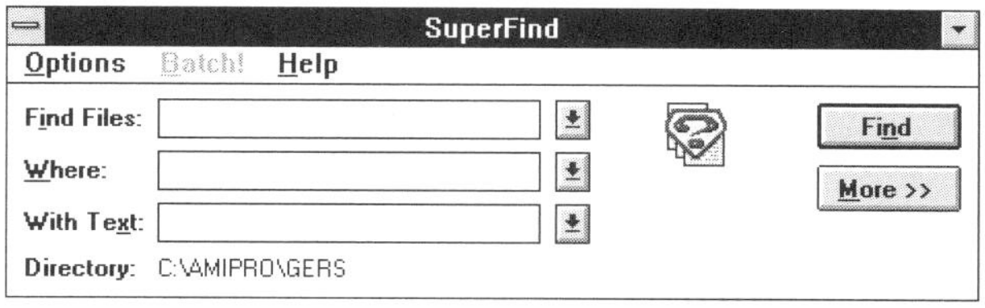

The SuperFind Dialog Box

Notice that three boxes are present in the dialog box: the first is for specifying which files you want to search for; the second for specifying where SuperFind should look; and the third for specifying text, if you wish SuperFind to search the contents of files for a word, phrase, or number. Understandably, this third type of search is often the lengthiest.

You can further define the search by choosing items from the Options menu. For example, you can enter a set of files to be searched and have SuperFind remember the set for future searches. Similarly, you can create a set of locations to be searched that will be remembered by SuperFind. The Batch! menu allows you to create a batch file for the files that SuperFind finds, but this option will not be covered here because it is beyond the scope of this book.

If you wish to restrict a search to files having specific file attributes, click on the More button. Clicking on More causes the SuperFind dialog box to expand, displaying new option boxes for file attributes, date and time of file creation, and file size, as shown in Figure 8.2.

To display search options for file attributes, date, time, or size:

▲ Click on the More button in the SuperFind dialog box. The dialog box appears similar to Figure 8.2.

To specify any of the file attributes or data options in a search, follow the procedures in *Including Attributes and Other File Data in the Search,* later in this chapter.

▼ *Figure 8.2. The Expanded SuperFind Dialog Box*

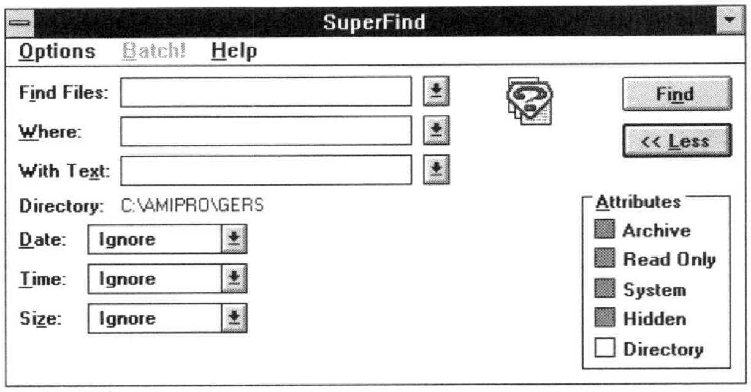

	SuperFind	▼
Options Batch! **Help**		

F**i**nd Files:

Where:

With Te**x**t:

Directory: C:\AMIPRO\GERS

Date: Ignore

Time: Ignore

Size: Ignore

Find

<< **Less**

Attributes
- Archive
- Read Only
- System
- Hidden
- Directory

TIP

The More button changes to Less when the SuperFind dialog box is expanded. By clicking on Less, you can hide the Date, Time, Size, and Attributes boxes again.

CHECK YOURSELF

Open the SuperFind dialog box and expand it to its full size. Then, change the dialog box back to its original size and exit SuperFind.

1. Choose File Find.

2. Click on the More button in the SuperFind dialog box.

3. Click on the Less button in the SuperFind dialog box.

4. Double-click on the SuperFind Control menu box, or choose Close from the Control menu.

Telling SuperFind Where to Look

SuperFind searches can be extensive or brief. You can narrow a search to one floppy drive or one subdirectory if you wish. On the other hand, you can search every directory on every drive if you really have no idea where a file or group of files is located. Of course, the narrower the search, the sooner the search will be done. So if you can eliminate even a few directories from the search, it will be to your benefit.

Norton Desktop provides you with *location sets,* which are predefined areas to be searched. For instance, one location set limits a search to the current directory only, while another limits the search to floppy drives. Figure 8.3 shows the location sets included with SuperFind. Using these predefined location sets can save you time by preventing SuperFind from searching areas you already know do not contain the files being sought.

If you want to narrow a search to a certain location, chances are that one of the location sets already represents that area. You can simply select the location set in the Where box.

To see which files are specified in a location set:

▲ Choose Search Sets from the Options menu.

▲ Click on the Location Sets option. The names of the predefined location sets appear on the left, and the corresponding areas to be searched are defined on the right, as shown in Figure 8.4.

To specify where SuperFind should search:

▲ Click on the Where box scroll button in the SuperFind dialog box.

▲ Select the appropriate location set by highlighting it in the Where box.

▼ *Figure 8.3. SuperFind Provides Nine Predefined Location Sets*

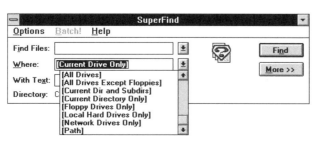

▼ *Figure 8.4. The Search Sets and Add Location Set Dialog Boxes*

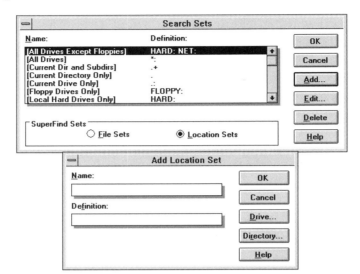

TIP

▲ If you want to limit the search to one particular drive or directory, you can type the letter or name in the Where box (for example, C:, or C:\AMIPRO\LETTERS).

▲ To search multiple drives, type a space after each drive letter and colon (for example, C: F: D:).

CHECK YOURSELF

Specify that you want all drives except floppies to be searched.

1. Click on the Where box scroll button in the SuperFind dialog box.

2. Select the [All Drives Except Floppies] location set from the Where pull-down list.

Creating New Location Sets

In some circumstances, none of the predefined location sets will adequately identify where you want SuperFind to search. In such cases, you can create a customized location set to be used. You can also save this location set for future searches. SuperFind can remember up to 16 location sets.

To create a customized location set:

1. Choose Search Sets from the SuperFind Options menu. The Search Sets dialog box appears. The Search Sets dialog box will be discussed in more detail in the next section.

2. Click on Location Sets. The Search Sets dialog box changes to show location sets, as shown in Figure 8.4.

3. Click on the Add button. The Add Location Set dialog box appears, as shown in Figure 8.4.

4. In the Name box, enter a descriptive name (up to 30 characters) for the location set (for example, Drives A and D).

5. Do one of the following to enter information in the Definition box:

   ▲ If you want to define drives only, click on the Drive button. The Select Drives to Search dialog box appears, as shown in Figure 8.5a. Mark the appropriate check box(es) in the Drive region or click on the drives individually. Corresponding drives become highlighted when you click on one of the drive check boxes, and drive letters representing the selected drives appear at the bottom of the box. Click the OK button. The selected drives now appear in the Definition box.

   ▲ If you want to define one directory only, click on the Directory button. The Select Directory to Search dialog box appears, as shown in Figure 8.5b. Scroll though the Directory box and click on the appropriate directory. Select the Include Subdirectories check box if you want to search subdirectories as well. Click the OK button. The directory now appears in the Definition box.

6. Click the OK button to save the new location set. The new set will appear in alphabetical order in the Name and Definition box.

7. Click the OK button to close the Search Sets dialog box.

▼ *Figure 8.5a. Select Drives to Search Dialog Box*

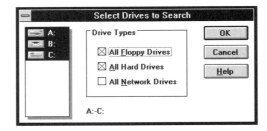

▼ *Figure 8.5b. Select Directory to Search Dialog Box*

You can create more complex location sets to meet your unique needs by following the guidelines above and using the existing Norton location sets as an example.

TIP

You can edit existing location sets by clicking on the Edit button in the Search Sets dialog box, then following procedures similar to those above for creating a new location set.

CHECK YOURSELF

Create a new location set to search floppy drive A.

1. Choose Search Sets from the SuperFind Options menu.

2. Click on Location Sets in the Search Sets dialog box.

3. Click on the Add button in the Search Sets dialog box.

4. In the Name box in the Add Location Set dialog box, type Floppy Drive A.

5. Click on the Drive button in the Add Location Set dialog box.

6. Click on floppy drive A in the Select Drives to Search dialog box, then click the OK button.

7. Click the OK button to save the new location set.

Telling SuperFind Where to Look

Telling SuperFind What to Search for

Now that you've told SuperFind where to search, it's time to tell it what to look for. A search can be as broad or narrow as you wish: from all database files to a few files created on a certain date after a specific time that are less than a designated size.

Norton Desktop provides you with a set of predefined *file sets* similar to the location sets just discussed. Each file set designates a particular group of files to be searched for, such as spreadsheet or program files. You can see the six available file sets and their related extensions in the Search Sets dialog box displayed in Figure 8.6.

▼ *Figure 8.6. The Search Sets Dialog Box, with File Sets Displayed*

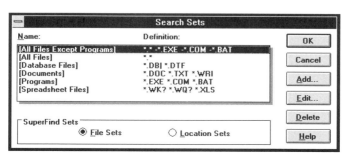

Finding Files by Name

You can search for files either by file name or by file contents. Follow the procedures below to perform a search based on file names. Later you'll learn how to search for files with certain text.

Selecting File Sets

To specify what files SuperFind should search for using a file set:

▲ Click on the Find Files box scroll button in the SuperFind dialog box. A pull-down list of file sets appears.

▲ Select the appropriate file set. The file set will now appear highlighted in the Find Files box.

CHECK YOURSELF

Specify that all files except programs be searched for.

1. Click on the Find Files box scroll button in the SuperFind dialog box.

2. Select the [All Files Except Programs] file set from the Find Files pull-down list.

Searching for Multiple and Customized Groups of Files

You can enter multiple groups directly in the Find Files box or in a file set, to be remembered for future searches. You might want to do this when searching for a group of files whose extensions are not associated with any software application and are not present in the existing file sets. You'll often want to use wildcard characters when specifying the groups to be searched for. For more on wildcard characters, refer to Chapter 3.

For example, if you used your initials (L.U.V.) as file extensions for a particular group of files, you could enter *.LUV in the Find Files box to search for those files.

You must follow certain guidelines when entering the file specifications. For example, to make SuperFind *not* search for a group of files, you place a hyphen (-) in front of the file specification.

If you plan to specify more than one group of files in the Find Files box or in the Definition box of the File Set dialog boxes, you must separate the specifications with one of the following separators (an example appears beside each separator):

Telling SuperFind What to Search for

▲ Space   (*.DOC *.SAM)

▲ Comma   (*.DOC,*.SAM)

▲ Plus sign   (*.DOC+*.SAM)

▲ Semicolon   (*.DOC;*.SAM)

▲ Hyphen (-)   (*.DOC-*.SAM)

The first four separators tell SuperFind to search for all of the listed groups. The hyphen, however, indicates that you do not want the group following the hyphen to be searched for. For example, if you want all files on a drive to be searched for except those with the extensions .WK? and .DB just this one time, you would type ***.*,-.WK?,-.DB** in the Find Files box. Or, to ensure that those files are never searched for, you could modify the [All Files] file set by typing **-.WK?,-.DB.** in the Find Files box.

CHECK YOURSELF

Modify the [Documents] file set so that it will search for files with the extension .SAM and not search files with the extension .BAK.

1. Click on the [Documents] file set in the Name box in the Search Sets dialog box.

2. Click on the Edit button.

3. In the Definition box, press the **Spacebar** after .WRI, then type ***.SAM -*.BAK**.

4. Click the OK button twice.

Creating New File Sets

The existing predefined file sets are quite general—all spreadsheets or all documents, for example. In all likelihood, you'll frequently search for a more specific group of files. If you are likely to search for these files often in the future, you should create a file set for this group so that you won't have to continually enter the file specifications in the Find Files box each time. As with location sets, SuperFind can remember up to 16 file sets.

To create a customized file set:

▲ Choose Search Sets from the SuperFind Options menu. The Search Sets dialog box appears.

▲ Click on the Add button. The Add File Set dialog box appears, as shown in Figure 8.7.

▲ In the Name box, enter a descriptive name (up to 30 characters) for the file set (for example, *Gone with the Rain* **Chapters).**

▲ In the Definition box, enter the name of the file or file specifications

▲ Click the OK button to save the new file set. The new set will appear in alphabetical order in the Name and Definition box.

▲ Click the OK button to close the Search Sets dialog box.

Editing File Sets

You might wish to modify one or more of the predefined file sets to include file extensions not currently associated with the file set. For example, the [Documents] file set is currently associated with the extensions .DOC, .TXT, and .WRI. But if you are running Ami Pro for Windows, your document files will not be searched for because Ami Pro documents have the extension .SAM, which the [Documents] file set is not currently associated with. Therefore, it would make sense to edit the [Documents] file set so that it will search for files with the extension .SAM.

▼ *Figure 8.7. The Add File Set Dialog Box*

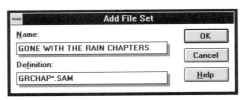

Additionally, you can remove a file extension from a file set. Using the same example, you would want to remove .DOC from the [Documents] file set since you aren't running Word for Windows. For very broad file sets, such as [All Files], you can instruct SuperFind *not* to look for a particular group of files by adding the extension you want ignored preceded by a hyphen. For example, if you don't want your backups included in an [All Files] search and your backups have the extension .BAK, you would enter **-*.BAK**.

Telling SuperFind What to Search for

To edit a file set:

▲ Click on the name of the file set you wish to modify in the Name box of the Search Sets dialog box.

▲ Click on the Edit button. The Edit File Set dialog box appears, showing the name and definition of the selected file set. (This dialog box is exactly the same as the Add File Set dialog box shown in Figure 8.7, except that the title is different.)

▲ In the Definition box, enter the new extension(s) to be associated or not associated with the file set.

▲ Click the OK button to save the new file set configuration.

▲ Click the OK button again to close the Search Sets dialog box.

TIP

You can quickly delete a file set or location set by selecting the set, then clicking on the Delete button. Be careful though—you won't get a second chance to confirm the deletion. If you accidentally delete a file set or location set, just click on Cancel so that the deletion won't be remembered. The set will show again the next time you open the Search Sets dialog box.

Finding Files with Specific Text

Remember the scenarios presented at the beginning of the chapter? A secretary is instructed to find every file—letter, contract, invoice, spreadsheet—that includes the name "Sosume, Inc." Also, an editorial assistant is told to find every chapter file that contains the word "nit-picky" and replace it with "petty." In these situations, you would specify a *text string* for SuperFind to find. A text string is simply any word, phrase, number, or a combination of words and numbers. So the secretary would enter "Sosume, Inc." in the With Text box, and the editorial assistant would enter "nit-picky."

This feature is ideal if you are looking for documents relating to a particular client, company, or invoice number. For instance, suppose you wanted to move all of your invoice files (.INV) sent to customer #777 to floppy drive A. After entering ***.INV** in the Find Files box, you would enter **777** in the With Text box, and SuperFind would place all of those files in a drive window. You could then move the files to the floppy disk in one step. You could also locate all letters dated March 21, 1990, all databases containing the name J. L. Peters, or all files containing the line "I eagerly await your reply."

To search for files that contain a specific text string:

▲ Choose File Find. The SuperFind dialog appears.

▲ Enter the text string in the With Text box.

Conveniently, the With Text box remembers the last four text strings you used, so you can select one later if you need to search for the text again.

TIP

When you search for text strings in the Find Files dialog box, you must also specify which files you want SuperFind to search. If you have no idea which files SuperFind should look through, just choose the [All Files] file set. Keep in mind, though, that this will be a lengthy search. If you neglect to specify any files in the Find Files dialog box, you'll get an error message telling you to enter a specification.

CHECK YOURSELF

Configure SuperFind to locate all program files on the current drive containing the number 123.

1. In the SuperFind dialog box, select the [Programs] file set from the Find Files pull-down list box.

2. In the Where pull-down list box, select the [Current Drive Only] location set.

3. In the With Text box, enter 123.

Including Attributes and Other File Data in the Search

As mentioned earlier, you can include file attributes, the date and time a file was created or last modified, and a file's size as part of the search criteria.

File Attributes

The available file attributes—Archive, Read Only, System, Hidden, and Directory—are discussed in detail in Chapter 3, with the exception of the Directory attribute. The directory attribute can give you a handy list of all directories and subdirectories on a drive—including their parent directories. When you use the Directory file attribute, you should choose [All Files] as the file set. The results of a directory search can be seen in Figure 8.8.

To display all directory names in a drive:

▲ Click on the More button in the SuperFind Dialog box. The dialog box appears similar to Figure 8.9.

▲ In the Attributes region, select the Directory check box.

▲ Select the [All Files] file set in the Find Files pull-down list box.

▲ Enter the appropriate drive letter in the Where box.

▲ Click on the Find button. SuperFind will list the directories in a SuperFind drive window.

▼ *Figure 8.8. Results of a SuperFind Directory Search*

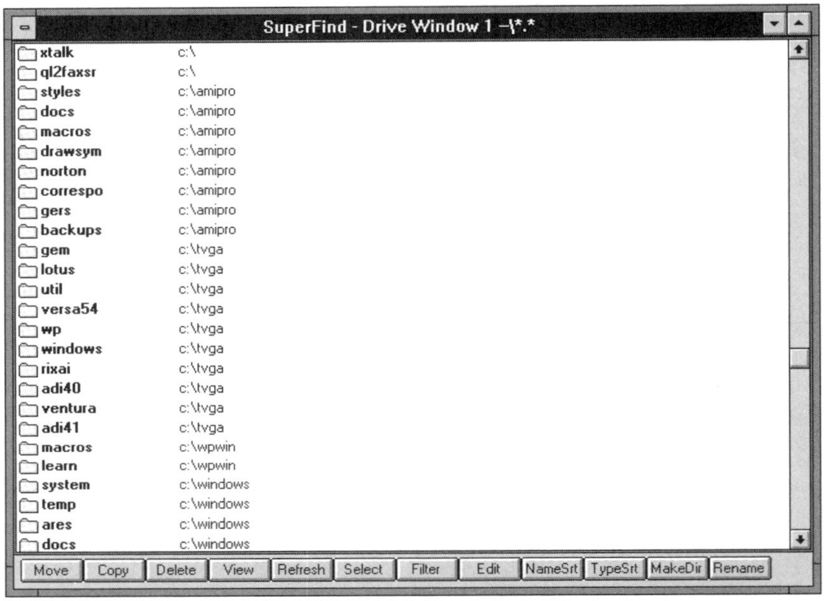

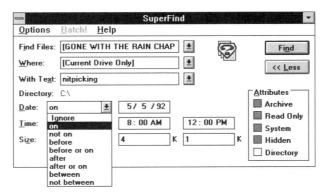

TIP

To print the directory list, click on Batch!, then press OK in the Create Batch dialog box. Then, enter the name FILELIST.BAT (or the appropriate name if you assigned a different one) in the Print dialog box.

▼ *Figure 8.9. Date Options in the SuperFind Dialog Box*

The attribute check boxes are three-state check boxes that can be clear, gray, or checked. These types of boxes are discussed in detail in Chapter 3, but here is a quick reminder of what each state means.

▲ Gray: Ignore the attribute in the search (files *with* or *without* the attribute will be searched for).

▲ Checked: Search for only those files that have the attribute.

▲ Cleared: Search for only those files that do *not* have the attribute.

If you wanted to search only for files that needed to be backed up, you would *check* the Archive check box; if you then wanted to eliminate read-only files from the search, you would *clear* the Read Only check box as well.

Keep in mind that the attributes refer to the files you have specified in the Find Files box. In other words, you cannot leave the Find Files box blank and check the System attribute check box (thinking that you would locate all system files). Instead, you would have to enter a specification in the Find Files box (such as the [Programs] file set), then check the System check box.

The Date Option

You can have SuperFind search for a file based on the date of the file's creation. However, an important point to keep in mind when specifying a date is that if the file was subsequently modified, the date that will be associated with the file is the date it was last modified, *not* its original creation date. For example, if you created the file MODIFY.ME on 3/2/92, then modified it on 6/23/92, the date that is significant to the search is 6/23/92. So when we refer to a file's creation date, it can also mean the date it was last modified.

Norton Desktop gives you a multitude of options for specifying date criteria. You can look for files created on a particular date, not created on a particular date, before that date, after that date, between that and another date, or not between that and another date. Figure 8.9 shows a list of the available date criteria options. If you are searching for files created *between* 2/7/91 and

1/25/92, files created on 2/7/91 and 1/25/92, plus all of the files created between the two dates, will be found. On the other hand, if you're looking for files with creation dates *not between* 2/7/91 and 1/25/92, files created before (not on) 2/7/91 and after (not on) 1/25/92 will be found.

When you choose any options except between, one box will appear to the right of the Date scroll box, as shown in Figure 8.9. When you choose the between or not between options, two boxes will appear, side by side. You must change each item in the date separately. For example, to change 5/31/92 to 6/3/90, you would double-click on 5 (so that it's highlighted) and type **6**, then double-click on 31 and type **3**, and finally double-click on 92 and type **90**.

To specify a date criterion for the search:

▲ Click on the Date scroll button in the SuperFind dialog box. A pull-down list appears, as shown in Figure 8.9.

▲ Select the appropriate date criterion. One or two boxes appear next to the Date box.

▲ Modify the date(s) accordingly.

TIP

SuperFind always remembers the last date, time, and file size entry you made.

The Time Option

The Time box works much the same way as the Date box, except that you are dealing with hours and minutes instead of months and days.

To specify a time criterion for the search:

▲ Click on the Time scroll button in the SuperFind dialog box.

▲ Select the appropriate time criterion from the pull-down list. One or two boxes appear next to the Time box.

▲ Modify the time(s) accordingly.

The Size Option

You can search for a file based on its size. This can be helpful, for example, if you want to move your largest files from a hard drive to a floppy diskette to free up disk space. You can look for files less than or greater than a certain size, or files between or not between two sizes. The Size box works like the Date and Time boxes. Sizes are measured by kilobytes.

To specify a size criterion for the search:

▲ Click on the Size scroll button in the SuperFind dialog box.

▲ Select the appropriate size criterion from the pull-down list. One or two boxes appear next to the Size box.

▲ Modify the size(s) accordingly.

CHECK YOURSELF

Specify a search for read-only files less than 3 kilobytes that were created before or on 8/21/91 between 8:00 a.m. and 12 noon.

1. In the SuperFind dialog box, click twice on the Read Only check box so that it is checked.

2. Select before or on in the Date box. Change the date to 8/21/91.

3. Select between in the Time box. Type **8:00 AM** in the first time box and **12:00 PM** in the second.

4. Select less than in the Size box. Type **3** in the K box.

Performing a Search

Now that you know how to define a search, you're ready to perform one. After you've told SuperFind what to look for and where to look, having it start the search is as easy as clicking on a button.

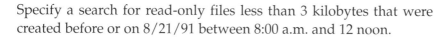

Telling SuperFind What to Search for

To start the search process after you've defined the search:

▲ Click on the Find button in the SuperFind dialog box.

When the search begins, the SuperFind icon (to the left of the Find button) becomes animated, moving to reflect the pace of the search. For example, when SuperFind is searching a large directory, the icon's pace usually slackens. The number of matching files found thus far in the search is displayed beneath the icon, as shown in Figure 8.10. The Directory data also changes quickly as the name of each directory currently being searched is displayed.

When the first file is found, a SuperFind drive window opens, and the file is listed inside. All subsequently found files are placed inside this drive window as well, as shown in Figure 8.10. When the search is done, everything stops moving, and the message "Search Done" appears below the total number of files that were found. Now you can perform any functions on the files in the SuperFind drive window that you would perform in

▼ *Figure 8.10. The SuperFind Dialog Box and Resulting Drive Window After a Search*

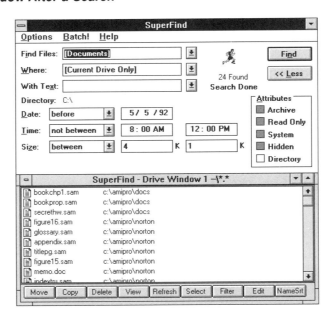

an ordinary drive window, such as moving, copying, assigning file properties, sorting, viewing, renaming, and deleting files. Notice that buttons for these features appear on the button bar at the bottom of the SuperFind drive window.

Performing a Search

TIP

Remember, files are moved, not merely copied, to a SuperFind drive window—they are removed from their original directories. This means that if you delete a file in the SuperFind drive window, that file is deleted from the disk drive. However, if you don't perform any functions on the files in the SuperFind drive window, the files are restored to their original directories.

Stopping a Search in Progress

When a search begins, the Find button changes to a Stop button. You can click on this button at any time to immediately terminate a search. If you click on Stop, the message "Search Aborted" appears beneath the total amount of files that were found before you canceled the search. If a SuperFind drive window already displays, it will continue to display after you abort the search.

To stop a search in progress:

▲ Click on the Stop button. The search is immediately terminated.

If you are running a minimized search (see "Searching in the Background"), double-click on the SuperFind icon to bring up the SuperFind dialog box again, then click on the Stop button.

Using the Options Menu

There are numerous features you can use to make a search more precisely meet your needs. Using selections from the Options menu, you can make searches for text case sensitive, change the SuperFind icon to a jogger, reuse a drive window, speed up a search, or have SuperFind search in the background while you work on other programs.

Case-Sensitive Search

SuperFind will not bother to check whether letters are uppercase or lowercase when it searches for a text string—unless you tell it to. For example, by default "Ms. S. S. Elizabeth" will be treated the same as "ms. s. s. elizabeth," or "mS. S. s. eLizabeth." In some cases, you can narrow the matching files found during a text string search if you make the search case sensitive.

To make a search case sensitive:

▲ In the SuperFind dialog box, choose Match UpperLowercase from the Options menu.

A check mark appears next to the menu command. To deactivate the case-sensitive command, simply select it again—the check mark will disappear.

The Running Man

You have the option to display either the SuperFind icon or the Running Man icon when a search is being executed.

To have the SuperFind icon change to the Jogger (or Running Man) icon:

▲ Choose Options Running Man in the SuperFind dialog box. You'll now see a jogger running in place every time a search is in progress (see Figure 8.10).

Choose Running Man again if you wish to restore the original SuperFind icon.

TIP

By default, the SuperFind icon is animated (i.e., it moves) while a search is in progress. When the search is over, the icon stops moving. This is helpful when a search is running minimized, because you can tell when the search is over just by looking at the icon. However, if you don't want the icon to move, choose Options Animation (the check mark will disappear).

Reusing the Drive Window

Each time SuperFind performs a search—even if it's exactly the same search it just performed—a new SuperFind drive window is opened. You'll notice that the drive windows are numbered. SuperFind does this to help you keep your search results organized. However, if you want the results of the next search to be placed in the same drive window used for your last search, you can tell SuperFind to do this for you.

To reuse the previous drive window:

▲ Choose Options Reuse Drive Window in the SuperFind dialog box.

Choose this menu command again if you wish to turn the feature off.

The Exclusive Search Command

When you choose the Exclusive Search menu command, SuperFind takes over your computer, so that your searches are done as quickly as possible. You cannot switch to other tasks, other programs cannot be running, and all animation stops. Basically, SuperFind suddenly has a one-track mind—namely, finding your files.

To speed up your search:

▲ Choose Options Exclusive Search in the SuperFind dialog box.

Choose this menu command again when you wish to return to the regular search mode.

Searching in the Background

Suppose you have to perform a long search (for example, perhaps you're searching through 800 files in search of the phrase "pay me soon, or else") and you don't want to tie up your computer while the search is performed. You can have SuperFind do all of its tedious work in the background, which means that while the search is being carried out you can continue to use Norton Desktop and Windows for other tasks, or even run other programs.

When you run a search in the background, the SuperFind dialog box will be reduced to an icon—to a jogger, if you selected Running Man—at the bottom of the desktop. While SuperFind works, you can still work in whichever programs you desire. The Running Man icon at the bottom of the screen in Figure 8.11 represents a SuperFind search running in the back-

▼ *Figure 8.11. SuperFind Working in the Background*

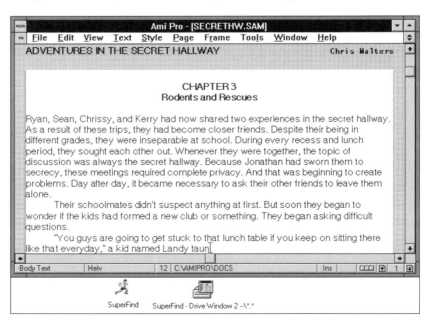

ground while an Ami Pro document is being edited. You'll know that the search is over when the Running Man quits running.

Using the Options Menu

To have SuperFind search in the background:

▲ Choose Options Minimized Search in the SuperFind dialog box. The next time you click on Find, the SuperFind dialog box will be minimized at the bottom of the desktop as SuperFind searches.

As before, choose the menu command again to turn off the minimize feature.

CHECK YOURSELF

Replace the regular SuperFind icon with the Running Man icon, and make a text search case-sensitive.

1. Choose Options Running Man in the SuperFind dialog box.

2. Choose Options Match UpperLowercase.

QUICK SUMMARY

Command	To Do This
File Find	Access the SuperFind dialog box.
SuperFind: Options Search Sets	Add, edit, and delete file sets and location sets.
SuperFind: Options Match UpperLowercase	Make a text string search case sensitive.
SuperFind: Options Running Man	Make the SuperFind icon show a picture of a running man.
SuperFind: Options Animation	Have the SuperFind icon move while a search is in progress.
SuperFind: Options Reuse Drive Window	Have SuperFind place results from the next search in the drive window created by the previous search.
SuperFind: Options Exclusive Search	Speed up the search. (Under this option, you cannot work in other programs while SuperFind searches.)

Command	*To Do This*
SuperFind: Options Minimized Search	Have SuperFind search in the background so that you can work on other programs as it searches.

PRACTICE WHAT YOU'VE LEARNED

Search in the background for all database files in your current directory and subdirectories that were created on or after 3/12/92, that contain the text string "Portland, OR", and that need to be backed up.

1. Choose File Find.

2. Choose [Database Files] in the Find Files pull-down list box.

3. Choose [Current Dir and Subdirs] in the Where pull-down list box.

4. In the With Text box, type **Portland, OR**.

5. Click on the More button.

6. Check the Archive attribute check box.

7. Choose after or on in the Date pull-down list box. Change the date to 3/12/92.

8. Choose Options Minimized Search.

9. Click on the Find button.

9

Using the Scheduler

It must be something in our nature that makes us feel like children whenever someone warns us not to miss a meeting, or to have a report done by a specific time. When we miss the appointment, or turn in the report late, we feel even more childish. Wouldn't you rather have your computer be responsible for reminding you of your important deadlines? Seeing a reminder flash on your screen is less irritating than hearing a grating voice warn you again not to forget the upcoming deadline. And certainly being greeted by a Scheduler dialog box informing you that an event has expired is more enjoyable than hearing the same news from the self-appointed office time-keeper. As for your reports, you can program Norton Scheduler to automatically run them for you daily, weekly, or monthly. In this chapter, you will learn how to:

▲ **Display timed messages**

▲ **Run programs and documents automatically**

▲ **Create automatic backups**

▲ **Edit, copy, and delete scheduled events**

An Overview of the Scheduler

You can take the alarm clock you brought to work last year home now. Thanks to the Scheduler you will even begin to build a reputation for handing in your reports in a consistent, timely manner.

The Scheduler lets you type in messages that will be displayed in the future to remind you of appointments to keep, tasks to do, phone calls to make, and so on. For example, if your child is getting off early from school today and you don't want to get so caught up in your work that you forget to pick him up, you can program the Scheduler to display a message before you need to leave.

Here's another example: A customer has made a complaint, and you've requested information to help clarify the matter. You'll need a message to run every day for the following few weeks, asking "Did you get the information on Mr. Paltry yet?" It would be hard to let the matter slip with such a constant reminder.

But that's only half of the Scheduler's function. It can also run programs automatically on a regular or a one-time basis. Isn't it nice to wake up to freshly brewed coffee every morning? The timer on your coffee maker gets the credit. And isn't it helpful to program your lights and TV to turn on at regular intervals when you are on vacation?

You can program the Scheduler to perform similar functions on your computer. For instance, if there is a certain daily report that you must submit at the end of each workday, you can configure the Scheduler to automatically generate the document file for you at 4:30 p.m. daily. Or imagine that you're leaving for a two-week vacation on August 22 and will need to have a monthly financial statement printed on September 1. The file containing the financial document is linked to a spreadsheet file that's updated on a daily basis, so you must wait until the first to print the report in order for the figures to be accurate. You could configure the Scheduler to open the financial report on September 1 (someone will turn your computer on). Then, as if by magic (but really with a couple of macros in place), you can update the link and print the file. Your boss might be a little impressed by your ghostlike abilities as he picks up the financial statement from your printer.

Starting the Scheduler

By default, Scheduler runs each time you start Windows, so if you configure Windows to start automatically each time your computer is turned on, Scheduler will automatically be running. You can easily tell whether the Scheduler is activated; the Scheduler icon will appear at the bottom of your desktop whenever Scheduler is running (unless you have purposely hidden the icon).

Scheduler

Chances are that the Scheduler is already running on your system. If you want to access the Scheduler window when the Scheduler is already running, double-click on the Scheduler icon. However, if you don't see the icon and want to start Scheduler, use the Tools menu.

To start Scheduler:

▲ Choose Tools Scheduler. The Scheduler window appears, as shown in Figure 9.1.

▼ *Figure 9.1. The Scheduler Window*

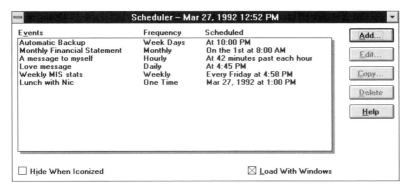

The Scheduler window lists all events that are to take place, how often they will occur, and when they will run. It also includes buttons for adding, editing, copying, and deleting events. Next to the word Scheduler on the title bar, the current date and time are displayed. Also, notice the two check boxes at the bottom of the window: the left check box allows you to hide the Scheduler when it is iconized (that is, minimized or reduced to an icon), and the right check box determines whether Scheduler will start each time Windows starts.

Iconizing the Scheduler

After you've started the Scheduler, you can iconize (minimize) it so that it doesn't take up so much space on the desktop. It's also handy to iconize the Scheduler because its icon is an active clock, as shown above. You can quickly check the time while working in any Windows program if you size your application window so that the bottom inch of Norton Desktop shows. Figure 9.2 shows an example of this: an Ami Pro file called CHAPTER9.SAM

▼ *Figure 9.2. Viewing the Scheduler Clock Icon While Working in Ami Pro*

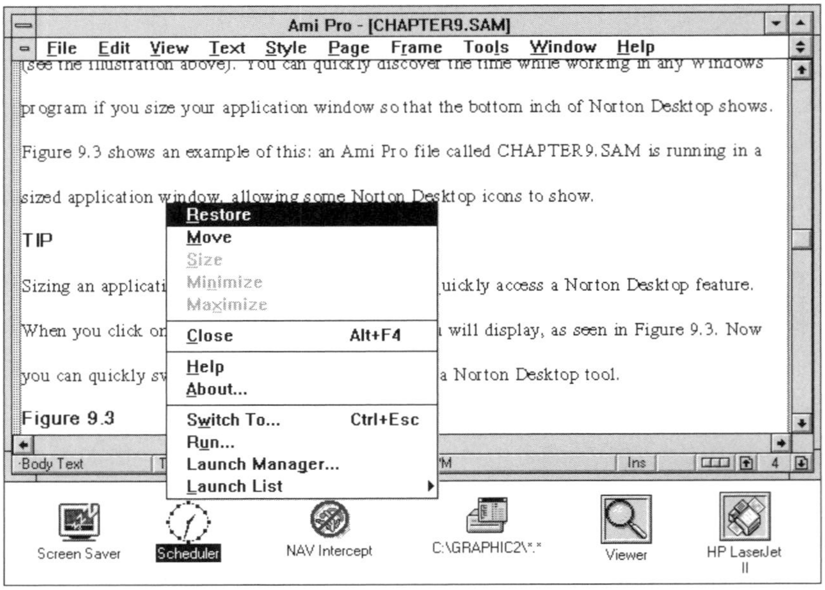

is running in a sized application window, allowing various Norton Desktop icons to show at the base of the screen.

TIP

Sizing an application window is also a great way to access a Norton Desktop feature quickly. By double-clicking on an icon for a Norton Desktop tool, you can quickly switch from the current document to the tool.

To iconize the Scheduler:

▲ Click on the Minimize button in the Scheduler window, or choose Minimize from the Control menu.

Perhaps your desktop is beginning to get littered with icons and you'd rather *not* see the Scheduler icon, even though you do want the Scheduler to be running. If so, you can hide the Scheduler icon.

To hide the Scheduler icon:

▲ Select the Hide When Iconized check box in the Scheduler window. The Scheduler icon will no longer appear on your desktop.

TIP

Remember, Scheduler will still be running even though the Scheduler icon is hidden. From now on you'll have to use the Scheduler command (accessed from the Tools menu) to add or edit events in the Scheduler window.

Closing the Scheduler

If you don't want the Scheduler to run at all, you must close it. If any one-time events were scheduled to run while the Scheduler was closed, the next time you start the Scheduler you'll be informed that these events have expired, as shown in Figure 9.3. If

---

▼ *Figure 9.3. You'll Be Notified of One-time Events That Expired While the Scheduler Was Closed*

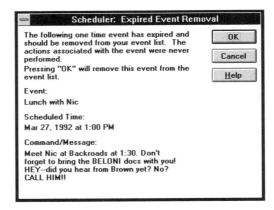

you wish to remove the expired events from the Scheduler, click the OK button in the Expired Event Removal dialog box. Perhaps, on the other hand, you want to reactivate some of these expired events. If so, click on Cancel instead, then edit the events to display again in the future.

To close the Scheduler:

▲ Double-click on the Control menu box in the Scheduler window.

or:

▲ Click on the Scheduler icon so that the Control menu is displayed (see Figure 9.2), then choose Close.

TIP

Remember, scheduled messages and programs will not run when the Scheduler is closed!

CHECK YOURSELF

Start, iconize, then close the Scheduler.

1. Choose Tools Scheduler. The Scheduler window appears.

2. Click on the Minimize button in the Scheduler window, or choose Minimize from its Control menu.

3. Click on the Scheduler icon so that the Control menu is displayed, then choose Close.

Adding a New Event to the Scheduler

There are two types of events you can schedule to run: a message and a software program. When scheduling a software program to run, you can specify a specific document file to open as well, so long as that file's extension is associated with the software program. (To make a file association, choose Associate from the File menu. If you need more details, refer to Chapter 5.) For example, you could start Lotus 1-2-3 alone, or Lotus 1-2-3 and a spreadsheet file called REPT0803.WK1.

Events can be scheduled to run once or on a regular basis, such as monthly, weekly, on week days, daily, or hourly. After a one-time event has run, it will disappear from the Events list in the Scheduler window.

Displaying Timed Messages

How do you keep track of the multitude of events that occur each working day? You could write them down in a planner, but what often happens is that by the time you get a chance to review the entries in that planner, half of the events have already expired. With Norton Scheduler, when you create a message that message will appear on your computer screen and remain there until you click the OK button—you can't continue to work until you've acknowledged the message. Figure 9.4 shows an example of a Scheduler message that appears each day at 4:45 p.m.

Each time a message runs, you'll hear a few beeps from your computer and the program you're currently working with will become frozen. A dialog box titled Scheduler: Event Notification appears at the top of your screen, as shown in Figure 9.4. This dialog box displays the message you entered in the Scheduler earlier and contains an OK button. To return to your work, you must first click the OK button; after you do, the message box disappears.

To create an event that displays a message:

▲ Click on the Add button in the Scheduler window. The Add Event dialog box appears, similar to Figure 9.5.

▲ In the Description box, type a brief description of the desired message.

▲ In the Type of Action region, click on Display Message.

▲ In the Message to Display box, enter the message you want to show at the designated time(s). The message can contain a maximum of 128 characters.

▼ *Figure 9.4. A Scheduler Message in Action*

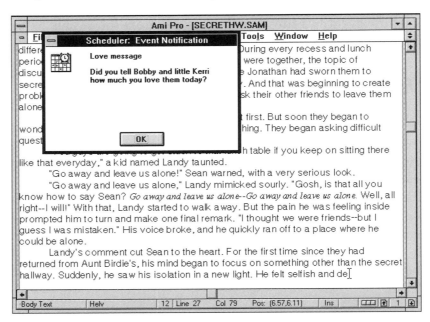

▼ *Figure 9.5. The Add Event Dialog Box When a Message Is Being Scheduled*

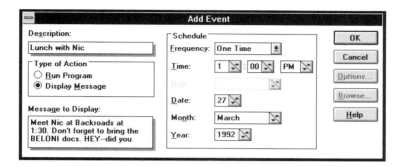

Adding a New Event to the Scheduler

▲ In the Schedule box, select the frequency of your message from the Frequency pull-down list box. You can choose from One Time, Hourly, Daily, Week Days, Weekly, and Monthly.

▲ In the Time box, click on the scroll buttons to set the desired hour and minutes. Also be sure to indicate AM or PM.

▲ Click the OK button. The new event will now appear at the bottom of the Events list in the Scheduler window.

TIP

By default, the Frequency box shows the One Time option. Also, the current day, month, year, and time are displayed in the respective option boxes. This makes it easy if you want to schedule a one-time event to run later that day: simply adjust the time, leaving the other values alone.

CHECK YOURSELF

Create a message called Good Morning that says "Good Morning! What would you like to work on today? How about a game of Reversi to get the old blood pumping? Solitaire?" Have the message display on week days at 8:05 in the morning.

1. Open the Scheduler window and click on Add.

2. In the Description box, type **Good Morning**.

3. In the Type of Action box, click on Display Message.

4. In the Message to Display box, type **Good Morning! What would you like to work on today? How about a game of Reversi to get the old blood pumping? Solitaire?**

5. In the Schedule box, select Week Days from the Frequency pull-down list box.

6. In the Time box, use the scroll buttons to set the hour to 8, the minutes to 05, and the last box to AM.

7. Click the OK button.

Running Programs Automatically

As mentioned earlier, you can schedule an application alone, or an application and an associated document to run at any given time. For example, perhaps you need to print a weekly management report each Friday afternoon. You might work on the report throughout the week and usually finish it midmorning on Fridays. Rather than print the report only to have something important come up later that needs to be included in it, you wait until the last moment on Friday afternoon. The only problem with this is that sometimes you get engrossed in a project, forgetting altogether about the report. Scheduler could solve this problem; it could open that document automatically each Friday at 4:58. Seeing the document on the screen will be your reminder to print it.

Each time an event occurs, a few beeps sound and the current program is interrupted as the scheduled program launches. The scheduled program can be set to run minimized if you don't want it to take precedence over the application that you're working on when the Scheduler kicks in. If so, you'll need to specify that the program be minimized when you create the event.

To create an event that runs a program:

▲ Click on the Add button in the Scheduler window. The Add Event dialog box appears, as shown in Figure 9.6.

▼ *Figure 9.6. The Add Event Dialog Box When a Program Is Being Scheduled to Run*

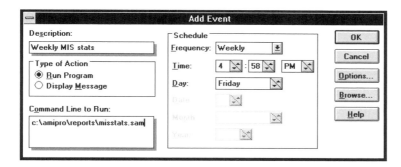

▲ In the Description box, type a brief description of the event.

▲ In the Command Line to Run box, enter the complete path and name of the program or document you wish to run. An example of a document specification is shown in Figure 9.6.

▲ Click on the Options button. If you want the program or document to run minimized, select Minimized in the Run Style box. If you wish to specify a startup directory, click on the Directory button. Select a directory and double-click the OK button. (As soon as the program runs, the directory you specified will become the default directory.)

▲ In the Schedule box, select the frequency of the event from the Frequency pull-down list box. The selection is the same as it is for messages: One Time, Hourly, Daily, Week Days, Weekly, and Monthly.

▲ In the Time box, click on the scroll buttons to set the desired hour and minutes. Also be sure to indicate AM or PM.

▲ Click the OK button. The new event will now appear at the bottom of the Events list in the Scheduler window.

TIP

You can use the Browse button to select the program or document name for the Command Line to Run box. Only program names will be shown in the Files box by default. If you wish to run a document, select All (*.*) in the List Files of Type box, then select the document. Remember that for this technique to work, the extension of the document file name has to be associated with the software application. Otherwise, you'll get an error message and the event won't run as scheduled. See Chapter 5 for more on file associations.

CHECK YOURSELF

Schedule a Reversi game (REVERSI.EXE) to start at 4:45 each Monday afternoon.

1. Open the Scheduler window and click on the Add button.

2. In the Description box, type **Reversi**.

3. In the Command Line to Run box, type **C:\WINDOWS \REVERSI.EXE**.

4. In the Schedule box, select Weekly from the Frequency pull-down list box.

5. In the Day box, select Monday.

6. In the Time box, click on the scroll button to set the hour to 4, the minutes to 45, and the last box to PM.

7. Click the OK button.

Editing, Copying, and Deleting Events

Just when you think you've got Scheduler to organize your whole life, things change. Don't worry; you can update Scheduler to reflect your changes—otherwise you might have messages going off weekly that are irrelevant or programs running daily that you aren't even working on anymore. When your schedule does change, you can edit, copy, and delete events in the Scheduler to meet your new needs.

Editing an Event

Perhaps you've mistakenly scheduled automatic backups to take place at an inconvenient time. The backup event begins at 4:00 p.m., but you'd really like it to take place at 5:00 p.m. Or, maybe Reversi always starts a few minutes later than you'd like it to. For whatever reasons, you can quickly edit an existing event to reflect your current needs.

To edit a scheduled event:

▲ In the Events list of the Scheduler window, select the event you wish to edit.

▲ Click on the Edit button. The Edit Event dialog box appears. This dialog box is exactly the same as the Add Event dialog box (see Figure 9.6), except that the title is different.

▲ Change the appropriate settings.

▲ Click the OK button.

Copying an Event

At times, you might want to create new events that are very similar to existing events. Instead of reentering entirely new messages or command line path names, you can copy the old event to make the new one. The event you copy from remains unchanged; in other words, you'll edit the copy, not the original. Suppose you're enjoying playing Reversi so much every morning that you'd also like to play it for a few minutes during lunch time every day. You could copy the existing event as a shortcut for creating the new one.

To add a similar event:

▲ Select the event you wish to make a copy of in the Events list in the Scheduler window.

▲ Click on the Copy button. The Copy Event dialog box appears. This dialog box is exactly the same as the Add Event dialog box (see Figure 9.6), except that the title is different.

▲ Change the settings to reflect the configuration you wish.

▲ Click the OK button.

TIP

You cannot access the Edit Event or Copy Event dialog boxes until you've selected an event in the Events box. The Edit and Copy buttons will remain dimmed until an event has been highlighted.

Deleting an Event

If you want to get completely rid of an event, simply delete it. But beware: you are not asked to confirm the deletion. After you click on the Delete button, the event is gone. There's no way around it; so if you accidentally delete an event, you'll have to re-create it from scratch.

To delete an event:

▲ In the Events list of the Scheduler window, select the event you want to delete.

▲ Click on the Delete button. The event is deleted.

CHECK YOURSELF

Change the Reversi event created earlier to start every week day at 8:00 a.m., then delete the event.

1. In the Events list of the Scheduler window, select Reversi.

2. Click on the Edit button.

3. Change the Frequency option from Weekly to Week Days.

4. Change the Time settings from 4:45 PM to 8:00 AM.

5. Click the OK button.

6. Select the Reversi event again.

7. Click on the Delete button.

QUICK SUMMARY

Command	To Do This
Tools Scheduler, or the Scheduler icon	Start the Scheduler, or open the Scheduler window if Scheduler is already running.
Scheduler: Load With Windows	Make the Scheduler start automatically every time Windows starts.
Scheduler: Hide When Iconized	Hide the Scheduler icon while Scheduler is running.
Scheduler: Add button	Schedule a new message or program event.
Scheduler: Options button	Specify that a program event run minimized.
Scheduler: Options Directory button	Specify a startup directory for a program event.
Scheduler: Edit button	Make changes to an existing event.
Scheduler: Copy button	Copy an existing event, as a shortcut to creating a new one.
Scheduler: Delete button	Permanently remove an existing event.

PRACTICE WHAT YOU'VE LEARNED

Create an event called Painting It, which will run Windows Paintbrush in the background at 9:30 a.m. daily. Then create a message to run 15 minutes earlier called Ready, Set, Paint!, which will get you prepared for the work you will do in the Paintbrush that day.

1. Open the Scheduler window by double-clicking on the Scheduler icon, or by choosing Tools Scheduler.

2. Click on the Add button in the Scheduler window.

3. In the Description box in the Add Event dialog box, type **Painting It.**

4. In the Command Line to Run box, type **C:\WINDOWS \PBRUSH.EXE**.

5. Click on the Options button.

6. Select Minimized in the Run Style box, then click the OK button.

7. In the Schedule box, select Daily from the Frequency pull-down list box.

8. In the Time box, use the scroll buttons to specify 9:30 AM.

9. Click the OK button. This event will now appear at the bottom of the Events list in the Scheduler window.

10. Click on the Add button in the Scheduler window.

11. In the Description box, type **Ready, Set, Paint!**.

12. In the Type of Action box, click on Display Message.

13. In the Message to Display box, type a message such as **What will you be painting today? Flowers? Cats? Landscapes? Think about it...**

14. In the Schedule box, select daily from the Frequency pull-down list box.

15. In the Time box, set the time to 9:15 AM.

16. Click the OK button. This event will now appear underneath the Painting It event in the Events list.

Preserving Your Monitor

Remember when your mom told you not to wear a certain facial expression too long, because if you did, your face might become perpetually configured that way (she didn't use those exact words)? She may have been making a good point—at least in an allegorical sense. If you told your computer not to wear the same, fixed screen image day after day or else its face might permanently resemble that screen setting—you'd be right. It's called screen "burn in," and over time it can ruin your screen's appearance, creating a ghostlike image on your screen. But Norton Screen Saver, also called the *Sleeper*, is burn-in's nemesis. The Sleeper lulls your screen to sleep whenever the action on your keyboard or mouse stops for a few minutes. Your screen's active dreams prevent burn-in from leaving its destructive mark. In this chapter, you will:

▲ **Launch Sleeper**

▲ **Sample the available sleep images**

▲ **Pick the image you want displayed on your screen**

▲ **Customize Sleeper**

▲ **Make Sleeper password-protected**

Sweet Dreams

Norton Screen Saver, or Sleeper, replaces whatever is on your screen with an animated image whenever you leave your computer idle for more than a few minutes. Leering eyeballs, fierce tornadoes, gliding fish, or a journey through the stars are just some of the *sleep images* you can choose from, and you can tell Sleeper which actions—such as moving the mouse or pressing a key—will reawaken your screen so that you can continue to work. In this chapter, we'll refer to the screen configuration that is present before Sleeper is activated as the *original display,* and the various images Sleeper uses to protect your screen as *sleep images.*

As with any Norton Desktop tool, you can determine how Sleeper should run. For instance, you decide how much time Sleeper waits before it replaces the original display with a sleep image. Perhaps you wish to configure Sleeper to display a sleep image 10 minutes after the last keystroke or mouse action takes place rather than five minutes (the default). You can also activate a sleep image instantly—a helpful option when someone walks up to your desk while you're working on a confidential document. And if you work with private material often, you can assign a password to Sleeper for even greater protection.

Launching Sleeper

If Sleeper is currently running on your system, perhaps you've noticed that each time your desktop is set up a message briefly flashes saying "Searching for Screen Savers. Please wait." This message displays because you cannot have two separate screen saver software programs running at the same time. Norton Desktop searches for other screen savers before starting Sleeper, to prevent more than one screen saver program from running. For instance, suppose you have a copy of After Dark installed on your system. You cannot run After Dark and Sleeper simultaneously. However, Sleeper automatically incorporates sleep images from such programs as After Dark, Intermission, and the Windows 3.1 screen saver program. So if you want to use an After Dark sleep image such as *Down The Drain*, you can select this image from the Savers box in the Sleeper window the same way you'd select a Norton Desktop sleep image.

*Launching
Sleeper*

When the Screen Saver is running, this icon appears at the lower-left side of the desktop:

Screen Saver

Seeing the Screen Saver icon on the desktop means that Screen Saver is running, but it does not automatically indicate that Sleeper is activated. There is an option in the Sleeper window that lets you disable Sleeper, even though Screen Saver remains running. So if you see the Screen Saver icon on the desktop, but sleep images are not appearing when they should, Sleeper has been disabled; you must open the Sleeper window, shown in Figure 10.1, to enable it. You can open the Sleeper window by double-clicking on the Screen Saver icon. If you don't see the Screen Saver icon (and you haven't purposely hid it), the program isn't running at all; you must use the Tools menu to start it.

▼ *Figure 10.1. Sleeper Window*

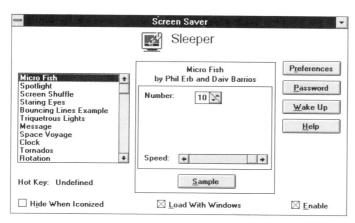

TIP

To hide the Screen Saver icon while Screen Saver is running, select the Hide When Iconized check box in the Sleeper window.

To start Screen Saver and enable Sleeper:

▲ Choose Tools Screen Saver. The Sleeper window appears, as shown in Figure 10.1.

▲ Check the Enable check box to activate Sleeper.

▲ Click on the Minimize button. The Screen Saver icon will now appear at the bottom left of the desktop.

TIP

If you want to have the Screen Saver automatically launched whenever Windows starts, select the Load With Windows check box in the Sleeper window.

Selecting the Sleep Image

Roving eyes, bouncing lines, trivia questions, roaming spotlights, a floating clock—these are only some of the images available in Sleeper. You'll have fun switching among the eighteen available sleep images.

Sleepy Choices

It's important that you know a bit about the setup of a sleep image before you select it, especially if you're concerned about someone accidentally or intentionally viewing your screen while you are gone. Some of the sleep images completely hide the original display, while others do not. Refer to Table 10.1 for a description of each image's options and confidentiality and additional helpful hints. See pages 202 and 203 for pictures of the images.

▼ *Table 10.1. Pictures, Options, and Confidentiality of Sleep Images*

Sleep Image	*Options (Comments)*	*Hide Entire Screen?*
Micro Fish	Select from four to 32 fish, and their speed. (The smaller the number of fish, the faster they will move across the screen.	Yes
Spotlight	Select from one to four spotlights, their size and speed.	No
Screen Shuffle	Select among tiny, small, medium, and large boxes, and their speed. (This image shuffles around bits of your screen.)	No
Staring Eyes	Select from 1 to 16 pairs of eyes, and their speed.	Yes
Bouncing Lines	Select one or two lines, and their speed.	Yes
Triquetrous Lights	Select from 16 to 256 lights, their size and speed, and whether they are shaded. (To achieve the closest resemblance to fireworks, choose 256 lights at maximum speed.)	Yes
Message	Have a personalized message displayed in a blimp, balloon, trailing a plane, or floating, scrolling, or flashing on its own. Also choose the font, size, style, and color of the message.	Yes
Space Voyage	Set the speed. (Maximum looks like you're on a warp drive journey!)	Yes
Clock	Choose between a regular clock or a digital display, and flashing, floating, or scrolling. Select size, color, and speed. (If you want a really spastic display, set tiny digital clock to floating at maximum speed—you'll get dizzy!)	Yes
Tornadoes	Select from 1 to 16 tornadoes, and their speed.	Yes
Rotation	Select from 1 to 48 large, compound, or vanishing shapes, and their speed. (For a free-flowing effect, choose 10 or less, regular. 48 large, compound, at maximum speed is a nice effect.)	Yes
Fading Away	Choose between dotted breakup and horizontal or vertical fading. Set the speed. (For optimum effect, choose Random Pixel Fading at medium speed.)	No
Animation Gallery	Select color and size. (Everything from a man walking backward to a teddy bear. The smaller the size, the slower they move across the screen.)	Yes
Art Gallery	Select color and speed. (Slowest speed gives a really nice effect.)	Yes
Trivia	Select from 20- to 70-point font size, and speed. (This is fun to observe with a co-worker.)	Yes
Spiro	Select from 1 to 16 spiral designs, centered and/or intersected. (Choose centered for a uniform effect.)	Yes
Killer Crayon	This is an actual game you play against the computer. (Click on Game Play for instructions.)	Yes
Starless Night	This is just a black screen.	Yes

Micro Fish

Triquetrous Lights

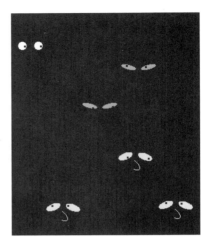

Staring Eyes

Spotlight

Space Voyage

Clock

Message

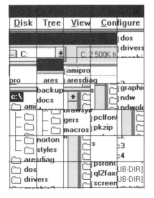

Screen Shuffle

Starless Night

Animation Gallery

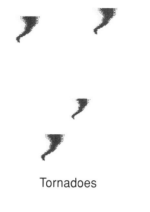

Tornadoes

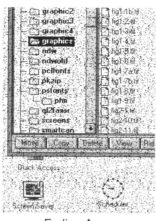

Fading Away

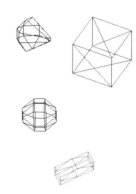

Rotation

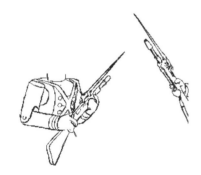

Art Gallery

TRIVIA – Who was the first Republican
President?

Trivia

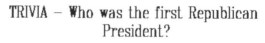

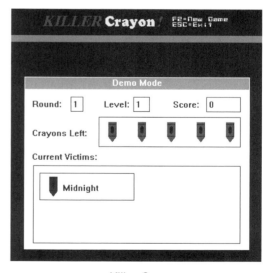

Killer Crayon

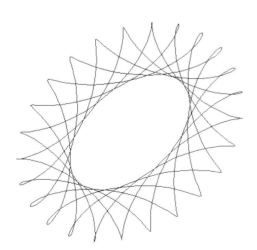

Spiro

Bouncing Lines

TIP

The Message image is ideal if someone normally uses the computer after you. You can type in a message to them that will be floating around on the screen when they arrive. Or if you're expecting someone shortly but need to leave your desk for a moment, display a message like "I'll be back in a minute--don't leave!"

Sleepy Sampling

Norton Desktop makes it easy for you to test drive any of the sleep images. Each time you select one in the Savers box in the Sleeper window, the large box in the middle of the window (the *sample box*) changes to reflect information on the current sleep image selection. For example, when you select *Micro Fish,* the sample box appears as it does in Figure 10.1. The name of the sleeper image, in this case Micro Fish, and the name of its developer(s), here Phil Erb and Daiv Barrios, appear at the top of the sample box. Any options you can modify appear in the middle of the sample box, and finally, a Sample button is located at the bottom of the sample box. Now, if you select *Spotlight,* the sample box changes to reflect information on the Spotlight image; if you select *Rotation,* the sample box information changes again; and so on.

There's a simple and quick way to see any of the sleep images in action. Simply highlight the image in the Savers box, then click on the Sample button. Your screen changes to the sleep image you selected. The sample box remains displayed as well, so that you can return to the original screen display by clicking the Restore button (which replaces the Sample button).

To sample a sleep image:

▲ In the Sleeper window, click on the sleep image you wish to sample in the Savers box. The selection is highlighted.

▲ Modify any of the options you wish to experiment with (located in the middle of the sample box). For instance, you may wish to increase or decrease the speed.

▲ Click on the Sample button. The screen displays the new image and the sample box appears in the middle of the screen.

▲ To return to the Sleeper window, click on Restore.

TIP

You can change any of the options in the sample box while you are viewing the sleep image. When you change an option, you will see immediate results. For example, if you decrease an image's speed, the objects will slow down instantly. Experiment with the sleep image during this one sample session to determine how you want the image configured.

CHECK YOURSELF

Sample *Triquetrous Lights,* changing the number of lights to 256 while you are watching the sample. Then, return to the original display.

1. In the Sleeper window, click on *Triquetrous Lights* in the Savers box.

2. Click on the Sample button. The screen switches to the image.

3. Double-click in the number box so that the current number is highlighted.

4. Type **256**. The number of objects changes instantly.

5. Click on Restore to return to the original screen display.

Making Your Selection

Now that you are aware of the different types of sleep images available and have sampled a few, it's time to make your selection.

To select a new sleep image:

▲ Open the Sleeper window.

▲ Click on the desired sleep image in the Savers box. The selection is highlighted.

▲ Make sure the Enable check box is selected.

▲ Click on the Minimize button.

Now, whenever a specific amount of time passes after you stop working on your computer, or whenever you drag the mouse to a certain corner of the screen, the sleep image you've chosen will display. To learn more about these features, read *Customizing Sleeper*, below.

Customizing Sleeper

You're writing an evaluation report on one of the employees in your department. Suddenly you hear this employee and a co-worker walking toward your office. Previously in a situation like this, you would have panicked, fumbled with the mouse to execute the Close command, and then wondered with a churning stomach why the screen display didn't disappear. When you realize you must have chosen the Save command, it's too late—the employees walk into your office. They wear strange looks as you jump out of your seat and sit on the keyboard, trying to block the screen. But in a similar situation with Sleeper running, you would simply drag the mouse to a corner on your screen to instantly hide the display. And when the coast was clear and you were ready to resume working on the document, you'd just click the mouse to restore the original display.

To set up these and other sleep functions, choose options in the Preferences dialog box, which can be accessed from the Sleeper window.

To access the Preferences dialog box:

▲ Click on the Preferences button in the Sleeper window. The Preferences dialog box appears, as shown in Figure 10.2.

▼ *Figure 10.2. Preferences Dialog Box*

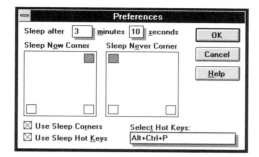

Specifying the Time Before Sleeper Appears

By default, Sleeper is set to display a sleep image five minutes after all action on your keyboard and mouse has stopped. However, you can set the time to any number of minutes and seconds you wish (between 10 seconds and 999 minutes, 59 seconds), though it's generally best not to specify less than three and a half minutes; otherwise, you may lose a screen display while pausing to read and mull over what you've written—which can become quite annoying. Also, if you set the option above 15 minutes, you'll begin to lose some of its beneficial effects.

To specify how long Sleeper should wait before displaying a sleep image:

▲ Double-click on the number in the Sleep after X minutes box, to highlight it.

▲ Type the new number of minutes you wish to specify.

▲ If you wish to change the number of seconds as well, double-click on the seconds box, then type the new number of seconds.

▲ Click the OK button.

Dream ON

You can make a sleep image appear instantly on the screen by dragging the mouse pointer to a corner that you have specified in the Sleep Now Corner box in the Preferences dialog box. By default, the upper-right corner of your screen is the Sleep Now Corner. This means that if you park the mouse pointer in the upper-right portion of your screen, a sleep image will immediately appear. You can change the Sleep Now Corner to the lower-right or lower-left corners of the screen; however, you cannot use the upper-left corner because by default this corner is reserved as the Sleep Never Corner (discussed later in this chapter).

To designate a Sleep Now Corner:

▲ Click on the desired square in the Sleep Now Corner. The square becomes shaded.

▲ Click the OK button.

TIP

Make sure that you drag the mouse pointer as far into the corner as you can, so that the pointer no longer appears on the screen. Then, release the mouse altogether. Otherwise, you might accidentally move the mouse, preventing the sleep image from appearing.

Hot Keys!

You can immediately trigger a sleep image by pressing a combination of keys that you have specified in the Select Hot Keys box.

To designate a key combination that will trigger a sleep image:

▲ Select the Use Sleep Hot Keys check box, if it is not already selected.

▲ Click on the Select Hot Keys box.

▲ Press the keys you wish to use in order, holding them down simultaneously (you should limit it to four keys). The keys will now appear in the Use Sleep Hot Keys check box.

▲ Click the OK button.

Now every time you press that key combination, a sleep image will appear. So make sure you select a combination that you will not use under ordinary circumstances.

Temporarily Disabling Sleeper

Suppose you are studying and reviewing complex data displayed on your screen. It would get very annoying if your screen saver was constantly appearing and disrupting your concentration. To prevent a sleep image from appearing, you can move the mouse cursor to the upper-left corner of your screen (the default). As long as the cursor remains parked there, Sleeper will be disabled and you can work uninterrupted.

To designate a Sleep Never Corner:

▲ Click on the appropriate square in the Sleep Never Corner. The square becomes shaded.

▲ Click the OK button.

TIP

If the Sleep Corners are not working, make sure the Use Sleep Corners check box in the Preferences dialog box is selected. If they still don't work, select the Enable check box in the Sleeper window and be sure to park the mouse pointer as far into the corner as you can.

Awakening Sleeper

After returning from lunch, you'd have to restart a program, open the document you were working on, and try to find where you left off. If you were using Sleeper, you could simply awaken your screen from its dreamy sleep to instantly display the document at the point where you left off before lunch. There are several options you can choose from to awaken Sleeper and instantly display your screen as it was before the sleep image appeared. You can configure Sleeper so that one or a combination of actions will awaken the screen. For example, you can provide that *only* pressing a key will snap your screen out of its dreams, or that pressing a key, clicking on the mouse button, or moving the mouse will awaken it.

To specify how to restore your screen:

▲ Click on the Wake Up button in the Sleeper window. The Wake Up Settings dialog box appears, as shown in Figure 10.3.

▲ Select one, two, or all three of the wake-up options you wish to use to restore a screen display.

▲ Click the OK button.

CHECK YOURSELF

Display a sleep image instantly by pressing **Alt+Ctrl+P**, then restore the original display by clicking on the mouse button.

1. Click on the Preferences button in the Sleeper window.

2. Make sure the Use Sleep Hot Keys check box is selected.

3. Click on the Select Hot Keys box.

4. Press the **Alt+Ctrl+P**, then click the OK button.

5. Click on the Wake Up button in the Sleeper window.

6. Select the Wake on Mouse Clicks check box if it isn't already. Click the OK button.

7. Press **Alt+Ctrl+P** to display the sleep image, then restore the original display by clicking on the mouse button.

▼ *Figure 10.3. Wake Up Settings Dialog Box*

Using a Password to Shield Your Screen

Using a Password to Shield Your Screen

Do you work on confidential material a lot? You really can't leave your desk and rely on a sleep image to shield the document you're working on. Any office "spy" who is clever enough can come along and move the mouse or click on a key to restore the confidential document you thought was protected. But you can leave your desk confidently if you assign a password to the Sleeper that must be entered before the original display will be restored.

If a password is assigned to Sleeper, and a sleep image is showing, when you attempt to restore the original display, a dialog box appears asking you to enter the password. If you enter it correctly and click the OK button, the original display is restored. If you enter it incorrectly, you get an error message telling you to try again. If you never attempt to enter a password, the dialog box remains on your screen. Thus, if you come back from lunch and see the password request dialog box displayed on your screen, you'll know that someone has been fooling with your computer. However, if you've set the sleep image to wake up on mouse movement, the password dialog box could have been triggered accidentally.

TIP

Remember, the Sleeper password does not prevent someone from rebooting your machine to access your files. However, it does prevent people from knowing what document you're working on, and from seeing the contents of that document.

If you work on a network you can use your network password, or you can create one of your own.

To assign a custom password to Sleeper:

▲ Click on the Password button in the Sleeper window. The Password dialog box appears, as shown in Figure 10.4.

▼ *Figure 10.4. The Password and Confirm Custom Password Dialog Boxes*

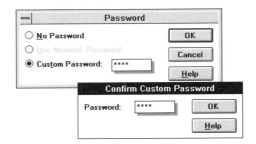

▲ Click on the Custom Password option.

▲ Enter the desired password. An asterisk (*) appears for each letter you type.

▲ Click the OK button. The Confirm Custom Password dialog box appears, also shown in Figure 10.4.

▲ Retype the password, then click the OK button.

TIP

To remove a password, choose the No Password option in the Password dialog box. A dialog box will appear, asking you to reenter the password. You must enter the password here before it will be removed.

QUICK SUMMARY

Command	To Do This
Tools Screen Saver, or the Screen Saver icon	Open the Sleeper window.
Sleeper: Sample Button	See what a sleep image looks like.
Sleeper: Preferences button	Specify how long Sleeper should wait before it displays a sleep image. Also, designate Sleep Corners and hot keys.
Sleeper: Wake Up button	Specify which actions will restore the original display.
Sleeper: Password button	Assign a password to Sleeper so that it won't restore the original display until the correct password has been entered.

PRACTICE WHAT YOU'VE LEARNED

By moving the mouse to the lower-right corner of the screen, instantly display the *Message* sleep image, after you have configured it to say "I'll be back in a minute—please wait!" inside the largest balloon available. Use a Courier font, 64-point, underlined, bold, italics, and in purple. Have the message continually move through the balloon at a medium speed.

1. Double-click on the Screen Saver icon to display the Sleeper window.

2. Click on the Preferences button.

3. Click on the lower-right corner of the Sleep Now Corner box.

4. Select the Sleep Corners check box, if it isn't already selected.

5. Click the OK button.

6. Click on *Message* in the Savers box.

7. In the top box of the sample box, type **I'll be back in a minute-- please wait!**

8. Choose *Courier* in the font box.

9. Choose *64* in the font size box.

10. Choose *Purple* in the color box.

11. Choose *UL Bld Itali* in the style box.

12. Choose *Dynamic* in the message movement box. (To make the message continually redisplay in the balloon.)

13. Choose *Balloon* in the object box.

14. Drag the mouse to the lower-right corner of your screen. The *Message* sleep image appears.

Using Special Symbols

You've just created a first-rate résumé complete with a variety of eye-catching fonts and different type sizes—printed on a laser printer to make it look even more professional. But there's a slight problem. To spell résumé accurately, you really need an accent over each *e*. So you pull out your black pen and try to draw straight, small, slanted lines above the e's. The result? A good job down the tubes.

Norton KeyFinder provides all of the special characters you'll ever need to use in your documents, in whatever fonts you're using. With KeyFinder, you can include characters such as é, Ó, Ô, or Ò in your document with just a few short steps. With KeyFinder, you'll see characters you never knew you could access. In this chapter, you'll learn how to:

▲ **Display characters for different fonts in the KeyFinder window**

▲ **Set KeyFinder window options**

▲ **Place characters into your documents**

▲ **Use shortcuts to move between KeyFinder and your documents**

An Overview of KeyFinder

At times, you'll need to use diacritical marks such as ñ, ü, or ç in your documents. There may even come a time when a ligature—two letters printed together, like Æ—needs to be added to a report you're working on. There's no need to go to a professional printer—with KeyFinder, you can insert these specialized characters yourself.

TIP

Warning: You may be unable to perform some of the procedures discussed in this chapter if you have different fonts installed on your system. Also, you might not be able to print some of the characters you import into your documents, depending on your printer's abilities.

KeyFinder displays all the characters available for each screen font (typeface) installed on your system. Although there are only a small number of characters available on the keyboard, fonts can have up to 256 characters. After you designate the desired font, KeyFinder places all available characters for that font in a table, where you can simply cut the symbol you're looking for and then paste it into your document. Figure 11.1 shows the KeyFinder window, with the character set for TimesNewRomanPS on display in the Character Table.

You'll start KeyFinder the same way you do most other Norton Desktop tools—by using the Tools menu.

TIP

Several of the table cells display the same character because fonts normally do not assign characters to all of the 256 available values. Other cells are blank because they represent certain key functions, such as Ctrl+P or Ctrl+[.

▼ *Figure 11.1. KeyFinder Window*

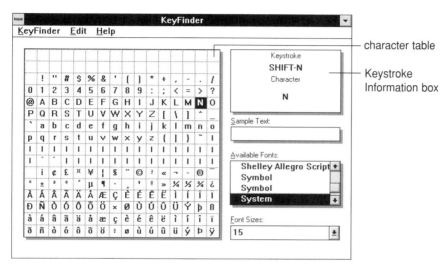

To start KeyFinder:

▲ Choose Tools KeyFinder. The KeyFinder window appears, as displayed in Figure 11.1.

Good news: you can throw away the lists of ASCII keystroke codes that will also enter a special character for you. The KeyFinder window shows all of a font's characters for you and identifies the keystrokes that will insert a character. For example, before, if you wanted to display "¼" in a document, you would press **Alt** while typing **0188**. Now, all you have to do is refer to the Keystroke Information box in the KeyFinder window to find the proper key combination. However, because of KeyFinder's ability to copy characters to the Clipboard, you probably won't use key codes as often as you'll use the cut and paste feature.

The KeyFinder window also contains a scroll box of the screen fonts installed on your system and a pull-down list of font sizes available for each font. A sample box is located at the right side of the KeyFinder window. You'll use this box to copy characters to the Clipboard (to paste into Windows documents later).

If you're likely to use special symbols periodically as you write a document, it would be a good idea to iconize the

KeyFinder window so that you can quickly redisplay the window whenever you need to use a special character (see *Shortcut Operations* near the end of this chapter); this will prevent you from having to continually close and reopen KeyFinder. The icon shown below will appear at the bottom of the desktop when you iconize the KeyFinder window. Double-click on this icon to redisplay the KeyFinder window.

KeyFinder

To iconize the KeyFinder window:

▲ Click on the Minimize button in the KeyFinder window.

When you're ready to close KeyFinder, either double-click on the Control menu box or choose Exit from the KeyFinder menu.

CHECK YOURSELF

Start KeyFinder, reduce it to an icon, then redisplay the KeyFinder window.

1. Choose Tools KeyFinder.

2. Click on the Minimize button in the KeyFinder window.

3. Double-click on the KeyFinder icon.

Selecting the Font and Font Size

You can display the available characters in the KeyFinder window for any screen font installed on your system. KeyFinder also lists all available sizes for that font that can be displayed on the screen (but not necessarily printed). The purpose of choosing a character in a particular font size is so that when you copy the character into a Document, it will be inserted in the proper size; you won't have to adjust it after it has been copied. For example, suppose you're using a 28-point Helvetica font in a document and want to insert a copyright symbol. You would choose Helvetica 28 in the KeyFinder window before cutting and pasting the copyright symbol into your document. When you select a font size in the KeyFinder window, the Character Table will not display the size you've chosen (there wouldn't be room!).

Selecting the Font and Font Size

TIP

You can see exactly what a symbol looks like in a certain type size by referring to the sample character displayed in the Keystroke Information box. Each time you change the font size (provided you're in regular mode and the Real Font Size option is turned on), the character will be shown in the new size in the Keystroke Information box.

Choosing a Font

Each time you start KeyFinder, the characters for the Windows default font, *System,* display in the Character Table. In the Available Fonts box, System is highlighted (see Figure 11.1). As mentioned earlier, all screen fonts installed on your system will appear in alphabetical order in the Available Fonts box. You can use the scroll buttons to move through the list to find the font whose characters you want to display.

TIP

Use any font that has the special character you want to use. If your application doesn't accept it, or if your application displays the special character but won't print it, try using the same character from a different font.

Notice that some of the fonts are displayed twice. Frequently one of the fonts will appear in bold and another in normal text.

To select a new font:

▲ Scroll through the Available Fonts box to locate the desired font, then click on the name of the font.

When you select a new font, the Character Table is immediately updated to show the new characters (you can see the table change column by column from left to right).

The Real Thing

By default, the Font Sizes box is not displayed in the KeyFinder window. To display it, you must turn on the Real Font Size option on the KeyFinder menu. We suggest you do this right now and leave this option turned on always. If you don't leave the Real Font Size option on permanently, you'll have to turn it on each time you want to select a different font size. Additionally, each time you copy a character to the Clipboard, that character will be copied in the largest available size for that font (usually 40 points), since the default font size is always a font's largest size. You'll then have to adjust the size once you've inserted the character into your document, which can be a headache.

To display the Font Sizes box:

▲ Choose Real Font Size from the KeyFinder menu. The Real Font Size option becomes checked, and the Font Sizes box appears at the lower-right corner of the KeyFinder window.

Choosing a Font Size

When you first open the KeyFinder window, the Font Sizes box displays *15*. Different fonts have different type sizes available, which can range from 2 to 40 points. Though you may be able to use a larger font in a word processor or desktop publisher, the largest size available in the KeyFinder window is 40 points. Whenever you select a new font in the Available Fonts box, the largest type size available for that font appears in the Font Sizes box. When you click on the Font Sizes scroll button, a pull-down

▼ *Figure 11.2. 28-Point Helvetica Font*

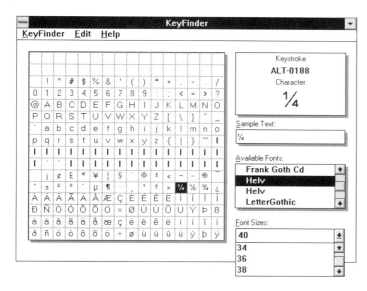

list of the available sizes for that font appears, as shown in Figure 11.2.

TIP

If your application does not have the ability to resize, make sure you select the correct size in KeyFinder.

To choose a new size for a font:

▲ Click on the Font Sizes scroll button to display a pull-down list of available sizes, as shown in Figure 11.2.

▲ Select the desired size. The new size will be displayed by the character appearing in the Keystroke Information box.

CHECK YOURSELF

Choose the Courier font in a 12-point type size.

1. Scroll though the Available Fonts box in the KeyFinder window to find Courier, then click on it.

2. Choose KeyFinder Real Font Size if the Font Sizes box is not already displayed.

3. Click on the Font Sizes scroll button, then choose *12* from the pull-down list that appears.

Setting the Options

Various options on the KeyFinder menu will change the appearance of the KeyFinder window. For example, you can change the orientation of the Character Table, alter the display format of the Keystroke Information box, and add or remove the Sample Text box.

A Table Swap

There are a lot of characters on display in the Character Table. After looking over several of the characters, your eyes may become character-blind. If so, changing the orientation of the table may help to make the characters more distinct once again. Rows will switch to columns and columns to rows. If you prefer this new orientation, you might choose to leave the table in that display format permanently.

To change the orientation of the Character Table:

▲ Choose KeyFinder Swap Orientation. The Swap Orientation option is checked, and the rows and columns of the table are transposed so that the first row becomes the first column, and so on, as shown in Figure 11.3.

Altering the Keystroke Information Box Display

If you've got a programmer's heart and are interested in finding out the decimal, hexadecimal, and octal ASCII values for a char-

▼ ***Figure 11.3. Changing the Orientation of the Character Table***

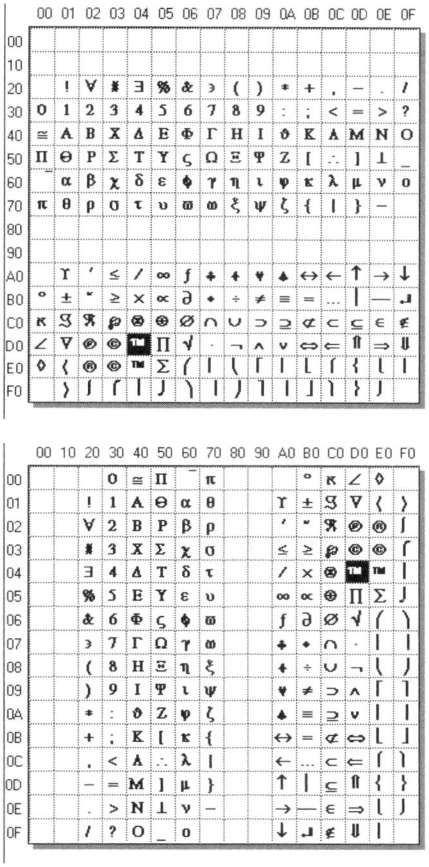

Setting the Options

acter, you can make it so these values are displayed in the Keystroke Information box. By default the Keystroke Information box displays only the selected character and the key combination that will insert that character into a document. However, if you set KeyFinder to programmer mode, you can display ASCII values in the Keystroke Information box as well.

To switch to programmer mode:

▲ Choose Programmer Mode from the KeyFinder menu. The Programmer Mode option is checked and the Keystroke Information box changes, as shown in Figure 11.4. Notice that

▼ *Figure 11.4. KeyFinder Window in Programmer Mode*

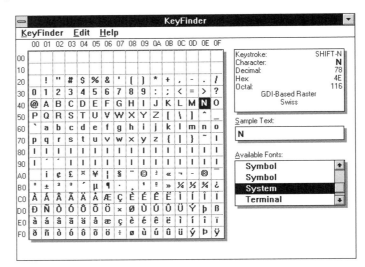

when the Programmer Mode is selected, the font type and family are displayed in the last two lines of the Keystroke Information box, in addition to the character, keystroke combination, and ASCII values.

▲ To switch back to regular mode, choose the Programmer Mode menu command again.

TIP

You can switch between regular and programmer modes quickly by double-clicking anywhere in the Keystroke Information box.

Notice that other features in the KeyFinder window change when you switch to programmer mode. For example, you won't be able to alter the size of a font because the Font Sizes box cannot be displayed in programmer mode. (Remember, this means that all characters will be copied in a font's largest size.) Also, the Character Table columns and rows are now labeled with numbers and letters.

TIP

To display control codes for ASCII values 0 through 31, choose KeyFinder Show ASCII. Now, instead of keystroke combinations, codes appear in the Keystroke Information box. For example, ESC will show rather than CTRL-[.

Displaying the Sample Text Box

If the Sample Text box does not presently appear in your KeyFinder window, we suggest you display it permanently, because this box must be displayed for characters to be copied to the Clipboard. The only reason you wouldn't need to display the Sample Text box would be if you always insert characters into your Windows documents using keystroke codes, rather than by cutting and pasting.

To display the Sample Text box:

▲ Choose KeyFinder Sample Text. The Sample Text option is checked and the Sample Text box appears in the KeyFinder window.

CHECK YOURSELF

Switch KeyFinder to programmer mode, swap the Character Table's orientation, then display the Sample Text box.

1. Choose Programmer Mode from the KeyFinder menu or double-click on the Keystroke Information box.

2. Choose KeyFinder Swap Orientation.

3. Choose KeyFinder Sample Text.

Choosing the Characters You Want to Use

Now that you know the basics of the KeyFinder window, you can select the character you want to appear in your Windows document. This is a three-step process: first you'll copy the character to the Sample Text box, then copy it to the Clipboard, and finally paste it into the document. In order to paste a copied character from the KeyFinder window into a Windows document, that character must appear in the Sample Text box. So when we speak of selecting a character, we're really referring to placing that character inside the Sample Text box, which you can do by double-clicking on that character. Contrary to what you may have supposed, the Copy Cell menu command does not copy a character to the Clipboard; it is merely another way you can place a character inside the Sample Text box.

To select one character:

▲ Using the Available Fonts box, choose a font that has the character you want to use.

▲ Choose the appropriate size in the Font Sizes box.

▲ Double-click on the character you want in the Character Table, or click on the character and choose Copy Cell from the KeyFinder Edit menu.

The character now appears in the Sample Text box and information on that character displays in the Keystroke Information box.

TIP

Some of the cells in the Character Table cannot be copied to the Sample Text box (usually ASCII characters 0 through 31). You'll hear a beep if you attempt to copy these cells.

At times, you might wish to copy multiple characters into a document. For example, if you know that you're going to need the ©, ®, and ø symbols in different parts of your document, you might copy and paste all of them at one time, then move them to the desired locations in your document later. When you have more than one character in the Sample Text box, all of the characters will be copied to the Clipboard in the order in which they appear in the Sample Text box. Even if you highlight only one of the characters in the Sample Text box, all of the characters will be copied to the Clipboard. If you change your mind and don't want to copy one of the characters in the Sample box, delete it (highlight the character, then choose Edit Delete) before following the procedures discussed later in *Copying Characters into Your Documents.*

Keep in mind that you can only copy multiple characters in the same font and size, because whenever you switch fonts any characters that already appear in the Sample Text box are switched to the equivalent characters in the new font. For example, if å—selected from the Helvetica font—is displayed in the Sample Text box, when you switch to the Symbol font, the å character changes to Symbol's å character, because both characters are located in the same cell in the Character Table.

To select multiple characters in the same font and size:

▲ Decide the order in which you wish the characters to appear in the document, then double-click on each character in turn. They will appear side-by-side in the Sample Text box in the order in which you've chosen them.

TIP

You can also move between characters in the Character Table using the Ctrl and arrow keys.

CHECK YOURSELF

Select these characters in 24-point Helvetica: ©, ®, and ø.

1. Choose the Helvetica in the Available Fonts box.

2. Choose 24 in the Font Sizes box.

3. Double-click on the © character.

4. Double-click on the ® character.

5. Double-click on the ø character. All three characters now appear in the Sample Text box.

Copying Characters into Your Documents

We've reached KeyFinder's most important function: inserting a character into a document. You can insert a special character into any application that runs in Windows, using either of the following methods:

▲ Cutting the character from the KeyFinder window, then pasting it into the document

▲ Typing the key combination associated with that character (for example, **Alt+0143**)

TIP

Warning! Using keystroke combinations might not always work for you. Many Alt+keystrokes are used by applications for special purposes. Also, for you to use some keystroke combinations, you must turn on NumLock. You'll have to work by trial and error.

In the second case, you'll still have to open KeyFinder to find out what key combination will insert the character you want, unless you already know that combination. Keep in mind that a special character will be assigned different keystroke combinations for different fonts. For example, though the copyright symbol (©) is usually inserted by typing **Alt+0169**, when you're using the Symbol font, you must type **Alt+0211** to insert the character.

Since you have to open the KeyFinder window anyway to find out a font's keystroke code, you'll generally end up copying and pasting more often than using a keystroke code to insert a character. An exception to this is if you use a special character quite frequently and soon memorize its code, simply by using it so much. For example, if you constantly insert the registered symbol (®) in Helvetica, pretty soon you may remember that typing **Alt+0174** will insert "®." There is an advantage to using character codes: the character is automatically inserted in the correct font and type size you're using.

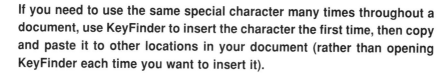

Copying Characters into Your Documents

TIP

If you need to use the same special character many times throughout a document, use KeyFinder to insert the character the first time, then copy and paste it to other locations in your document (rather than opening KeyFinder each time you want to insert it).

To insert a character in your document using a code combination:

▲ Select the character in the KeyFinder window following the guidelines discussed earlier (if you don't know the key combination yet).

▲ Write down or remember the keystroke combination listed in the Keystroke Information box.

▲ Place the insertion point where you want the character to appear in the document.

▲ Press **Alt** and the appropriate numbers. The character will appear immediately after the insertion point.

Remember, this might not always work because a program may preempt certain key combinations.

To insert a character in your document by cutting and pasting:

▲ Select the character in the KeyFinder window following the guidelines discussed earlier. The character will appear in the Sample Text box.

▲ Highlight the character in the Sample Text box by double-clicking on it.

▲ Choose Cut or Copy from the Edit menu. (Cut removes the character from the Sample Text box, whereas Copy leaves it there.)

▲ Place the insertion point where you want the character to appear in the document.

▲ Use the application's paste menu command to insert the character. The character will appear immediately after the insertion point.

TIP

For some applications, to be able to change the size of a new character, you'll first need to change its font.

CHECK YOURSELF

Insert the trademark (™) character (in the Symbol font) into a Windows document using the key combination.

1. Select the character in the KeyFinder window.

2. Write down Alt and the number 0212, as listed in the Keystroke Information box.

3. Place the insertion point where you want the character to appear in the document (the Symbol font must be the current font).

4. Press the **Alt+0212**. The character will appear after the insertion point.

Shortcut Operations

Have you ever used a certain technique to accomplish a function only to learn later that there was a much simpler way to achieve the same result? We want to make sure you're familiar with a couple of simple ways to switch between KeyFinder and your Windows application so that inserting special characters won't be a chore. When your screen is set up like this, you can quickly access other Norton features as well without having to exit the current program.

When you first start a program, an application window appears with a document window inside of it. Notice that there are two Maximize/Minimize buttons on the application window. Clicking on the bottom one reduces the size of the *document* window, while clicking on the top button reduces the size of the *application* window. The top button is the one you'll use to make accessing Norton Desktop features easier. When you click on the top Maximize/Minimize button, the application window becomes smaller, as shown in Figure 11.5. Clicking on the top button lets you see the Norton tools (or at least part of them) that appear at the bottom of the Norton desktop.

If only part of each icon is visible, reduce the size of the application window by dragging the bottom edge up an inch or

Shortcut Operations

▼ *Figure 11.5. Sized Down Application Window*

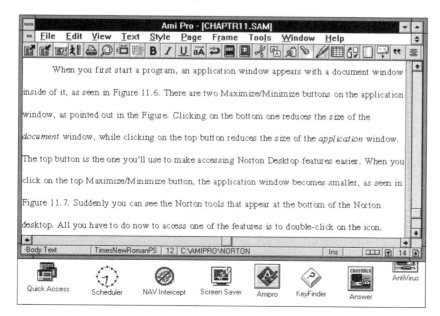

two. Now, all you have to do to access one of the features is to double-click on its icon. For example, you could double-click on the KeyFinder icon each time you want to insert a special character. Then, after you've cut the character from KeyFinder, you could reduce the window to an icon once again and paste the character into the current document, without having to close or reduce the document window.

This works well if the KeyFinder icon already appears at the bottom of the desktop. But what happens if you haven't started KeyFinder yet? Starting KeyFinder (or any tool feature for that matter) also becomes a simple task when you size down the application window. Any time you reduce the size of an application window, you can immediately access the Norton Desktop menu bar without having to close or reduce the application. To see an example of how this looks, review Figure 11.6. All you have to do is click at the very top of your screen (on the line that displays "Norton Desktop"), and the Desktop menu bar becomes active.

▼ **Figure 11.6. Norton Desktop Menu Shows when You Click Above the Application Window**

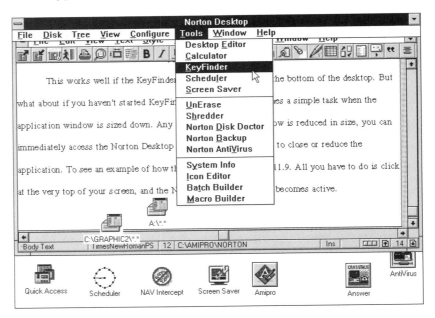

Notice that reduced drive windows for drives C and A appear on top of the Ami Pro application window. Whenever you click on the Norton Desktop title bar, all iconized drive and group windows that are located *underneath* the application window come to the surface along with the Norton Desktop menu bar. Now you can quickly open a drive window as well without having to close or minimize the current application.

**Shortcut
Operations**

TIP

If the Norton Desktop menu doesn't appear when you click at the top of the screen, the top border of the application window may be too high. Move the upper sizing bar down to lower the top border of the application window, then try clicking at the top of the screen again. The Norton Desktop menu bar should show now.

QUICK SUMMARY

Command	To Do This
Tools KeyFinder	Start KeyFinder.
KeyFinder icon	Open the KeyFinder window (after KeyFinder has already been started and minimized).
KeyFinder Real Font Size	Display the Font Sizes box in the KeyFinder window so that you can copy a character in a specified size.
KeyFinder Swap Orientation	Transpose the columns and rows in the Character Table.
KeyFinder Programmer Mode	Display ASCII values and the font type and family in the Keystroke Information box.
KeyFinder Show ASCII	Cause ASCII codes instead of keystroke combinations to appear in the Keystroke Information box.
KeyFinder Sample Text	Display the Sample Text box, which must be displayed to copy characters to the Clipboard.
KeyFinder: Edit Copy Cell	Place a character in the Sample Text box.
KeyFinder: Edit Delete	Delete a character from the Sample Text box.

Command	*To Do This*
KeyFinder: Edit Cut	Remove a character from the Sample Text box and place it on the Clipboard (from where it can later be pasted into a Windows document).
KeyFinder: Edit Copy	Copy a character from the Sample Text box to the Clipboard (from where it can later be pasted into a Windows document).

PRACTICE WHAT YOU'VE LEARNED

Paste the "Ç" and "é" characters (System, 16 points) into a Windows document.

1. Choose Tools KeyFinder.

2. Choose KeyFinder Real Font Size (if the Font Sizes box is not already displayed).

3. Choose 16 in the Fonts Sizes box.

4. Choose KeyFinder Sample Text (if the Sample Text box is not already displayed).

5. Double-click on "Ç."

6. Double-click on "é."

7. Highlight the two characters in the Sample Text box.

8. Choose Edit Cut.

9. Place the insertion point in the proper location in the document.

10. Use the application's paste feature to insert the characters into the document.

Norton AntiVirus

A *computer virus* is a computer program that copies itself to other programs, causing certain unwanted effects whenever that program is run. Viruses can be dangerously destructive (such as the Jerusalem-B virus, which wipes out all of your program files each Friday the 13th) or terribly annoying (such as the Keypress virus, which causes keystrokes to repeat on the screen, so that if you press Q, you'll get QQQQQ).

With Norton AntiVirus running, you won't need to panic the next time you hear that a virus may ransack your hard drive soon. It's as if you have your own biochemist installed on your computer system, continually checking your disk drives, ready to warn you of any occurrences and equipped to destroy the invaders. In this chapter, you will be introduced to Norton AntiVirus, and will learn how to:

▲ **Scan drives, directories, and files for viruses**

▲ **Repair, delete, and reinoculate infected files**

▲ **Reinoculate an entire drive**

▲ **Update virus definitions**

What Is a Virus?

The term *virus* is accurately applied: a computer virus affects your computer the same way a flu virus affects your body. If exposed to a computer virus, your computer has a significant chance of becoming infected, much like you can become infected when exposed to a flu virus. While a flu virus may give you a sore throat or high temperature, a computer virus may cause your computer to do strange things like repeat keystrokes or delete files you never told it to delete.

The two types of viruses even spread similarly. If you share a pen with someone who's carrying a flu virus, that virus might be transmitted into your body via your contaminated hand. Likewise, if you share a disk file that has a virus in one of its program files, your computer will be infected with the virus when you copy the contaminated file onto your hard drive. However, the virus is harmless until you run the infected application.

Generally, these files are created by computer hackers—some vengeful, others looking for a laugh. Sometimes they're high school computer whizzes that hook onto a network system and wreak havoc with their destructive computer codes. Other times they're college kids looking for a way to show off their advanced computer prowess. Unfortunately, a lot of time and expense has been wasted as the price of their fun.

There are two main types of viruses: program infectors and boot sector/partition table infectors. The types of viruses we've discussed thus far would be classified as *program infectors*—viruses that infect executable files (those with the extensions .EXE, .COM, .SYS, .DRV, or .OVL). *Boot sector/partition table infectors* attack either the master boot program on a hard disk or the boot sector program on a floppy disk (these are the programs that allow your disks to start up DOS correctly).

Some computer hackers have become quite good at creating "smart" viruses. You've heard of stealth bombers? Well, stealth viruses can be just as deadly to your computer. *Stealth viruses* are classes of viruses that can actually hide themselves from discovery programs or fight back when attempts are made to analyze or delete them. However, in the majority of cases, Norton AntiVirus is able to effectively detect and destroy the viruses.

What Is a Virus?

An Overview of Norton AntiVirus

Norton AntiVirus knows how to find and eliminate all of the approximately 1,000 known program and boot sector/partition table viruses. Unknown viruses are protected against as well; Norton AntiVirus checks to see if any changes have been made to your program and boot-up files. If any changes have been made, this could signify the handiwork of an unknown virus.

The first time you scan a disk, Norton AntiVirus assigns certain information to each of the executable files on the disk. This information, called *inoculation data,* outlines the configuration of the program file and will be used by Norton AntiVirus to verify the file's integrity later on. When a file has been assigned inoculation data, that file is now considered an *inoculated file.* The next time you open the inoculated file, Norton AntiVirus checks the file against its inoculation data. If any differences exist, Norton AntiVirus takes this to mean that an infection has occurred, and will respond accordingly.

Norton AntiVirus works in two ways: first, you can direct AntiVirus to find and destroy viruses on a drive, directory, or file; second, AntiVirus automatically scans for viruses in the background each time you boot or reboot your computer or copy a file (only if you configure AntiVirus to do so). When working in the background, AntiVirus will alert you if it finds any infected files.

Using AntiVirus

Norton AntiVirus scans all program files that you load onto your computer. It not only detects viruses, it destroys them as well, either by removing the virus from an infected file or by deleting that file. When AntiVirus detects a virus, it displays a dialog box that identifies the name of the infected file (including its path) and the name of the virus present in that file. You can then tell AntiVirus to repair the file. If this isn't possible, you should delete the file and later replace it with a clean copy from the original program disk. However, if you have upgraded or made changes to a program file yourself and therefore know that the file has not been infected by an unknown virus (as AntiVirus will assume since it considers any changes to a program file the work of an unknown virus), you can reinoculate the file (i.e., update its inoculation data), rather than have AntiVirus try to repair or delete it.

You can designate which files AntiVirus should scan. It can scan an entire disk drive; or, if you don't need to scan all the files on a drive, it can look over a single directory as well. In some situations, you may wish to scan only one file. For example, if you've just received a ShareWare file over your modem, it is strongly advised that you scan that file for viruses. Files sent over modems are usually the most susceptible to virus contamination.

TIP

To keep your system virus-free, make sure you scan all floppy disks before using them and all files that you copy onto your hard disk.

Before you scan a drive, directory, or file, you must open the Norton AntiVirus window, which you can do using the Tools menu or the AntiVirus tool icon.

To start Norton AntiVirus:

▲ Choose Norton AntiVirus from the Tools menu.

or:

▲ Double-click on the AntiVirus tool icon. The Norton AntiVirus window appears, as shown in Figure 12.1.

▼ *Figure 12.1. Norton AntiVirus Window*

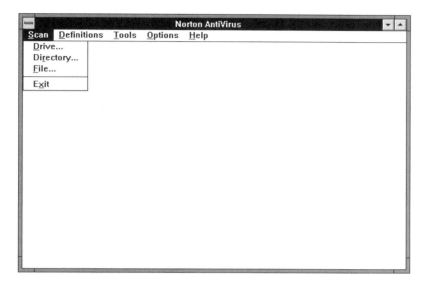

Scanning a Drive

If a virus has infected a file, you should scan the entire drive the file is located on to make sure other program files on that drive have not been infected as well. You can scan all types of disk drives, including hard, floppy, network, RAM, CD-ROM, and Bernouilli drives. Virus Clinic lets you scan one drive or any combination of drives.

To scan a drive:

▲ Choose Scan Drive from the Norton AntiVirus window. The Scan Drives dialog box appears, as shown in Figure 12.2.

▲ In the Drives box, click on each drive you wish to scan.

▲ If you wish to scan all drives of a particular type, you can select the check box for this type of drive in the Drive Types area.

▲ Click the OK button. The scan process begins.

AntiVirus first scans your computer memory for viruses, displaying the Memory Scan dialog box as it searches. Then, it

▼ *Figure 12.2. The Scan Drives Dialog Box*

scans the designated drive(s) for viruses; when it is finished, AntiVirus displays the results in the Scan Results dialog box (see Figure 12.5). To find out what to do if infected files are found, refer to *After the Scan,* later in this chapter.

TIP

AntiVirus performs a memory scan only the first time you scan during a Windows session. If it finds a virus in your computer's memory, it stops the scan process. You must immediately use Norton's Fix-It disk to eradicate the virus.

Scanning a Directory

It is advisable to scan a directory if you have just decompressed a set of files that have been placed into a new directory, or after you have installed a new software program onto your hard drive (software programs are copied into one directory).

To scan a directory:

▲ Choose Scan Directory from the Norton AntiVirus window. The Scan Directory dialog box appears, as shown in Figure 12.3.

▲ In the Drive box, click on the drive containing the directory to be scanned.

▲ In the Directory box, click on the name of the directory you wish to scan.

▼ *Figure 12.3. Scan Directory Dialog Box*

▲ If you *don't* wish to include subdirectories in the scan, deselect the Include Subdirectories check box (which is selected by default).

▲ Click the OK button. The scan process begins.

AntiVirus scans the designated directory for viruses; when it is finished, AntiVirus displays the results in the Scan Results dialog box (see Figure 12.5). To find out what to do when infected files are found, refer to *After the Scan,* later in this chapter.

Scanning a File

If you frequently download files via modem, you'll really appreciate that AntiVirus automatically scans files that you copy to your hard drive. You won't have to feel uneasy any longer when copying a file onto your computer—a file that has possibly been copied to many other computers and possibly is infected. Norton AntiVirus truly takes the scare out of ShareWare software.

However, there may be times when you want to scan a single file yourself. You can do so quite easily.

To scan a file:

▲ Choose Scan File from the Norton AntiVirus window. The Scan File dialog box appears, as shown in Figure 12.4.

▼ *Figure 12.4. Scan File Dialog Box*

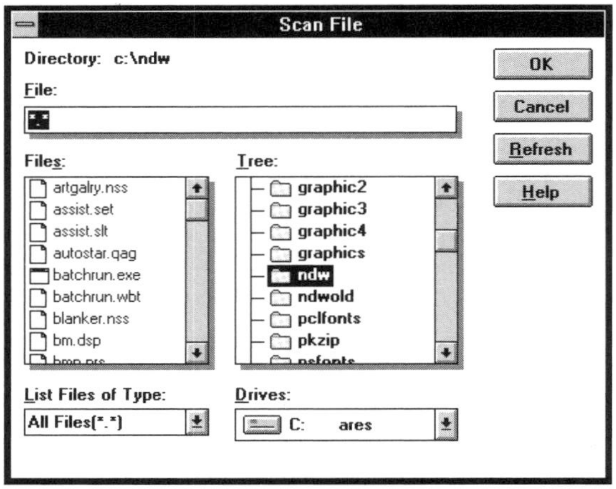

▲ In the File box, type the name of the file you want scanned, including its path. Alternatively, you can use the Drives, Tree, and File boxes to designate the desired file.

▲ Click the OK button. The scan process begins.

TIP

If you can't find the file you're looking for in the Scan File dialog box, try clicking on the Refresh button to update the drive information. You need to do this especially when working with multiple floppy disks.

AntiVirus scans the designated file for viruses; when it is finished, AntiVirus displays the results in the Scan Results dialog box (see Figure 12.5). To find out what to do if the file is infected, refer to the next section, *After the Scan*.

CHECK YOURSELF

Scan all floppy drives for viruses.

1. Double-click on the AntiVirus tool icon or choose Tools Norton AntiVirus.

2. Choose Scan Drive.

3. In the Drive Types area, select the All Floppy Drives check box.

4. Click the OK button.

After the Scan

If an infected file is found after Norton AntiVirus scans a drive, directory, or file, you can tell AntiVirus to repair the file. In most cases, AntiVirus will successfully remove the virus from the file. However, if elimination of the virus is not possible, you should have AntiVirus immediately delete the file. The only exception to this rule is when AntiVirus detects a virus only because you have modified a program file (in which case, AntiVirus considers the new file configuration the work of an unknown virus). If you know that no virus is present, you can reinoculate the file, meaning you can have AntiVirus erase the old inoculation information it stored on the file and replace it with updated inoculation data.

Once a scan is complete, the Scan Results dialog box displays a summary of the scan, as shown in Figure 12.5. The summary tells you how many files were scanned and verifies that

▼ *Figure 12.5. Scan Results Dialog Box when No Viruses Were Found*

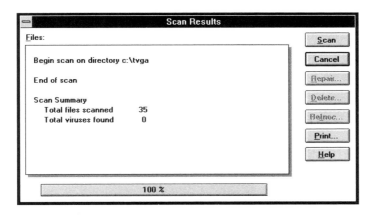

no viruses were found. If infected files were found, their names (including paths) are displayed in the Scan Results dialog box. The name of the virus that has contaminated the file is identified underneath the name of each infected file. If a known virus has been identified, you should repair the file. If an unknown virus has been identified, you should delete the file (it is not possible to repair a file containing an unknown virus), *unless* you've just upgraded or modified the file, in which case you should reinoculate it.

To repair an infected file:

▲ In the Scan Results dialog box, click on the name of the infected file you wish to repair.

▲ Click on the Repair button. The Repair Files dialog box appears.

▲ Click on Repair to eliminate the virus in the infected file, or click on Repair All to remove viruses from all of the repairable files located in the Scan Results dialog box.

TIP

If the file you selected for repair cannot be fixed, the Repair button in the Repair Files dialog box will remain dimmed. Be sure to delete the file in this case so that it will not infect other files on your computer.

Underneath the name of each previously infected file, the Scan Results dialog box displays a message saying that the file has been repaired.

To delete an infected file:

▲ In the Scan Results dialog box, click on the name of the infected file you wish to delete.

▲ Click on the Delete button. The Delete Files dialog box appears.

▲ Click on Delete to delete the infected file, or click on Delete All to delete all of the infected files located in the Scan Results dialog box. A message box appears asking you to confirm the deletion.

▲ Click the OK button.

Underneath the name of each deleted file, the Scan Results dialog box displays a message saying that the file has been deleted.

To reinoculate a file:

▲ In the Scan Results dialog box, click on the name of the infected file you wish to reinoculate.

▲ Click on the Reinoc button. The Reinoculate Files dialog box appears.

▲ Click on Reinoc to reinoculate the infected file, or click on Reinoc All to reinoculate all of the files located in the Scan Results dialog box that are identified as containing unknown viruses.

Underneath the name of each reinoculated file, the Scan Results dialog box displays a message saying that the file has been inoculated.

CHECK YOURSELF

You've just upgraded several program files and are told (in the Scan Results dialog box) that they contain unknown viruses. Reinoculate the files identified as containing unknown viruses.

1. In the Scan Results dialog box, click on the name of an infected file.

2. Click on the Reinoc button. The Reinoculate Files dialog box appears.

3. Click on Reinoc All.

Repairing Boot Sectors

One of the scary aspects of boot sector viruses is that they can infect your boot sector even when you simply *attempt* to boot from an infected disk—data disks as well as program disks (remember, here we're talking about *booting* from a data disk, not using the data files on the disk).

When you try to boot or download from a disk contaminated with a virus, a loud siren goes off in your CPU (computer processing unit—that is, your computer). Then, a dialog box appears on your screen warning you that the disk contains a virus in its boot sector. You must try to repair the boot sector of that disk *before* attempting to use it again.

To repair an infected boot sector or partition table:

▲ Following the directions under *Scanning a Drive* earlier, scan the disk containing the infected boot sector or partition table.

▲ In the Scan Results dialog box (see Figure 12.5), select the virus and click on the Repair button. If this button is dimmed, it means the file is not repairable; you must use the Fix-It disk to try to remove the virus.

▲ In the Repair Files dialog box, click on Repair. Again, if this button is dimmed, you must try to use the Fix-It disk to repair the infected boot sector or partition table.

TIP

If you did not just acquire a floppy disk whose boot sector is infected, it's a good idea to scan all of your other floppy disks to discover where the boot sector or virus originated. Likewise, you should scan all floppy disks for viruses whenever a partition table has been contaminated.

CHECK YOURSELF

When you attempt to download from floppy drive A, a siren goes off and a dialog box appears saying the floppy disk contains a virus in its boot sector. Try to repair the boot sector.

1. Choose Scan Drive from the Norton AntiVirus window.

2. In the Drives box, click on drive A.

3. Click the OK button. The scan process begins and the Scan Results dialog box appears.

4. In the Scan Results dialog box, select the virus and click on the Repair button.

5. In the Repair Files dialog box, click on Repair.

Repairing Boot Sectors

Reinoculating a Drive

Each drive contains an inoculation file that stores information about all of the drive's files that Norton AntiVirus scans. You should plan on updating this inoculation file periodically, especially if you upgrade or modify your program files often or if you regularly reorder your directories and files. Whenever you upgrade or move files, the inoculation data pertaining to the altered files becomes outdated. Your inoculation file may soon grow large with invalid information. Thus, it is helpful to replace the outdated inoculation file with a new, current one.

Keep in mind, however, it is not *imperative* that you update the inoculation file. However, if you don't, over time the file may start to use up a lot of your disk space. You can reinoculate one drive or a combination of drives at a time.

To replace the outdated inoculation file with a new inoculation file:

▲ In the Norton AntiVirus window, choose Tools Uninoculate. The Uninoculate Drives dialog box appears, as displayed in Figure 12.6.

▲ In the Drives box, click on the drive you wish to reinoculate. If you wish to reinoculate all drives of a certain type, select the appropriate check box in the Drive Types box.

▲ Click the OK button. The old inoculation file is removed.

▲ In the Norton AntiVirus window, choose Options Global. The Global dialog box appears, as shown in Figure 12.7.

▼ *Figure 12.6. Uninoculate Drives Dialog Box*

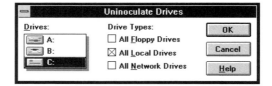

▼ *Figure 12.7. Global Dialog Box*

▲ Select the Detect Unknown Viruses check box and the Auto Inoculate check box, if they are not already checked, then click the OK button.

▲ In the Norton AntiVirus window, choose Scan Drive. The Scan Drives dialog box appears.

▲ In the Drives box, click on the drive you wish to reinoculate. If you are reinoculating all drives of a particular type, select the check box for the type of drive in the Drive Types area.

▲ Click the OK button. A new inoculation file is created for each reinoculated drive.

CHECK YOURSELF

Reinoculate drive C.

1. In the Norton AntiVirus window, choose Tools Uninoculate.

2. In the Drives box, click on drive C.

3. Click the OK button. The old inoculation file is removed.

4. Choose Options Global and make sure the Detect Unknown Viruses check box and the Auto Inoculate check box are selected in the Global dialog box.

5. Choose Scan Drive.

6. In the Drives box, click on drive C.

7. Click the OK button. A new inoculation file is created for drive C.

Reinoculating a Drive

Updating Norton AntiVirus

Norton AntiVirus contains definitions—actual values that make up a virus—on each of the known viruses so that it can identify and eradicate all known viruses from your files. When you purchased Norton Desktop for Windows, each currently known virus was defined in Norton AntiVirus and searched for during all scans. However, new viruses develop on a regular basis, while others become obsolete. For Norton AntiVirus to work effectively, you must update the virus definitions in AntiVirus so that new viruses are searched for and old viruses are removed from the scan. There are various ways to discover the names and definitions of new viruses.

▲ If you have a modem, you can use Symantec's Bulletin Board Service by dialing (408) 973-9598 and then downloading the latest virus definitions update.

▲ If you don't have a modem but do have a fax machine, you can use the Faxline service, which provides free listings of new viruses and their definitions. Call (310) 575-5018, available 24 hours a day. However, if you use this option, you will have to delete old viruses and add new definitions manually, since you'll only get a printout of virus definitions.

▲ If you have neither a modem nor a fax machine, you can call Symantec at (800) 343-4714 ext. 756 to order a floppy disk that contains the latest virus definitions file. You can receive updates on a quarterly basis. (There is a small fee for this service.)

TIP

It isn't imperative that you delete old virus definitions; however, leaving outdated virus definitions in AntiVirus will slow down its processing time.

If you receive updated virus definitions in a file by using the modem or by purchasing a virus definitions floppy disk from Symantec, you can enter the new definitions very easily using the Load File dialog box. When you copy this file into AntiVirus, it replaces the old file, meaning that all outdated viruses are removed and all current virus definitions are now present in Norton AntiVirus.

To load a new virus definitions file into AntiVirus:

▲ In the Norton AntiVirus window, choose Definitions Load from File. The Load from File dialog box appears, as displayed in Figure 12.8.

▲ In the File box, type the name of the new virus definitions file, including its path. Alternatively, you can use the Drives, Tree, and Files boxes to designate the desired file.

▲ Click the OK button. The virus definitions list is now updated.

▼ *Figure 12.8. Load from File Dialog Box*

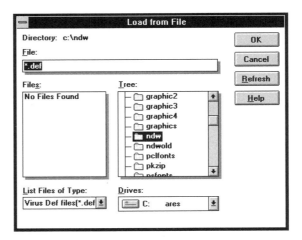

▼ *Figure 12.9. Modify List Dialog Box*

Updating Norton AntiVirus

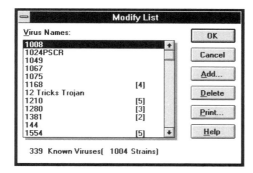

To add virus definitions manually:

▲ In the Norton AntiVirus window, choose Definitions Modify List. The Modify List dialog box appears, as shown in Figure 12.9.

▲ Click on the Add button. The Add Virus Definition dialog box appears, as shown in Figure 12.10.

▲ In the Name box, type the name of the virus.

▲ In the Length box, type the length of the virus. (This information will be specified along with the virus definition.)

▲ In the Checksum box, type the checksum value. (This information will be specified along with the virus definition.)

▼ *Figure 12.10. Add Virus Definition Dialog Box*

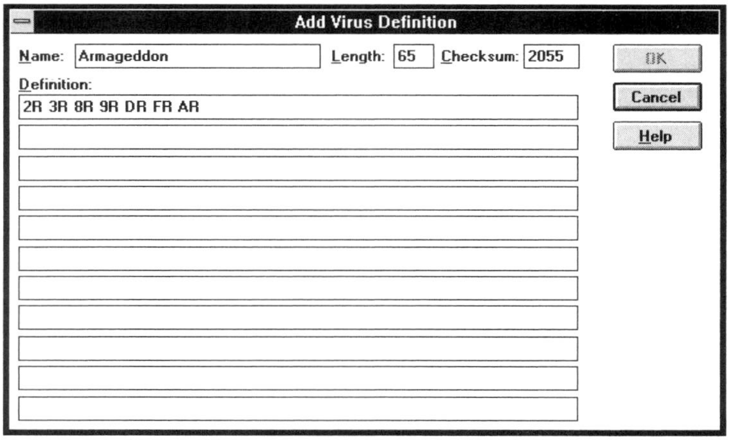

▲ In the Definition box, type the definition of the virus, following the pattern displayed in the Add Virus Definition dialog box in Figure 12.10 (that is, sets of two characters separated by spaces). Press **Tab** to move to a new line when you have reached the end of the current line.

▲ Click the OK button. You are returned to the Modify List dialog box.

TIP

You can print the virus definitions list by clicking on the Print button in the Modify List dialog box. Using a printed list may be helpful if you are trying to locate all outdated viruses.

To delete virus definitions:

▲ In the Modify List dialog box, click on the name of an outdated virus in the Virus Names box.

▲ Click on the Delete button. You are asked to confirm the deletion.

▲ Click on Yes.

▲ Repeat the above three steps to delete all other outdated viruses.

▲ Click the OK button. The new viruses are now included in Norton AntiVirus and the old virus definitions no longer exist.

CHECK YOURSELF

Load a new virus definitions file called 16all06.def located on floppy drive B.

1. In the Norton AntiVirus window, choose Definitions Load from the File menu.

2. In the File box in the Load From File dialog box, type **B:\16ALL06.DEF**.

3. Click the OK button.

QUICK SUMMARY

Command	To Do This
Options Global	Set AntiVirus options, such as having AntiVirus check for unknown viruses.
Tools Norton AntiVirus, or the AntiVirus tool icon	Start Norton AntiVirus, or open the Norton Anti-Virus window, if AntiVirus is already running.
Scan Drive	Have AntiVirus scan a drive for viruses.
Scan Directory	Have AntiVirus scan a directory for viruses.
Scan File	Have AntiVirus scan a file for viruses.
Tools Uninoculate	Replace the old inoculation file with a new one.
Definitions Load from File	Load a new virus definitions file into AntiVirus.
Definitions Modify List	Add and delete virus definitions manually.

PRACTICE WHAT YOU'VE LEARNED

Scan a directory called INFECTED (not including its subdirectories) for viruses, then repair an infected file called CONTAMIN.ATE.

1. Choose Tools Norton AntiVirus to open the Norton AntiVirus window.

2. Choose Scan Directory from the Norton AntiVirus window.

3. In the Drive box, click on the drive containing the directory to be scanned.

4. In the Directory box, click on infected.

5. Deselect the Include Subdirectories check box.

6. Click the OK button. The scan process begins.

7. In the Scan Results dialog box, click on contamin.ate.

8. Click on the Repair button. The Repair Files dialog box appears.

9. Click on Repair to eliminate the virus.

Customizing Norton Desktop

Do these issues sound familar: *Why isn't the Rename button on the drive window button bar? I use it all the time!* Or, when exiting Norton Desktop and you're stopped with: "This will end your Windows session," *Gee, I think that's why I double-clicked on the Control-menu button.* You can get rid of the prompts that question you whenever you use the mouse to move, copy, or print files, if you want. You can also add, remove, or change the order of menu items, as well as allocate whichever commands you wish to the drive window button bar. You can even assign a shortcut key to a desktop item icon that will run the represented program when you enter the correct key combination. In this chapter, you will learn many ways to customize Norton Desktop items to meet your needs, including configuring:

- ▲ **Drive, tool, and desktop icons**
- ▲ **Quick Access**
- ▲ **Drive windows**
- ▲ **The Control menu**
- ▲ **Confirmation options**
- ▲ **File name prompts**

Drive, Tool, and Desktop Icons

You can modify drive, tool, and desktop icons to accommodate your needs more precisely. We already covered in Chapter 1 how to place drive icons on the left or right side of the desktop, how to display or not display the drive and tool icons you wish, and how to put your desktop icons in order instantly or on a regular basis. But there are other items you can adjust as well.

TIP

Remember, to make any of the changes discussed in this chapter apply to future sessions of Norton Desktop, you must save the new configuration. You can do this by choosing Tools Save Configuration in the Configure Preferences dialog box. Otherwise, all changes you make will apply only to the current Norton Desktop session.

Preventing Drive Windows from Showing

You can arrange it so no one can access drives from Norton Desktop that are not selected in the Configure Drive Icons dialog box (the drives can be accessed from other applications, however). For example, if you're hooked to a network but do *not* select network drives in the dialog box, you will not be able to open a network drive window. For instance, suppose that your hard drive is C, your floppy drives are A and B, and your network drives are E, F, and Q. If you do not select the E, F, and Q drives in the Configure Drive Icons dialog box and turn on the option that limits access to selected drives only, when you choose the Window Open Drive Window menu command, only the A, B, and C drives will be listed in the Drive box. Further, all drive boxes in all dialog boxes (such as Browse scroll boxes) would let you choose only from the hard and floppy drives.

To limit access to drives:

▲ Choose Configure Drive Icons. The Configure Drive Icons dialog box appears, as shown in Figure 13.1.

▼ *Figure 13.1. Configure Drive Icons Dialog Box*

Drive, Tool, and Desktop Icons

▲ Select the Allow Access to Selected Drives Only check box.

▲ Deselect any drives you don't want to be accessible.

▲ Click the OK button. (Save this configuration if you wish to make it permanent.)

Displaying Icon Control Menus

By default, when you click once on a drive, tool, or desktop icon, a Control menu is displayed, as shown in Figure 13.2. Remember, when you double-click on an icon, it opens the associated feature, whether that's a drive window, the Viewer, or a software program; so unless you're likely to change icon properties often, you may wish to disable the Control menus from drive and tool icons.

▼ *Figure 13.2. Clicking Once on a Drive, Tool, or Desktop Icon Displays Its Control Menu*

TIP

You can't disable Control menus from desktop icons, because the only way to delete a desktop icon is by choosing Close from its Control menu.

To determine whether or not an icon's Control menu shows:

▲ Choose Configure Preferences. The Configure Preferences dialog box appears (see Figure 13.16 toward the end of this chapter).

▲ Click on the Advanced button. The Advanced dialog box appears, as shown in Figure 13.3.

▲ Deselect the Drive/Tool Icon Control Menu check box if you want to disable the Control menus; select the box if you want the Control menus to show.

▲ Click the OK button twice. (Save this configuration if you wish to make it permanent).

Changing an Icon's Label

Perhaps you wish to add your own personal touches to your desktop. Making icon labels more meaningful is a good way to start. If you've configured your icons to display Control menus, changing an icon's label will be easy. Follow the steps below to change drive and tool icon labels. The procedures for changing desktop icon labels are discussed in Chapter 2.

To change a drive or tool icon's label:

▲ Click once on the drive or tool icon to display its Control menu (see Figure 13.2).

▲ Choose Label from the Control menu. The Edit Label dialog box appears, as shown in Figure 13.4.

▲ In the Label box, type the name of the new label.

▲ Click the OK button. (Save this configuration if you wish to make it permanent.)

▼ *Figure 13.3. Advanced Dialog Box*

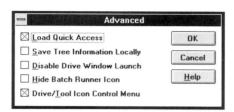

▼ *Figure 13.4. Edit Label Dialog Box*

Changing a Tool Icon's Graphic

Another way to add a personal touch to your desktop is by choosing your own graphics for the tool icons. There is a huge assortment of graphics to choose from, many of which will identify a tool's function just as well as the default graphic. For example, there are several graphics from which you can choose to change the magnifying glass displayed in the Viewer icon.

To change a tool icon's graphic:

▲ Click once on the tool icon whose graphic you want to change. The Control menu will appear (see Figure 13.2).

▲ Choose Icon from the Control menu. The Choose Icon dialog box appears.

▲ Follow the instructions in Chapter 2 for details on selecting a new icon.

▲ Click the OK button. (Save this configuration if you wish to make it permanent.)

TIP

If you ever wish to change the graphics of all group, desktop, and tool icons back to their original (default) graphics, open the Configure Quick Access dialog box (for details, see Quick Access, later in this chapter) and click on the Reset Icons button.

Desktop Icon Shortcut Keys

You can assign a special key combination, consisting of the Ctrl key plus another key to any of your desktop program or document icons so that whenever you enter this key combination, the corresponding program or document will run.

To assign a shortcut key combination to a desktop icon:

▲ Click once on the icon to display its Control menu (see Figure 13.2).

▲ Choose Properties from the Control menu. The Properties dialog box appears.

▲ Click on the Options button. The Options dialog box appears, as shown in Figure 13.5.

▲ Click on the Shortcut Key box.

▲ Press **Ctrl** as you type another key. Both keys will appear in the Shortcut Key box (review Figure 13.5).

▼ *Figure 13.5. Options Dialog Box*

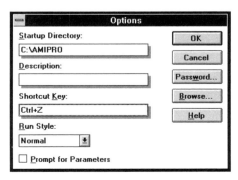

▲ Click the OK button twice. (Save this configuration if you wish to make it permanent.)

TIP

Make sure you don't assign a key combination that has already been assigned to a different item. If you select uncommon keys, such as Z, Q,], or +, you'll usually be safe. If you select a key combination that's already in use, the program doesn't tell you so, but you'll find out when you try to use that key combination and it doesn't work!

CHECK YOURSELF

Prevent all floppy drives from being accessed, then change a Printer tool icon's label to "My Printer." Make your changes permanent.

1. Choose Configure Drive Icons.

2. Select the Allow Access to Selected Drives Only check box.

3. Deselect the All Floppy Drives check box, then click the OK button.

4. Click once on Printer tool icon to display its Control menu.

5. Choose Label from the Control menu.

6. In the Edit Label dialog box, type **My Printer** in the Label box, then click the OK button.

Quick Access

Quick Access is covered in depth in Chapter 2; however, the ways that you can configure it are discussed here. With the exception of making Quick Access load at startup (which is discussed in Chapter 2), you will use the Configure Quick Access dialog box to specify all custom settings. You worked with the

Configure Quick Access dialog box briefly before when you designated group icons to be arranged automatically.

To configure Quick Access:

▲ Choose Configure Quick Access. The Configure Quick Access dialog box appears, as shown in Figure 13.6.

▲ Make any of the changes specified in the sections below.

▲ Click the OK button. (Save your configurations if you wish to make them permanent.)

Choosing the Group View

There are three different ways you can view icons in a group. *Icon view* displays a graphic and a label for each icon. *List view* displays the same items but also shows an icon's description, if you created one; icons are listed in rows rather than columns in list view. *Toolbox view* only displays a graphic for each icon, so you had better know your icon functions well if you choose this view. In Chapter 2 you learned how to designate a view style for one group and to change all existing groups to that view style. However, you can also specify that all subsequently created groups be configured in a particular view style, using the Configure Quick Access dialog box.

▼ *Figure 13.6. Configure Quick Access Dialog Box*

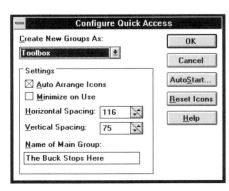

TIP

For more details and illustrations on each of the three view types, read Rearranging Groups in Chapter 2.

To designate a default view style:

▲ In the Configure Quick Access dialog box, choose the default view style in the Create New Groups As pull-down list box.

Minimizing Groups

By default, when you open a group item the group window containing that group item remains open on the desktop. If you wish, you can reduce a group window to a desktop icon automatically whenever you open one of the group's items.

To iconize group windows after items are chosen:

▲ In the Configure Quick Access dialog box, select the Minimize On Use check box.

Spacing Group Icons

If you are using the icon view style for your groups, you can specify how far apart group items are placed from each other, which will be significant if you've turned on the Auto Arrange Icons option, or when you choose the Window Arrange Group Icons menu command. If you usually place icons where you want them, you don't need to bother with this option.

Spacing is measured by *pixels,* which are the smallest measurements used to build an image. By default, both horizontal and vertical spacing are set to 75 pixels. You can lessen or increase either of these settings by using the appropriate spin buttons in the Settings box. Pixel measurements for both horizontal and vertical spacing can be set from 1 to 256, though you will probably not like the results of using vertical spacing below 65 pixels. If you'd like to have your icons arranged in two columns, set horizontal spacing to 164 pixels.

To change the spacing of group icons:

▲ In the Configure Quick Access dialog box, click on the upper or lower spin buttons for the Horizontal Spacing box to raise or lower the number of pixels.

▲ Click on the upper or lower spin buttons for the Vertical Spacing box to raise or lower the number of pixels.

TIP

To see the results of new space settings immediately, choose Window Arrange Group Icons while a group is open.

Renaming the Quick Access Group

Another way you can personalize your desktop is by assigning the Quick Access group a different name. Perhaps it would help you to remember that Quick Access holds all of your other groups if you named it "The Buck Stops Here," or "The Group of Groups." You can call the Quick Access group whatever you want, and from then on that name will appear on the title bar. Keep in mind, however, that "Quick Access" will remain on the Configure menu, and the Configure Quick Access dialog box *won't* change to Configure The Group of Groups dialog box.

To rename the Quick Access group:

▲ In the Configure Quick Access dialog box, type the desired name in the Name of Main Group box.

Making a New Group the AutoStart Group

In Chapter 5 you learned that you can drag whichever program and document icons you wish to the AutoStart (StartUp if running Windows 3.1) group to automatically launch those programs and open the corresponding document files. If one of your Quick Access groups contains the programs and/or documents you want started each time you begin a Windows session, you can simply make this the AutoStart group. Changing the AutoStart group will save you from having to drag a bunch of icons to the existing AutoStart group.

To make a new group the AutoStart group:

▲ Click on the AutoStart button in the Configure Quick Access dialog box. The Select AutoStart Group dialog box appears, as shown in Figure 13.7.

▲ Scroll through the Group box to locate the group you want to designate as the startup group. The check box is selected for the group you've chosen.

▲ Click the OK button.

TIP

The group you designate as the new AutoStart group retains its original name. While it becomes the new startup group, it is not named as such.

Drive Windows

Norton Desktop leaves you a lot of room to customize your drive windows by letting you determine which commands will appear on the button bar. You can set up a drive window just

▼ *Figure 13.7. Select AutoStart Group Dialog Box*

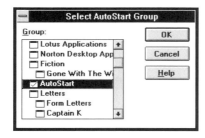

the way you want it—the view pane showing, a maximized window, and so on—and then save this configuration as a default so that all subsequent drive windows will appear this way. Additionally, there are options for speeding up the tree pane display and preventing program and document files from being launched from a drive window.

Designing the Button Bar

Chapter 3 introduced you to the drive window button bar, and Chapter 5 showed you how to use the command buttons. You can configure the button bar to include whichever commands you desire—replace old commands with new commands, or just switch the order of the existing commands. This latter option can be helpful if you normally display rather small drive windows, because when there isn't enough room in the drive window to display all of the buttons, those farthest right are not shown. For example, if you rename files frequently, you could move the Rename button, which is presently the twelfth command button, far enough to the left—perhaps to the second or third button—so that it will always show.

There are a total of 14 command buttons; however, the only screen mode that will display all 14 buttons is Super VGA. Even if you maximize a drive window in regular VGA mode, only 12 buttons will appear. The 14 default command buttons are displayed in the Configure Button Bar dialog box, as shown in Figure 13.8.

You can establish button commands for any of the available menu commands. You can even place such tool commands as Format Diskette and the Macro Builder on the Button Bar, as shown in Figure 13.9.

All Norton Desktop menu commands appear in the Menu Item scroll box in the Configure Button Bar dialog box, as shown in Figure 13.8. After you select a menu command, you can then assign it to a new button by clicking on that button. When you assign a menu command to a new button, the old command is deleted and the new command shows in its place.

▼ *Figure 13.8. Configure Button Bar Dialog Box, Showing the Default Command Buttons*

Drive Windows

TIP

Be careful when placing repeat submenu commands on the button bar, such as All, Some, and Invert, which exist for both Select and Deselect menu commands. After you assign one of these commands to a button, you should edit its name to make its function clearer (for example, change Some to DesSome or SelSome, depending on the function).

▼ *Figure 13.9. New Button Bar Configuration in the Configure Button Bar Dialog Box*

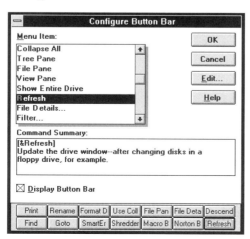

To add new command buttons to the Button Bar:

▲ Choose Configure Button Bar. The Configure Button Bar dialog box appears, as displayed in Figure 13.8.

▲ Scroll through the Menu Item box to locate the command you want to add.

▲ Click on the menu command so that it becomes highlighted. A summary of the menu command's function now appears in the Command Summary box, as shown in Figure 13.8.

▲ Click once on the command button (located at the bottom of the dialog box) that you want to assign the new command to. The name of the new command appears on the button you indicated. Remember, when you assign a new command to a command button, the command previously listed on that button will be deleted. However, you can reestablish it on a different button.

▲ Add any other new commands you wish following the steps above.

▲ Click the OK button. (Save your configuration if you wish to make it permanent.)

TIP

If you wish to switch the order of existing command buttons, first decide in which order you want the buttons to appear, then follow the above steps to place each command where you want it, in turn. There is no way to physically move buttons around; you'll have to overwrite existing buttons to switch the button bar order.

CHECK YOURSELF

Add the following menu commands in order to the button bar: The first four commands should now match those in the button bar in Figure 13.9.

1. Choose Configure Button Bar.

2. Select Print in the Menu Item box, then click on the Move button.

3. Select Rename in the Menu Item box, then click on the Copy button.

4. Select Format Diskette in the Menu Item box, then click on the Delete button.

5. Select Use Collapsible Tree in the Menu Item box, then click on the View button.

6. Click the OK button.

Making Command Names More Meaningful

You can also change the names that appear on the button in the button bar. You'll find that this is helpful when you add a new command like Norton Backup, which, by default, is written on the button as "Norton B," because there is only room for about eight characters on each button. Since "Norton B" does not clearly indicate the function of the command button, you could assign a more descriptive name, such as "BackUp," as shown in Figure 13.10. Compare the buttons in Figure 13.9 with those in Figure 13.10. The buttons in Figure 13.9 show how command buttons are named by default when you select the corresponding func-

▼ *Figure 13.10. Making the Command Button Names More Meaningful*

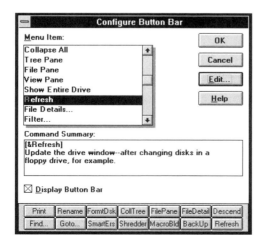

tions; the buttons in Figure 13.10 have been edited to display more meaningful names.

You'll use the Edit Button Bar Text dialog box, shown in Figure 13.11, to edit button names. This dialog box displays the names of all the current command buttons in the order in which they appear on the button bar, labeling them in rows from A to N.

TIP

Changing the name of a command button has no effect on the function of the command. For example, if you edit the Rename button to read as "Print," you will still bring up the Rename dialog box when you click on that command button. You must follow the steps discussed earlier if you want to change the function of a button.

To edit the name of a command button:

1. Click on the Edit button in the Configure Button Bar dialog box. The Edit Button Bar Text dialog box appears, as shown in Figure 13.11.

2. Click on the box that contains the name of the button you wish to change.

3. Type in a new name.

4. Repeat steps 2 and 3 if you want to change other command button names.

5. Click the OK button. The new names appear instantly on the sample button bar in the Configure Button Bar dialog box. (Save your configuration if you wish to make it permanent.)

▼ *Figure 13.11. The Edit Button Bar Text Dialog Box*

TIP

If you want to remove the button bar from the drive window altogether, deselect the Display Button Bar check box in the Configure Button Bar dialog box, then click the OK button. Remember to save your configuration if you wish to remove the button bar permanently.

CHECK YOURSELF

Edit the names of the last two buttons you created in the previous Check Yourself exercise to appear as they do in Figure 13.10.

1. Click on the Edit button in the Configure Button Bar dialog box.

2. Click on the C box, which contains "Format D," then type **FormDsk**.

3. Click on the D box, which contains "Use Coll," then type **CollTree**.

4. Click the OK button. The new names appear instantly on the sample button bar in the Configure Button Bar dialog box.

Changing the Default Appearance of the Drive Window

Usually when you open a drive window, the window occupies about a quarter of the desktop, the tree and file panes are showing, and the directory tree is not collapsible. However, you can create a new default drive window that has different settings. For example, you might wish your drive windows to be larger, to show only the tree pane, and to use a collapsible tree. You could create a default window that's designed accordingly so that from now on, whenever you open a new drive window, it will include these features.

Specifying the Panes

As mentioned earlier, by default the tree and file panes are shown whenever you open a drive window. However, you can make it so only one or the other is displayed in your drive windows by default. You cannot specify that the view pane be shown automatically; this pane must be selected after a drive window is opened.

To specify the default panes for the drive window:

▲ Open a drive window. Use the View menu to turn on or off the appropriate panes.

▲ Choose Configure Save Configuration.

Changing the Drive Window's Size

A new default size for the drive window can be set in two ways. You can either open a drive window, set it to the appropriate size you want, then choose the Use Current option in the Configure Drive Window dialog box; or you can use the sizing buttons in this same dialog box to set the default size.

To create a new default size for the drive window:

▲ Choose Configure Drive Window. The Configure Drive Window dialog box appears, as shown in Figure 13.12.

▲ Adjust the Size option buttons to the desired size, or click on the Use Current option if you have sized an active drive window to the default size you wish.

▲ Click the OK button. (Save this configuration if you wish to make it permanent.)

▼ *Figure 13.12. Configure Drive Window Dialog Box*

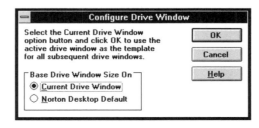

Choosing a Tree Style

Drive Windows

Directory trees can operate in two ways: they can either have all directories and subdirectories on a drive permanently showing or they can have collapsible branches so that subdirectories can be hidden and then redisplayed. The first method displays directory tree information faster than the second and is the default drive window tree style. However, you may prefer to be able to expand and collapse the directory tree for more efficient organization. By using the Configure Drive Window dialog box, you can specify that a collapsible directory tree be used in the default drive window.

TIP

Although using a collapsible tree will slow down the display process, you will never have to use the Refresh command button to update a drive's information, as you must do when using the default tree style. With a collapsible tree, when you copy or move directories from one drive to another, the new directory information is displayed instantly.

To use a collapsible directory tree style in the default drive window:

▲ Choose Configure Drive Window. The Configure Drive Window dialog box appears (see Figure 13.12).

▲ Deselect the Use Directory Tree Information check box.

▲ Click the OK button. (Save this configuration if you wish to make it permanent.)

TIP

If you work on a network drive but do not use a collapsible tree, make sure you specify that directory tree information is to be saved in the Norton Desktop directory rather than on the network drives. To do so, choose Configure Preferences Advanced and select the Save Tree Information Locally check box. Save this configuration to make the change permanent.

Preventing Launching from Drive Windows

If you share your computer with others or work on a network drive and are concerned about file security, you can disable the feature that allows you to launch files from a drive window (by double-clicking on them) and to create desktop items by dragging files from the drive window to the desktop—icons that can later be used to launch the files. To disable launching from drive windows, you use the Advanced dialog box accessed through the Configure Preferences dialog box.

To prohibit launching from drive windows:

▲ Choose Configure Preferences. The Configure Preferences dialog box appears (see Figure 13.16 at the end of this chapter).

▲ Click on the Advanced button. The Advanced dialog box appears (see Figure 13.3).

▲ Select the Disable Drive Window Launch check box.

▲ Click the OK button twice. (Save this configuration if you wish to make it permanent.)

CHECK YOURSELF

Make the default drive window size the size of the currently opened drive window and cause all drive windows to use collapsible directory trees.

1. Open a drive window and set it to the appropriate size.

2. Choose Configure Drive Window.

3. Click on the Use Current option.

4. Deselect the Use Directory Tree Information check box.

5. Click the OK button.

6. Choose Configure Save Configuration.

The Control Menu

By default, the Control menus for all of your Windows applications contain the Launch List, Launch Manager, and Run menu commands. You can quickly run a program by selecting an application from the Launch List, which contains a list of programs that you've specified with the Launch Manager. Another way to run a program using the Control menu is by using the Run command (refer to Chapter 5 for more on the Run command).

If you wish, you can remove any of these items from the Control menu. Additionally, you can specify that the Task List appear on the Control menu. (The Task List contains all currently running programs in Windows.) You can use this list to quickly switch between open applications.

To determine which items will be placed on all Windows applications' Control menus:

▲ Choose Configure Control Menu. The Configure Control Menu dialog box appears, as shown in Figure 13.13.

▲ Select the Task List check box if you wish this item to be placed on the Control menu.

▲ Deselect the check boxes for the other items if you don't wish one or more of them to appear on the Control menu.

▲ Click the OK button. (Save this configuration if you wish to make it permanent.)

▼ *Figure 13.13. The Configure Control Menu Dialog Box*

CHECK YOURSELF

Make the Task List appear on all Windows Control menus.

1. Choose Configure Control Menu.

2. Select the Task List check box.

3. Click the OK button.

4. Choose Configure Save Configuration.

Password-protecting Your Menus

If you want to make sure you're the only person who can switch the type of menus being used (that is, short, full, and custom menus) and edit those menus, you can assign a password to the Configure Load Menu and Configure Edit Menus commands so that no one can access the respective dialog boxes until the correct password is entered. You'll assign the password in the Set Password dialog box. If you later want to change or disable the password, you can do so in the Change Password dialog box (which is the same dialog box as the Set Password dialog box, only with a different name).

TIP

A password can contain up to 20 characters and can include letters (lower- and uppercase), numbers, the characters assigned to the number keys (accessed by pressing the Shift key), and spaces.

To assign a password to the Configure Menu commands:

▲ Choose Configure Menu Password. The Set Password dialog box appears, as shown in Figure 13.14a.

▲ Type the password in the New Password box, then click the OK button. An asterisk (*) appears for each letter you type.

▼ *Figure 13.14a. Set Password Dialog Box*

▼ *Figure 13.14b. Verify Password Dialog Box*

▲ Type the password again in the Confirm Password box.

▲ Click the OK button.

Now whenever the Configure Load Menu and Configure Edit Menus commands are selected, the Verify Password dialog box will appear, shown in Figure 13.14b.

To change a password:

▲ Choose Configure Menu Password. The Change Password dialog box appears (this is the same dialog box as the Set Password dialog box seen in Figure 13.14a).

▲ Type the password in the Old Password box, then click the OK button.

▲ Type the new password in the New Password box.

▲ Type the new password again in the Confirm Password box.

▲ Click the OK button.

TIP

To disable password protection, follow the steps for changing a password, but instead of entering a new password, click the OK button. A dialog box appears asking you whether you want to delete the password. Click Yes and the Menu commands will no longer require a password to be run.

CHECK YOURSELF

Assign the password "Just U & Me" to the Configure Menu commands.

1. Choose Configure Menu Password.

2. Type **Just U & Me** in the New Password box, then click the OK button.

3. Type **Just U & Me** again in the Confirm Password box.

4. Click the OK button.

Confirmation Options

Norton Desktop is configured to prompt you to confirm certain actions that have serious consequences or that you may have accidentally chosen. In other words, you're given a second chance to confirm your action. As it stands, every time you use the mouse to perform functions such as moving and copying files, you are prompted to confirm the move or copy. If a file you're moving or copying to a new location will overwrite a file with the same name, you are asked whether you really want to overwrite that file. Also, whenever you delete a file or a subdirectory (the directory itself—not its files), you are asked to confirm the delete. If you try to print a file that is not associated with any software application, you are notified that this is an unassociated file and asked whether you still want to print the file. Finally, you're probably quite familiar with the prompt that says you're about to exit Windows, after you have double-clicked on the Control menu button to do just this. If you want, you can make it so this and all of the other confirmation prompts no longer appear.

We suggest that you leave the Delete prompt operative. It's easy to delete one or more files unintentionally, and though you can use SmartErase to restore the files, you might not realize you deleted the wrong files until months later.

You can disable the Subtree Delete prompt, which prompts you only when you are deleting a subdirectory (not its files). Since you can't delete a subdirectory that still contains files, the consequences of accidentally deleting an empty subdirectory are minimal.

We also suggest you leave the Mouse Operation prompt intact. When dragging multiple files, it's easy to end up dragging files you didn't intend to—perhaps the selected files weren't showing in the drive window at the time. The confirmation prompt also verifies that you're moving rather than copying, or vice-versa, which can be helpful.

You should definitely leave the Replace prompt operative. When you copy files frequently between hard and floppy drives, over time you're likely to get a few if not several overwrite warnings. The results of accidentally and unknowingly overwriting the most recent version of a file with an older version of that file can be disastrous.

The Unassociated Print and Exit Norton Desktop prompts can be disabled without any serious consequences. An unassociated file can still be printed if the prompt is unchecked. Keep in mind, though, that you'll lose any formatting codes, meaning the print job will be rather generic.

You probably get tired of seeing the confirmation prompt each time you quit Windows; however, sometimes you may double-click on the Norton Desktop Control menu box thinking that you are double-clicking on an application's Control menu box. The prompt can save you from time wasted starting up Norton Desktop again. If you do decide to disable this confirmation prompt, and later exit Norton Desktop accidentally, you don't have to fear that the work you've done will be lost; you'll be notified of any open applications before leaving Windows and can save your work then.

Confirmation Options

▼ *Figure 13.15. Configure Confirmation Dialog Box*

Configure Confirmation

☒ Delete   OK
☒ Subtree Delete
☒ Replace   Cancel
☒ Mouse Operation
☐ Unassociated Print   Help
☐ Exit Norton Desktop

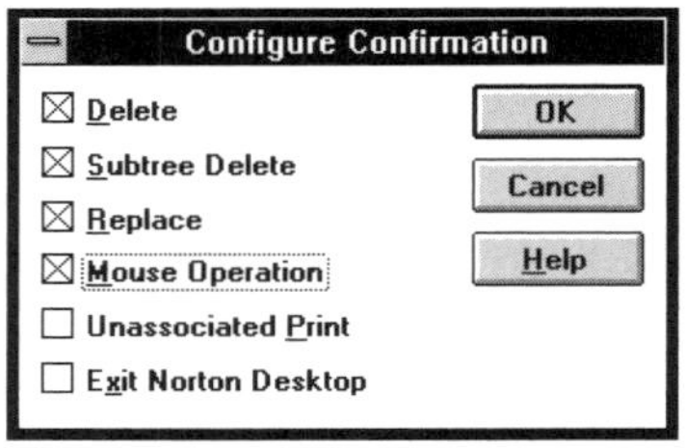

To determine which confirmation prompts are activated:

▲ Choose Configure Confirmation. The Configure Confirmation dialog box appears, as shown in Figure 13.15.

▲ Leave selected the check boxes of the options you wish to remain operative.

▲ Select the check boxes of the options you wish to disable.

▲ Click the OK button. (Save this configuration if you wish to make it permanent.)

CHECK YOURSELF

Disable the prompt that appears whenever you exit Windows.

1. Choose Configure Confirmation.

2. Select the Exit Norton Desktop check box.

3. Click the OK button.

4. Choose Configure Save Configuration.

File Name Prompts

When you select a file before choosing the File Delete and File Print commands, a dialog box appears that displays the name of the selected file so that you can confirm the operation. You can also have similar dialog boxes displayed before editing or viewing a file. Or if you want to speed up your operations, you can make it so no dialog boxes appear. You'll use the Configure Preferences dialog box to specify the prompts you wish to show or not to show.

We suggest that you leave the Delete File option operative, for the same reasons we cited in the previous discussion on confirmation prompts. The Print File prompt can spare you from printing a file you never intended to print, so it can be valuable at times. On the other hand, there's really no need to be queried about a file you wish to view; if the wrong one appears, you can quickly display the correct one. Finally, whether you decide to display a dialog box before editing a file really depends on how often you use the Editor and whether you think this is a helpful step.

To determine which prompts will show before performing file operations:

▲ Choose Configure Preferences. The Configure Preferences dialog box appears, as shown in Figure 13.16.

▲ In the Prompt for Filename box, select the check boxes for the types of operations you would like to have a dialog box appear for before performing the operations.

▲ Deselect any check boxes for file operations you don't want to be prompted about.

File Name
Prompts

▼ *Figure 13.16. Configure Preferences Dialog Box*

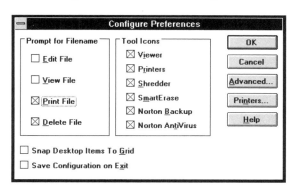

▲ Click the OK button. (Save this configuration if you wish to make it permanent.)

TIP

Remember that if an operation's corresponding check box is deselected, the action will be performed automatically on a selected file or group of files, without confirmation from you.

CHECK YOURSELF

Have a dialog box appear before you edit a file.

1. Choose Configure Preferences.

2. In the Prompt for Filename box, select the Edit File check box.

3. Click the OK button.

4. Choose Configure Save Configuration.

QUICK SUMMARY

Command	*To Do This*
Configure Drive Icons	Prevent certain drives from being accessed from Norton Desktop.
Configure Preferences	Enable or disable prompts for file names when editing, viewing, printing, and deleting.
Configure Preferences Advanced	Display or hide icon Control menus, specify that files cannot be launched from drive windows, and specify that directory tree information be saved in the Norton Desktop directory.
Configure Quick Access	Specify a view type (icon, list, or toolbox), set the spacing of items in group windows, or rename the Quick Access group.
Configure Quick Access AutoStart	Make a new group the AutoStart group.
Configure Button Bar	Add new commands to the button bar, switch the order of existing names, or edit the button bar names.

Command	*To Do This*
Configure Drive Window	Create a new default size for a drive window or make the default drive window display a collapsible tree.
Configure Control Menu	Determine which commands will be placed on all Windows applications' Control menus.
Configure Menu Password	Assign, change, or disable a password to the Configure Load Menu and Configure Edit Menus commands.
Configure Confirmation	Specify whether confirmation prompts will appear when certain file functions are performed.

PRACTICE WHAT YOU'VE LEARNED

Assign the shortcut key combination Ctrl+Z to one of your desktop items. Then, change the name of the Quick Access group to "My Main Group," and assign Toolbox view to all of your future group windows.

1. Click on the desktop icon to display its Control menu.

2. Choose Properties from the Control menu. The Properties dialog box appears.

3. Click on the Options button. The Options dialog box appears.

4. Click on the Shortcut Key box.

5. Press **Ctrl+Z**, then click the OK button twice.

6. Choose Configure Quick Access.

7. Type **My Main Group** in the Name of Main Group box.

8. Choose Toolbox View in the Create New Groups As box.

9. Click the OK button.

10. Choose Configure Save Configuration.

Backing Up a Group of Files

Though you may think it will never happen to you, someday your hard disk will probably crash. An electrical surge, a mechanical failure, fire—whatever the cause, all of the files you've spent the past few years working on could disappear. If you don't have backups for those files, it could be disastrous.

Backing up files not only protects your valuable work, but it also helps to free up hard disk space. After you've backed up a group of files that you no longer use but don't want to lose, you can safely delete them from your hard disk and use the freed space for new documents. With good backup software such as Norton Backup, your backup process can be smooth and efficient. This chapter tells you about basic backup concepts, as well as:

▲ **How to use the Backup Window**

▲ **How to select the files to be backed up**

▲ **How to run the backup**

▲ **How to create a setup file**

Basic Backup Concepts

If you don't have some kind of plan for backing up your files, pretty soon you'll have floppy disks everywhere containing who knows what backup files. You'll be hesitant to reuse any of them because you're not sure which files you'd be overwriting. And restoring a backed-up file becomes a task you dread to attempt—where do you start?

To back up your files quickly and efficiently, you must develop a consistent backup strategy. The one you select will depend on the amount of file activity on your system (that is, how often you create and/or edit files), and on how much risk you're willing to take with your work.

Before discussing the various types of backup strategies, we must first introduce you to backup flags, which are an essential part of the backup picture.

Backup Flags

Attached to each file is a *backup flag*. Whenever you create a new file or modify an existing one, its backup flag is raised. Essentially, this flag (when raised) indicates that the file has been modified since the last time it was backed up. Here's a typical scenario involving a file and its backup flag:

▲ You create a new file. When you do, the operating system automatically raises the backup flag for that file.

▲ Sooner or later you back up the file, along with several others. When this happens, the file's backup flag is lowered, indicating that the file has been backed up.

▲ Sometime after the backup, you edit the file. When you do, the backup flag is automatically raised again, indicating that the file has been modified since it was last backed up.

As you may guess, file backup flags are an indispensable part of the overall backup picture.

Backup Strategies

The type of backup strategy you select depends on how frequently you modify your files and how much of your work you care to put at risk. For example, if you edit your files very infrequently, you may be willing to get by with a backup once a week. On the other hand, if you frequently create new files or edit existing ones, you may want to perform a daily backup.

Many files or directories don't need to be backed up. For example, most program files don't change, so there's little reason to back them up. If you do have a disk crash, you can always reinstall the programs from the original disks. There are some exceptions: some program files do change when you customize a program, and you may want to back them up to save having to recustomize the program. Some examples of this are files with the extension .INI that are part of most Windows programs.

A Simple Backup Strategy

About the simplest backup strategy you can adopt is to perform a *total backup of your entire hard disk* periodically. Although the simplest in concept, this approach has several disadvantages:

▲ A total backup requires a lot of time, during which both you and the computer may be unavailable for any other activity.

▲ Depending on the number and size of files on your hard disk, a total backup may require a great many floppy disks.

▲ Many files are unnecessarily backed up. For instance, most program files don't need to be backed up regularly, as discussed above.

To reduce the magnitude of these disadvantages, you'll probably be tempted to perform this type of backup infrequently— perhaps every week, or even less often. The problem then becomes that you risk all of your work between each pair of backups. For instance, if you do weekly backups every Friday afternoon, but this week your hard disk crashed Friday morning, all of your work for the past week will be lost!

A Better Approach: Using Selective Full Backups

You can reduce the problems associated with total backups by selecting which files you want to back up each time. For example, if your program files are stored on drive C and your data files on drive D, you could periodically perform a backup of just the files on drive D. Using Norton Backup's terminology, this is called a *full backup*—even though you're not backing up the entire disk drive. In the following sections, we'll contrast full backups with other types of backups.

Although faster than total backups (which copy every single file on all hard disks), full backups are nevertheless time consuming. They require a large number of floppies, and they put at risk all of your work between backups. Again, you won't want to perform a daily full backup because of the time and disks required.

TIP

Don't confuse a full backup with a total backup, which is a backup of all hard disk files. A full backup copies all files you have specified.

A Still Better Approach: Using Differential Backups

To help alleviate the disadvantages of relying strictly on full backups, you can vastly improve the situation by combining full backups with more frequent *differential backups.*

Here's how a differential backup works: periodically—say once a week—you perform a full backup of selected files. These might be all of your data files, which are on drive D. Then, once a day you perform a *differential backup,* which backs up only those files created or modified since the last full backup.

How does Norton Backup know which files have been changed or created since the last full backup? By looking at the backup flag for each file. What we didn't mention before is that when you perform a full backup, the backup flag of each file that's backed up is lowered. Subsequently, as you change any of these files or create new ones, their backup flags are raised. When a differential backup is performed, only those files (from among those you select—such as all the files in drive D) whose flags are raised are backed up.

Basic Backup Concepts

TIP

When you perform a differential backup, none of the backup flags are lowered, which is why each differential backup copies all the files modified since the last full backup.

To illustrate how this full backup/differential backup system works, suppose you do a full backup every Monday morning, but the rest of the week you perform a differential backup each morning. Table 14.1 shows which files are backed up when.

Here are a couple of important points to keep in mind about this type of backup strategy:

▲ Each day, the differential backup is larger than the one for the previous day, because the number of modified files increases. In other words, each differential backup includes all the files saved in the previous differential backup. Thus, the previous differential backup disks are then redundant (but should be kept for extra protection).

▲ Your entire set of files is protected by (1) the most recent full backup and (2) the most recent differential backup. If your hard disk crashes, you can recover by first restoring all the

▼ *Table 14.1. Full/Differential Backups*

Day	Backup Type	Files Backed Up That Morning	Files Changed That Day
Monday	Full	All selected files	FileA, FileB
Tuesday	Differential	FileA, FileB	FileC, FileD
Wednesday	Differential	FileA, FileB, FileC, FileD	

files from the most recent full backup, then those from the most recent differential backup.

▲ Whenever you perform a new full backup, all of the previous differential backup disks can then be released for reuse.

Another Backup Strategy: Using Incremental Backups

The combination of full and differential backups is a powerful and effective technique for safeguarding your work. However, it has one disadvantage: The differential backup for each day is larger than the previous one, and by the end of the week in an environment with heavy file usage, a great many floppies could be needed for the differential backup.

To alleviate this problem, you can use daily incremental— instead of differential—backups, combined with periodic full backups. When an *incremental backup* is performed, the flag of each backed-up file is lowered. The significance of each backed-up file's flag being lowered is that each incremental backup copies all files that have been created or modified since either the last full or the last incremental backup; all of the incremental backups between pairs of full backups form a complete backup set. In other words, you must save all of the incremental backup diskettes between successive full backups. (By contrast, you only need to save the diskettes used for the last differential backup.)

To illustrate this strategy, suppose that you perform a full backup each Monday morning, and the rest of the week you perform an incremental backup each morning. Table 14.2 shows which files will be saved each day.

▼ *Table 14.2. Full/Incremental Backups*

Day	Backup Type	Files Backed Up That Morning	Files Changed That Day
Monday	Full	All selected files	FileA, FileB
Tuesday	Incremental	FileA, FileB	FileC, FileD
Wednesday	Incremental	FileC, FileD	

Backup Cycles

A complete *backup cycle* is the period of time during which you perform one full backup and then a set of either incremental or differential backups. For instance, if you perform a full backup of Group "A" files on the first and fifteenth days of the month and perform differential backups every other day in between, the backup cycle is two and a half weeks long. Likewise, if you perform a full backup each Monday, and incremental backups on Tuesday through Friday, the backup cycle would be a week long.

You'll need to decide which type of backup cycle to implement. The best type for you will depend on your work habits, how much time you can spend on backing up your files, and the number of floppy disks you wish to use for the backups. Table 14.3 offers some advice about when to use the different backup types.

Types of Backup Media You Can Use

For each backup you perform, a group of files (called a *backup set*) is created and placed on a backup medium. Though we often refer to floppy diskettes when discussing storage of your

▼ Table 14.3. Using the Different Backup Types

Backup Type	When to Use	Advantages	Disadvantages
Full	Weekly, monthly, or on some other regular basis	Copies all the files you select; necessary for full protection	Time consuming; requires many floppies
Incremental	Between full backups; use this or differential backups when file activity is high	Requires fewer diskettes than differential backups	Requires more floppies than for differential backups; restoring a group of files is more complicated than with differential backups
Differential	Between full backups; use this or incremental backups when file activity is high	Simplifies the restore process following a disk crash, because each set of differential backup disks contains all the files changed since the last full backup	Each differential backup is larger than the prior one up to the next full backup

backup files, other types of media can be used as well. You can use the following types of backup media to store your files:

▲ Floppy diskettes

▲ DOS devices, such as network drives or Bernouilli hard drives (which are removable hard disks)

▲ Tape drives formatted as DOS devices

CHECK YOURSELF

You usually work with the same files each day, and you'd prefer to minimize the number of backup floppies to be filed. Which backup style should you use and why?

▲ Differential. Each set of differential backup floppies includes all the backup information on the previous set, so you need only save the most recent differential backup (although for extra safety you should save the most recent two or three sets).

Starting Up Norton Backup

When you start Norton Backup, the Backup window appears on the desktop. You will do all of your backup work from this window. Norton Backup can be started in two ways, as described below.

To start Norton Backup:

▲ Double-click on the Backup tool icon.

or:

▲ Choose Norton Backup from the Tools menu. The Backup window appears, as shown in Figure 14.1.

The Backup window allows you to select files for a backup, set various backup options, and start the backup. There are three

▼ *Figure 14.1. Basic Backup Window*

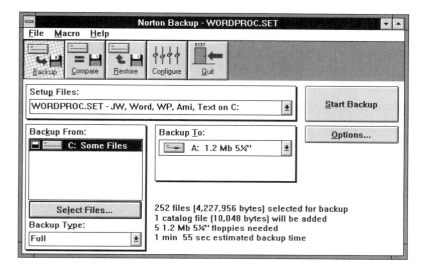

levels of the Backup window: Preset, Basic, and Advanced. When you first open the Backup window, the Basic program level will be chosen by default. Figure 14.1 shows what the Backup window looks like at the Basic program level.

In this chapter we'll concentrate on using the Basic level, which has sufficient flexibility for the majority of backup situations. If the Basic level isn't selected when you start up Norton Backup, you can easily switch to it.

To switch to the Basic level:

▲ Make sure the Norton Backup window is displayed.

▲ Click on the Configure button.

▲ When the next window appears, click on the scroll button for the box labeled Program Level, then click on the Basic option.

▲ Click on the Backup button to return to the Backup window.

Table 14.4 describes the functions of the different components of the Basic Backup window.

▼ Table 14.4. Backup Window Components

Component	This Lets You
File menu	Load and save setup files. Print the contents of the current setup file.
Macro menu	Run one macro per setup file.
Setup Files box	Choose the setup file you want to back up.
Backup From box	Choose which drives to back up.
Select Files button	Choose the directories and files you want backed up.
Backup Type box	Choose the type of backup, from: Full, Incremental, Differential, Full Copy, or Incremental Copy.
Backup To box	Choose where the backup set will be created.
Start Backup button	Start the backup process.
Options button	Modify the way the backup is performed.

Notice also that underneath the Backup To box, the number of selected files and their total byte size are displayed. If you are backing up to a floppy drive, the number of floppy diskettes and the estimated time length of the backup are also displayed.

TIP

If you've selected the data compression options in the Basic Backup Options dialog box, the number of floppies needed for the backup will usually be less than the number specified in the Backup window.

CHECK YOURSELF

Start Norton Backup and display the Basic level in the Backup window.

1. Double-click on the Backup tool icon, or choose Tools Norton Backup.

2. Click on the Configure button.

3. Click on the scroll button for the box labeled Program Level, then click on the Basic option.

4. Click on the Backup button to return to the Backup window.

Selecting the Files to Be Backed Up

Selecting the Files to Be Backed Up

The first step in performing a backup is to select the files you want to copy. When you first start up Norton Backup, a group of files is usually preselected for backup. Typically, this group includes all the files on drive C. To begin, you should *deselect* these files, as follows:

▲ Look in the box labeled Backup From, which lists the available drives on your system. If any of the drive names is followed by the label "All Files" or "Some Files," move the cursor to that drive name, then click *with the right mouse button,* until the label disappears. This deselects any files on this drive previously selected for backup.

When you have finished with this step, you can start with a "clean slate," selecting only those files you want to be backed up.

To select files for a backup:

▲ Click on the name of the drive that contains the files you want to back up.

▲ Click on the Select Files button. The Select Backup Files window appears, as shown in Figure 14.2. The Select Backup Files window displays two panes, similar to those shown in the drive windows. You can select either individual files or entire directories for backup.

▲ To select a file, first click on the name of the directory containing that file. Then, use the *right mouse button* to click on the file name. Notice that as you do, a black box appears next to the file name, indicating that it's selected for backup.

▲ To select an entire directory of files for backup, click on that directory name with the right mouse button. Again, notice that a black box appears next to the directory name, indicating that it's been selected.

▼ *Figure 14.2. Select Backup Files Window*

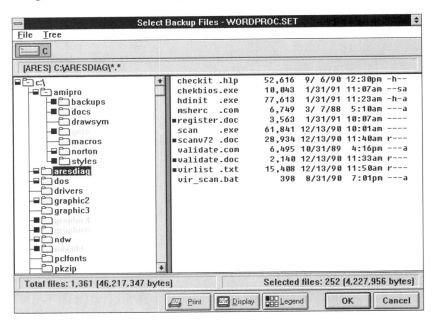

▲ To select a group of contiguous files or directories, hold down the right mouse button as you drag the mouse over the file or directory names.

▲ To deselect a file or directory that you previously selected, click on it again with the right mouse button.

▲ To understand the status of a particular file or directory, you can review the meaning of its associated selection icon, which is the little box to the left of any selected files and directories (see *Understanding the Selection Icons* below). You can also use the *information cursor,* which is explained below.

▲ Using the previous five steps, select as many different files and/or directories as you wish.

▲ Click the OK button.

You can select files for backup from more than one disk drive. For each drive, click on its name in the Norton Backup window, then follow the above steps to select additional files and directories.

Understanding the Selection Icons

Small boxes called *selection icons* appear next to all directories and files that you have selected. They also can appear next to the drive names in the Norton Backup window. These icons can appear in different shadings: some are clear, some are gray, some are black, and some half one shade and half another. In the file pane, only solid black or completely clear boxes will appear. Each of the different box settings indicates particular information about the drive, directory, or file. You can easily find out what each box stands for in the Backup Selection Legend dialog box shown in Figure 14.3, which appears after you click on the Legend button located at the bottom of the Select Backup Files window.

To review the meanings of the selection icons:

▲ Click on the Legend button at the bottom of the Select Backup Files window. The Selection Legend dialog box appears, as shown in Figure 14.3.

The Selection Legend dialog box tells you what a selection icon means, but it doesn't tell you, for example, why a file that

▼ *Figure 14.3. The Selection Legend Dialog Box*

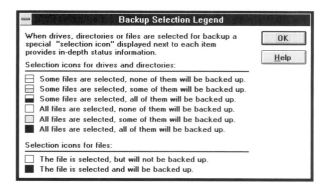

has been selected won't be backed up. There is a simple way to find this information. When you move the mouse pointer to the immediate left of *any* file name in the file pane or to the left of a directory icon in the tree pane, the cursor changes from an arrow to the *information cursor,* shown below.

If you click on the mouse button when the information cursor is showing next to a directory, a Backup Directory Selection Information dialog box appears, similar to the top one in Figure 14.4. This box gives you information about the directory, including the total number of files the directory contains, how many of those files are selected for backup, and how many of those selected will be backed up.

If you click on the mouse button while the information cursor is next to a file, a Backup File Selection Information dialog box appears, similar to the bottom box in Figure 14.4. This box lists the name of the respective file and states whether it will be backed up. If a file is selected that won't be backed up, this box will tell you why the file won't be backed up. For example, the file in Figure 14.4 won't be backed up even though it's selected because it's a system file, and system files have been excluded from the backup.

▼ *Figure 14.4. Backup Selection Information Boxes*

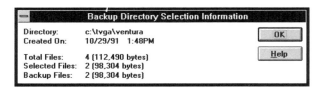

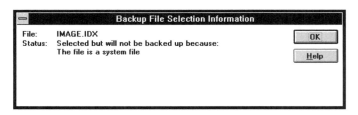

Customizing the Select Backup Files Window

The display of files in the Select Backup Files window can be manipulated in various ways. For instance, you can determine what information about the files is shown, such as file attributes, size, date, and time. Additionally, the files can be sorted by name, extension, size, date, or attributes. You can even filter the file pane to show only certain groups of files. You'll do all of this in the Display Options dialog box shown in Figure 14.5, which can be accessed by clicking on the Display button located at the bottom of the Select Backup Files window.

TIP

You can also view any file in the file display by clicking on that file, then choosing View from the File menu in the Select Backup Files window.

To configure the display of files:

▲ Click on the Display button in the Select Backup Files window. The Display Options dialog box appears, as shown in Figure 14.5.

▲ In the Display box, select the check boxes for the file data you want displayed.

▼ *Figure 14.5. Display Options Dialog Box*

```
┌─────────────────────────────────────────────────────┐
│ ▭                  Display Options                    │
├─────────────────────────────────────────────────────┤
│ ┌─Display──────┐  ┌─Sort Files By──┐    ┌───────┐   │
│ │ ☒ File Size  │  │ ◉ File Name     │    │  OK   │   │
│ │ ☒ File Date  │  │ ○ File Extension│    ├───────┤   │
│ │ ☒ File Time  │  │ ○ File Size     │    │ Cancel│   │
│ │ ☒ File Attributes│ ○ File Date    │    ├───────┤   │
│ │              │  │ ○ File Attributes│   │ Help  │   │
│ │              │  └─────────────────┘    └───────┘   │
│ ┌─Other────────────────────────┐                     │
│ │ □ Group Selected Files       │                     │
│ │ □ Show Directories Above Files│                    │
│ │ File Filter:                 │                     │
│ │ [*.*                       ] │                     │
│ └──────────────────────────────┘                     │
└─────────────────────────────────────────────────────┘
```

▲ In the Sort Files By region, click on the appropriate option (by default, files are sorted by name).

▲ To display only certain groups of files, in the Other region, enter the file specifications in the File Filter box for groups of files you wish to be displayed (you can use wildcard characters, as discussed in Chapter 4).

▲ If you want all files that are selected to appear together at the top of the file pane, select the Group Selected Files check box. (Selecting this check box can be helpful if you have only a few files selected in a large directory.)

▲ If you want the directories listed at the top of the file pane, select the Show Directories Above Files check box.

▲ Click the OK button. The file pane reflects the new settings.

TIP

You can print the file pane listing by clicking on the Print button located at the bottom of the Select Backup Files window.

CHECK YOURSELF

Sort the Select Backup Files file pane by file size.

1. Click on the Display button in the Select Backup Files window.

2. In the Sort Files By box, click on the File Size option.

3. Click the OK button. The file pane instantly reflects the new settings.

Setting the Backup Options

Before performing a backup, you may want to change some of the backup options, which determine exactly how the backup is

▼ *Figure 14.6. The Basic Backup Options Dialog Box*

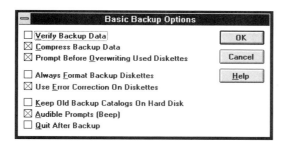

performed. When you click on the Options button in the Norton Backup window, the Basic Backup Options dialog box appears, as shown in Figure 14.6.

Table 14.5 outlines the functions of the eight available options to help you decide whether to turn the options on or off. It also points out certain options you should leave on to optimize the backup process.

▼ *Table 14.5. The Basic Backup Options*

Option	*Function When Turned On*
Verify Backup Data	Data on the hard disk is compared with data on the backup diskette to verify accuracy.
Compress Backup Data	Speeds up the backup process and lessens the amount of diskettes needed for the backup. Recommended you select this option.
Prompt Before Over-writing Used Diskettes	Warns you that the floppy diskette you inserted for backup already contains data and will be overwritten if you continue with the backup. Recommended you select this option to prevent erasing valuable diskettes.
Always Format Backup Diskettes	Forces all diskettes to be formatted. Helpful if you reuse old backup diskettes. Recommended you select this option to save you time.
Use Error Correction On Diskettes	Helps compensate for possible damage to the backup diskette when restoring backup files. Recommended you leave this option selected.
Keep Old Backup Catalogs On Hard Disk	Leaves old catalogs stored on the hard disk. However, since you can quickly retrieve a catalog from the backup set, we recommend you deselect this option to save hard disk space.

▼ *Table 14.5. The Basic Backup Options (continued)*

Option	Function When Turned On
Audible Prompts (Beep)	Causes a beep to sound whenever message is displayed on the screen during the backup progress.
Quit After Backup	Immediately closes Norton Backup after the backup process is completed. Recommended you select this option to save you time and keystrokes.

To set the Basic options:

▲ Make sure the Basic program level is displayed in the Backup window.

▲ Click on the Options button. The Basic Backup Options dialog box appears, as shown in Figure 14.6.

▲ Select the check boxes of the options you wish to activate, and deselect the check boxes of options you wish to turn off.

▲ Click the OK button. The selected options will now be in effect.

CHECK YOURSELF

Set the options so that your backup files are compressed and the program warns you against overwriting diskettes that already contain data.

1. Make sure the Basic program level is selected.

2. Click on the Options button.

3. Select the Compress Backup Data check box.

4. Select the Prompt Before Overwriting Used Diskettes check box.

5. Click the OK button.

Selecting the Backup Type

*Selecting the
Backup Type*

Before running a backup, you must select which type you want performed. For a review of backup types, see *Backup Strategies* earlier in this chapter.

To select the backup type:

1. Click on the arrow to the right of the Backup Type window.
2. Click on the backup type, as follows:

   ▲ **Full:** Back up every file you have previously selected.

   ▲ **Incremental:** Of the files you've selected, back up only those created or changed since the last full or incremental backup.

   ▲ **Differential:** Of the files you've selected, back up only those created or changed since the last full backup.

   ▲ **Full Copy:** Back up all the files you've selected, but do not lower the backup flags.

   ▲ **Incremental Copy:** Same as a Differential backup.

Running the Backup

After you've selected the files you want to back up, the backup options, and the backup type, you're ready to have Norton Backup go to work. Before you start a backup, make sure you have enough diskettes on hand to store all of the data, and be ready to label each diskette. Remember to review the information below the Backup To box to discover how many diskettes you'll need (if you will be backing up to a floppy drive). Also, keep in mind that if you're compressing the backups, fewer diskettes than listed will be required.

To perform the backup:

▲ Using the Backup To box, select where you want the backup to be written.

▲ Click on the Start Backup button. The Backup Progress dialog box appears, as shown in Figure 14.7.

▲ If you haven't already inserted the first diskette, insert it now to begin the backup.

The Backup Progress window displays information about the backup and updates it as the backup progresses. Pay attention to the information in the upper-left corner; the drive boxes will tell you when you need to insert the next diskette. If you wait more than 15 seconds, an alert box will appear telling you to insert the next diskette. A beep will sound as well if you have turned on the Audible Beep option in the Basic Backup Options dialog box.

TIP

Do not wait for the drive light to turn off before you insert a new diskette— because it won't. You may feel strange pulling out and inserting diskettes while the drive light is on (and rightly so), but don't be alarmed; this is normal for Norton Backup.

▼ *Figure 14.7. Backup Progress Dialog Box*

Backup Progress		
Now Backing Up	c:\amipro\backups	

Drive A:		Setup	wordproc.set
Drive B:		Catalog	wordproc.cat
Complete	16%	Session	cc20410a.ful

	Estimated	Actual		
Disks	4	1	Backup Time	0:18
Files	259	28	Your Time	0:01
Bytes	4,287,629	702,099	Compression	1.3:1
Time	1:56	0:19	Settings >>	Cancel

After you remove each diskette, make sure you label it with the Catalog and Session names, which are located in the upper-right corner of the Backup Progress window. Also, note the sequence number of the diskette if more than one diskette was used.

CHECK YOURSELF

Perform a backup to drive A.

1. Click on drive A in the Backup To box.

2. Click on the Start Backup button.

3. Insert the first diskette. The backup progress begins.

4. Click on Cancel to end the backup process.

Creating a Setup File

It would be a terrific nuisance if every time you wanted to perform a backup on the same group of files you had to go through all the steps for selecting those files. Fortunately, Norton Backup allows you to save all the details about a particular backup in a *setup file.* A setup file contains all the details about performing a backup: the files to be selected, the type of backup to be performed, where the backup is to be written, and other backup options. Once you've created a setup file, you can use it each time you want to perform a backup on that group of files.

Norton Backup comes with a few preconfigured setup files. These setup files are listed on the Backup window in the Setup Files pull-down list box. However, unless you're very lucky, these preconfigured setup files probably won't be useful to you, and you'll have to create your own.

To create a new setup file, you first set up Norton Backup just as though you were about to perform a backup: select the files to be backed up, the backup options you want, the backup

---

▼ *Figure 14.8. Save Setup File Dialog Box*

```
┌──────────────────────────────────────────────────────┐
│ ▬                    Save Setup File                   │
│ Dir:    c:\ndw                              ┌────────┐ │
│                                             │   OK   │ │
│ File Name:                                  └────────┘ │
│ │JPLETTRS.SET│                              ┌────────┐ │
│                                             │ Cancel │ │
│ Description:                                └────────┘ │
│ │Letters to JP CORP on C:                 │┌────────┐ │
│                                             │  Help  │ │
│                                             └────────┘ │
│ Files:                    Directories:                 │
│ ┌──────────────┐          ┌──────────────┐             │
│ │assist.set    │          │[..]          │             │
│ │dbase.set     │          │[-a-]         │             │
│ │default.set   │          │[-b-]         │             │
│ │full.set      │          │[-c-]         │             │
│ │sprdsht.set   │          │              │             │
│ │wordproc.set  │          │              │             │
│ └──────────────┘          └──────────────┘             │
└──────────────────────────────────────────────────────┘
```

type, and where the files are to be copied to. Then, you create the new set file to save all of your selections.

To create a setup file:

▲ Select the files you want to back up.

▲ Select the type of backup you want performed.

▲ Using the Options button on the Norton Backup window, select the backup options you want.

▲ Select the disk drive (or other medium) to be used for the backup.

▲ Choose File Save Setup As. The Save Setup File dialog box appears, as shown in Figure 14.8.

▲ In the File Name box, type a name for the new setup file. Make sure you use the extension .SET.

▲ In the Description box, type a description for the new setup file.

▲ Click the OK button. The new setup file will now be displayed in the Setup Files box in the Backup window.

CHECK YOURSELF

Create a new setup file called PROJECTS.SET with the description "All Ami Projects on C:" to back up all files in the PROJECTS directory.

1. Configure the Backup window just the way you want it.

2. Choose File Save Setup As.

3. In the File Name box, type **PROJECTS.SET**.

4. In the Description box, type **All Ami Projects on C:**, then click the OK button.

Creating a Setup File

Using an Existing Setup File to Perform a Backup

Once you've created a setup file, you can use it to perform a backup quickly on the files specified in that file. For example, you might create a setup file called DAILY.SET to perform a daily differential backup of all your data files on drive D. To use this setup file, you select it in the Norton Backup window, then run the backup.

If necessary, you can make changes before running the backup. For example, you might want to deselect certain files from the backup, or you might want to perform the backup to a floppy drive that's different from the one named in the setup file.

To perform a backup with a setup file:

▲ Make sure the Norton Backup window is displayed.

▲ In the Setup Files list box, click on the setup file you want to use.

▲ Click on the appropriate backup medium in the Backup To box, if it is not already showing.

▲ If necessary, change any of the backup options specified by the setup file (these all appear in the various backup window boxes after you select the setup file).

▲ If necessary, you can modify the selection of files to be backed up by clicking on the Select Files button and selecting or deselecting the files you want.

▲ Make sure you have your diskettes ready, then click on the Start Backup button.

▲ Label each diskette with the catalog name, session name, and sequence number.

QUICK SUMMARY

Command	To Do This
Tools Norton Backup, or the Backup tool icon	Start Norton Backup.
Backup window: Select Files button	Select certain files or directories to back up.
Backup window: Options button	Modify the way a backup is performed.
Backup window: Start Backup button	Begin the backup process.
Backup window: File Save Setup As	Create a new setup file.

PRACTICE WHAT YOU'VE LEARNED

Perform a backup of the SPRDSHT.SET setup file to floppy drive B.

1. Make sure the Norton Backup window is displayed.

2. Click on SPRDSHT.SET in the Setup Files box.

3. Click on drive B in the Backup To box, if it is not already showing.

4. If necessary, change any of the backup options specified by the setup file (these all appear in the various backup window boxes after you select the setup file).

5. If necessary, you can modify the selection of files to be backed up: click on the Select Files button and select or deselect the files you want.

6. With diskettes ready, click on the Start Backup button.

7. Label each diskette with the catalog name, session name, and sequence number.

Verifying Your Backups

What a horrible feeling you'd experience if you found out—after having deleted the originals from your hard drive a long time ago—that some of your backup files were not recorded properly, and that you're now unable to restore certain important files. Although this type of crisis could happen, Norton Backup provides a way to help prevent it from ever occurring.

The Compare feature verifies that a backup set contains exact replicas of the original files, which ensures that the backups can be restored at any time in the future and lets you shelve your diskettes with calm assurance. The Compare feature also lets you determine which files on a hard disk have changed since a given backup set was created—information that can be useful before restoring files. In this chapter, the Compare feature is covered in detail, including information on:

- ▲ **The Compare window**
- ▲ **Setting Compare options**
- ▲ **Selecting the files to be compared**
- ▲ **Canceling and pausing a Compare in progress**

The Compare Window

Just as you can work at three different program levels in the Backup window, you can run a Compare from a Preset, Basic, or Advanced Compare window. However, in this book we'll cover using the Compare feature only at the Basic level, which should serve you well enough in nearly all situations.

Before going on, make sure that the Norton Backup window is displayed, and that the Basic level is selected.

To open the Compare window at the Basic level:

▲ Start up Norton Backup by clicking on the Backup icon on the Norton Desktop.

▲ Click on the Configure button, and make sure that the Program Level option is set to Basic. If it isn't, click on the scroll button for the Program Level box, then click on Basic.

▲ Click on the Compare button to display the Compare window, as shown in Figure 15.1.

▼ *Figure 15.1. Compare Window*

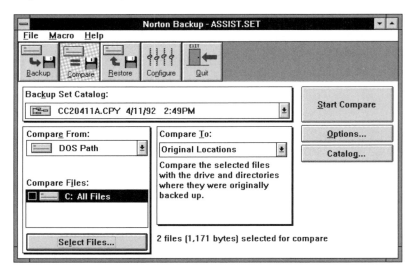

You use the Compare window to select files and set various options to compare against criteria that you specify. Table 15.1 outlines the various components of the Compare window and explains their functions.

Notice that underneath the Compare To box, a description of the current selection is given. You can choose from Alternate Drives, Directories, or a Single Directory to compare the backup set with. When you choose any of these three options, the information below the Compare To box changes to tell you information about that option. For example, if you choose Single Directory, the box asks you to type the name of the directory to be compared. For more on the Compare To box, read *Compared To What?*, later in this chapter.

At the bottom of the Compare window, you are also shown how many files are selected to be compared and their total number of bytes.

The Compare Window

▼ *Table 15.1. Compare Window Components*

Component	*This Lets You*
Backup Set Catalog box	Choose the backup set you want to compare. (The catalog name is used to identify the backup set.)
Compare From box	Specify which disk drive will be used to read the backup set.
Compare Files box	Select all files on the drive(s) that were backed up.
Select Files button	Choose the directories and files you want compared in the event that you don't want to compare all of the files in the backup set.
Compare To box	Designate where files to be compared with the backup files are located (usually in the original location).
Start Compare button	Start the Compare process.
Options button	Determine whether beeps will sound during the Compare and whether to quit Norton Backup after the Compare.

CHECK YOURSELF

Open the Compare window and set it to the Basic level.

1. Open the Backup window, then click on the Configure icon located at the top of the Backup window.

2. Click on the scroll button for the Program Level box, then click on Basic.

3. Click on the Compare button to display the Compare window.

Setting the Options

You can customize two options for the Basic program level when comparing from a floppy diskette. You can determine whether beeps sound during the compare, and whether to quit Norton Backup automatically after the Compare is completed.

To set Compare options:

▲ Make sure you are at the Basic Compare level in the Compare window.

▲ Click on the Options button. The Basic Compare Options dialog box appears, as shown in Figure 15.2.

▲ Select the Audible Prompts (Beep) check box if you want to have beeps accompany Compare messages.

▼ *Figure 15.2. The Basic Compare Options Dialog Box*

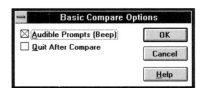

▲ Select the Quit After Compare check box if you want to exit Norton Backup immediately after the Compare.

▲ Click the OK button. Selected options will now be in effect.

CHECK YOURSELF

Make Norton Backup automatically close after you run a Compare.

1. Make sure you are at the Basic Compare level in the Compare window.

2. Click on the Options button.

3. Select the Quit After Compare check box.

4. Click the OK button.

The Backup Catalog

Every time you perform a backup, Norton Backup creates a *catalog* for that backup, which is a file containing information about the files that were backed up. If more than one diskette is used for a backup set, the catalog file is stored on the last diskette of the backup set. The backup catalog is essential to restoring backed-up files; you must specify the catalog name before Norton Backup can retrieve the files from the backup set. For this reason, it is essential that you write the name of the catalog directly on each diskette used in a backup set. A catalog contains the following information on the backed-up files:

▲ Directory structure of the backed-up hard drive

▲ Name, size, and attributes of each directory and file

▲ Total amount of files

▲ Total size of the backup

▲ Setup file name

▲ Date the backup was performed

In addition to regular catalogs, *master catalogs* keep track of all backup catalogs performed during a backup cycle. Whenever a full, incremental, or differential backup is performed for the first time on a setup file, a master catalog is created and will be active until you perform the next full backup.

The master catalog includes the backup catalogs for the full backup and the related incremental backups, or the full backup and the most recent differential backup. For instance, when you use a weekly backup cycle, with the full backup being created on Monday and incremental backups every other weekday, a master catalog is created on Monday when the full backup is done. This master catalog will keep track of all the incremental backup catalogs that will be created the rest of the week. When the next full backup is created (on the next Monday), a new master catalog will be created.

You might wonder how a catalog name will possibly help you identify what files are included in the backup set. After all, CC10521B.INC or CD21130.FUL might not mean much to you at first glance. However, each character in a catalog name refers to a particular aspect of the backup set. Therefore, it will help you to know how the catalog name is created, especially since part of the name includes the date the backup was performed. If you don't remember the catalog name of a backup set you wish to restore, but you do remember that the backup set was created on September 23, 1992, there's a good chance you'll be able to locate the correct backup set by its catalog name.

Here is what each character in a catalog name refers to. We'll use the catalog CD21130A.FUL as an example.

Character	Meaning
C	The first drive backed up in the backup set.
D	The last drive backed up in the backup set.
2	The last digit of the year in which the backup set was created.
11	The month in which the backup set was created.
30	The day on which the backup set was created.

Character	Meaning
A	The sequence (order) of the backup. (This only applies if there are two backups of the same type created on the same day on the same drives.)
.FUL	Indicates a full backup was performed. The extension .INC refers to an incremental backup, .DIF to a differential backup, and .CPY is either a full or an incremental copy.

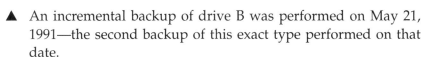

The Backup Catalog

When translated, catalog CD21130A.FUL means that a full backup of drives C and D was performed on November 30, 1992—the first backup of this exact type performed on this date.

CHECK YOURSELF

What does the catalog CC10521B.INC tell you about the backup set it represents?

▲ An incremental backup of drive B was performed on May 21, 1991—the second backup of this exact type performed on that date.

Selecting the Files to Be Compared

If you want to compare all of the files in a backup set, usually you'll choose the appropriate catalog name in the Backup Set Catalog box and then begin the Compare. The catalog for the most recent backup you performed will be displayed in the Backup Set Catalog box when you first open the Compare window. The catalogs are configured in the Backup Set Catalog box in such a way that all backup sets in a particular backup cycle branch out from the master catalog.

There may be times, however, when the catalog you're looking for is not displayed in the Backup Set Catalog box. In this case, you can use the Catalog menu to load the catalog.

To choose a backup set to be compared:

▲ In the Compare window, click on the Backup Set Catalog scroll button to display a pulldown list of catalog names.

▲ Click on the catalog name of your choice. The catalog will now appear in the Backup Set Catalog box.

TIP

If many catalogs are stored on your hard disk, you may have difficulty selecting the correct one to use for a compare. If so, you can instead retrieve the catalog directly from the backup set itself by following the steps below. If the catalog you want to compare is not listed in the Backup Set Catalog box, you can retrieve it from the set of backup disks (or other media) you want to compare.

To retrieve a catalog from a backup set:

▲ Choose Catalog Retrieve. The Retrieve Catalog dialog box appears, as shown in Figure 15.3.

▲ In the From box, select the disk drive containing the backup set.

▲ Click the OK button.

▲ As indicated next on the screen, make sure that the *last* disk of the backup set is in the disk drive, then click the OK button.

▼ *Figure 15.3. Retrieve Catalog Dialog Box*

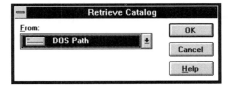

▲ If you see a message asking you if it's okay to overwrite a catalog, click the OK button. (This message means that Norton Backup knows where the catalog is on the hard disk, and that it will overwrite that file with the catalog on the floppy disk.)

▲ The catalog on the floppy will now be copied to the hard disk. When the copy is finished, the Select Backup Set dialog box appears, and the name of the catalog just retrieved is highlighted.

▲ Click the OK button.

Selecting the Files to Be Compared

TIP

If you want to compare the backup sets of an entire backup cycle, select the master catalog in the Backup Set Catalog box. Master catalogs always have the extension .CAT.

Selecting Drives to Be Compared

After you have selected the correct backup catalog, all the drives that were backed up and therefore listed in the catalog will be displayed in the Compare Files box. To compare all of the files on a drive, select that drive. If you want to compare only some of the files on a drive, follow the procedures in the next section.

To select all files on a drive to be compared:

▲ Double-click on the appropriate drive name in the Compare Files box (or click on the drive name with the right mouse button). A selection icon appears next to the drive, indicating that all files have been selected for comparing.

To select multiple drives, repeat the above step. To deselect a drive, double-click on the drive again.

Selecting Only Certain Files to Be Compared

Perhaps you don't want to compare *all* of the files in a backup set. In such a situation, you'll use the Select Files button, then choose the files to be compared in the Select Compare Files window, shown in Figure 15.4. To select files to be compared, follow the same procedures given in Chapter 14 for selecting backup files.

TIP

Make sure the correct catalog is displayed in the Backup Set Catalog box before you click on the Select Files button.

To use the Select Compare Files window:

▲ In the Compare window, display the appropriate catalog in the Backup Set Catalog box.

▲ Click on the Select Files button. The Select Compare Files window appears, as shown in Figure 15.4.

▼ *Figure 15.4. Select Compare Files Window*

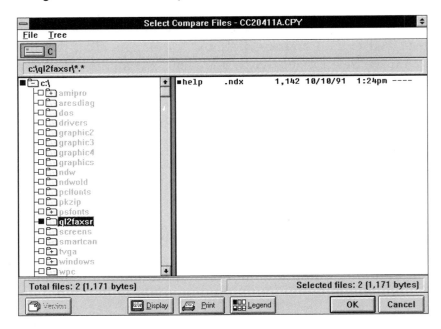

▲ Select the files you want to be compared, or deselect those you don't want to be compared.

▲ Click the OK button.

TIP

When comparing incremental backups while a master catalog is loaded, there may be more than one version of a file. If a file has more than one version, the Version button will become active when you position the cursor over that file name, letting you know that multiple versions exist. Click on the Version button while it's active to get a list of the different file versions, then click on the version you want.

CHECK YOURSELF

Select all files specified in a backup set on drives C and D to be compared.

1. Double-click on the C: drive in the Compare Files box.

2. Double-click on the D: drive in the Compare Files box.

Compared to What?

Usually, you'll compare backed-up files to the original files located on the same drive and in the same directory as when they were backed up. However, perhaps you've changed your directory structure, or perhaps you're comparing with files on a different computer. In this case, selecting Original Locations in the Compare To box won't work. Instead, you can choose from the following three options:

▲ *Alternate Drives:* All files to be compared are checked against files on a drive or drives other than the one the original files were backed up from. During the Compare, a dialog box appears, asking you to enter the name of the new drive and, if applicable, a path name.

▲ *Alternate Directories:* Each directory to be compared is checked against a directory other than the one from which the original files were backed up. During the Compare, a dialog box appears asking you to enter the name of the new directory.

▲ *Single Directory:* All files to be compared, regardless of their original drives and directory, are checked against a single directory. A dialog box appears during the Compare asking you to enter the name of the new directory.

Running the Compare

Though you can run a Compare at any of the three program levels, in this book we'll focus only on the Basic level.

To perform a Compare:

▲ Have the backup set material (diskettes, tapes, and so on) on hand.

▲ Open the Backup window if it is not already open, then click on the Compare icon located at the top of the Backup window. Make sure the Compare window is set at the Basic level. (To be sure, click on the Configure icon, then make sure that the program level is set to Basic.)

▲ Click on the Backup Set Catalog scroll button to display a pull-down list of available catalogs, then click on the one you wish to compare. If the catalog is not listed in the box, load it from the backup set itself, following the procedures discussed earlier under *Selecting the Files to Be Compared.*

▲ Click on the Compare From scroll button, then click on the medium containing the backup set you wish to compare (such as floppy drive B).

▲ In the Compare Files box, double-click on the drive(s) you want to compare. This selects all files (specified in the backup set) on that drive.

▲ If you want to select only some of the files in the backup set to be compared, first make sure that the drive is *not* selected (double-clicking on it if necessary), click on the Select Files button, select the files you want to compare, then click the OK button.

▲ If you are not comparing the backup set to files in their original location, click on the Compare To scroll button, then click on the location containing the files you wish to compare the backup set with.

▲ Click on the Start Compare button. The Compare process begins and the Compare Progress window appears, as shown in Figure 15.5.

Running the Compare

TIP

If the Start Compare button is dimmed, then no files have been selected. You must double-click on the drive to select all the backup files to be compared or use the Select Compare Files window to select some of the backup set files.

The Compare Progress window looks like and works similarly to the Backup Progress window. Pay attention to the information in the top left pane, which will tell you when to insert another diskette (if necessary). This area also continually dis-

▼ *Figure 15.5. Compare Progress Window*

Compare Progress			
Now Comparing	c:\ql2faxsr		
Drive A:	Insert diskette #1	**Setup**	assist.set
Drive B:		**Catalog**	dbase.cat
Complete	0%	**Session**	cc20411a.ful

	Estimated	Actual		
Disks		0	**Compare Time**	0:00
Files	2	0	**Your Time**	0:27
Bytes	1,171	0	**Corrections**	0
Time		0:27		Cancel

plays the percentage of the Compare that is completed until the job is finished.

CHECK YOURSELF

Compare all files in a backup set called CC20411A.FUL, located on floppy drive A, with the original files, which are located in the original location on the C drive.

1. Insert the first floppy diskette in drive A.

2. Make sure that you're at the Basic program level. Click on catalog CC20411A.FUL in the Backup Set Catalog box.

3. Click on floppy drive A in the Compare From box.

4. In the Compare Files box, double-click on the drive C.

5. Click on the Start Compare button.

Comparing Immediately After Backup

The best time to run a Compare is immediately after you have performed a backup. Then you can put away your backup media, assured that the backup was successful.

To perform a Compare immediately after backup:

▲ Click on the Compare icon. The Compare window appears.

▲ Double-click on each drive in the Compare Files box.

▲ Click on the Start Compare button.

After Compare Has Finished

At the end of the Compare process a dialog box appears, telling you how many files were selected for the Compare and how many files were actually compared. You can prevent this dialog box from appearing and automatically exit Norton Backup each time a Compare has been completed by choosing the Quit After Compare option in the Compare Options dialog box.

CHECK YOURSELF

Perform a Compare immediately after a backup.

1. Click on the Compare icon. The Compare window appears.

2. Double-click on each drive in the Compare Files box.

3. Click on the Start Compare button.

Canceling or Pausing a Compare in Progress

You can pause a Compare while it's running or cancel it altogether before it's finished. Use the Cancel button in the Compare Progress window (see Figure 15.5) to both pause and terminate a Compare.

To pause a Compare in progress:

▲ Click on the Cancel button in the Compare Progress window. An alert box appears asking you if you're sure you want to cancel the Compare.

▲ Click on No to reactivate the Compare.

To cancel a Compare in progress:

▲ Click on the Cancel button in the Compare Progress window. An alert box appears asking you whether you're sure you want to cancel the Compare.

▲ Click on Yes. The process is canceled, the Compare Progress window closes, and you're returned to the Compare window.

QUICK SUMMARY

Command	To Do This
Compare icon	Open the Compare window.
Catalog Load	Load a catalog that is not listed in the Backup Set Catalog box.
Options button	Select Compare options.
Start Compare button	Start the Compare process.
Select Files button	Select only certain files in a backup set to be compared.
Compare Progress: Cancel button	Pause or cancel a Compare in progress.
Catalog Retrieve	Load a catalog that's currently located on a floppy diskette onto the hard drive.

PRACTICE WHAT YOU'VE LEARNED

Run a Compare of the most recent backup set from floppy drive B. Then pause the Compare process temporarily before it's finished.

1. Insert the first floppy diskette in drive B.

2. Open the Backup window if it is not already open, then click on the Compare icon located at the top of the Backup window. Make sure the Compare window is set at the Basic level.

3. Click on drive B in the Compare From box.

4. In the Compare Files box, double-click on drive C.

5. Click on the Start Compare button. The Compare Progress window appears.

6. Click on the Cancel button in the Compare Progress window.

7. Click on No in the alert box that appears as soon as you are ready to reactivate the Compare.

Restoring Files from Your Backups

What would be the purpose of backing up files if you couldn't restore them later? Norton's Restore feature lets you recover your backups quickly. You can choose to recover all the files in a backup set or only some of them. And if you ever turn on your computer only to see a frightening DOS message that reads "General Failure error" or "Disk boot failure," you can use Norton Restore to restore the disk data from your backup sets after you have your computer repaired—if Norton Utilities or Norton Disk Doctor can't recover all of the data for you. In this chapter, you will learn about Norton Restore and the Restore window, including how to:

▲ **Set Restore options**

▲ **Select the files to be restored**

▲ **Run the Restore at the Basic program level**

▲ **Recover from a hard disk failure**

The Restore Window

Just as you can work at three different program levels in the Backup window, you can run a Restore from a Preset, Basic, or Advanced Restore window. However, in this book we'll cover using the Restore feature only at the Basic level, which should serve you well enough for most situations.

Before going on, make sure that the Norton Backup window is displayed, and that the Basic level is selected.

To open the Restore window at the Basic level:

▲ Start up Norton Backup by clicking on the Backup icon on the Norton Desktop.

▲ Click on the Configure button, then make sure that the Program Level option is set to Basic. If it isn't, click on the scroll button for the Program Level list box, then click on Basic.

▲ Click on the Restore button to display the Restore window, as shown in Figure 16.1.

▼ *Figure 16.1. Basic Restore Window*

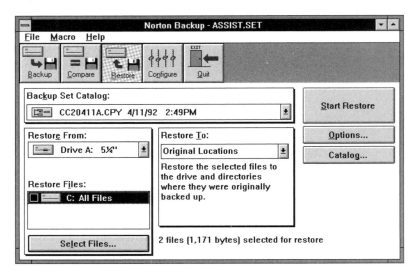

The Restore window lets you select files to be recovered, set various options, and start the Restore process. Table 16.1 outlines the various components of the Restore window and explains their functions.

Notice that underneath the Restore To box, a description of the box's current selection is given. Rather than restore the backed up files to their original location, you can place them in a different drive or directory if you wish. When you place them in a different drive or directory, the data below the Restore To box changes to tell you what information you'll need to provide, such as a drive or directory name, before the Restore can be performed. For example, if you choose Single Directory, you are asked to type the name of the directory where the restored files should be placed. For more on choosing the location to restore your files to, see *Where to Restore?*, later in this chapter.

At the bottom of the Restore window, you are also shown how many files are selected to be restored and their total number of bytes.

The Restore Window

▼ **Table 16.1. Restore Window Components**

Component	This Lets You
Backup Set Catalog box	Choose the backup set you want to restore. (The catalog name is used to identify the backup set.)
Restore From box	Specify where the backup set to be restored is located.
Restore Files box	Select all files on the drive(s) that were backed up to be restored.
Select Files button	Choose the directories and files you want restored in the event that you don't want to restore all of the files in the backup set.
Restore To box	Designate where files to be restored will be placed (usually back in the original location).
Start Restore button	Start the Restore process.
Options button	Set various Restore options.

CHECK YOURSELF

Open the Restore window and set it to the Basic level.

1. Open the Backup window, then click on the Configure icon located at the top of the Backup window.

2. Click on the scroll button for the Program Level box, then click on Basic.

3. Click on the Restore button to display the Restore window.

Setting the Options

You can customize several options when you restore files from a floppy diskette. For example, you can determine whether beeps sound during the Restore process, and whether to quit Norton Backup automatically after the Restore is completed. Some of the options are similar to the Backup and Compare options discussed in Chapters 14 and 15, respectively, except that they relate to the Restore process. To get information on each of the Restore options, click on the Help button in the Basic Disk Restore Options dialog box. On-line help will tell you what effects will result when you turn on any of the Restore options.

To set Restore options:

▲ Open the Restore window and set it to the Basic level, as described earlier.

▲ Click on the Options button in the Restore window.

▲ The Basic Restore Options dialog box appears, as shown in Figure 16.2.

▲ Select the check boxes of the options you want to activate; deselect the check boxes of the options you don't want activated.

▲ Click the OK button. The selected options will now be in effect.

▼ *Figure 16.2. Basic Restore Options Dialog Box*

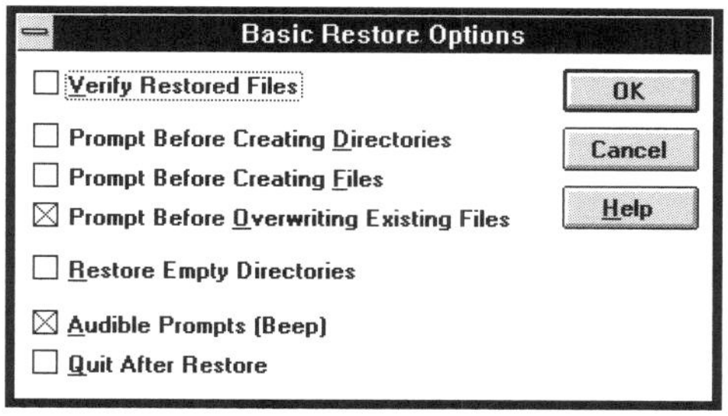

Setting the Options

CHECK YOURSELF

Make Norton Backup automatically close after you run a Restore.

1. Make sure you are at the Basic level in the Restore window.

2. Click on the Options button.

3. Select the Quit After Restore check box.

4. Click the OK button.

Selecting the Files to Be Restored

Before you can restore files from a backup set, you'll need to know its catalog name. If you want to restore all of the files in a backup set, you'll usually choose the appropriate catalog name in the Backup Set Catalog box and then begin the Restore. The catalog name for the most recent backup you performed will be displayed in the Backup Set Catalog box when you first open the Restore window. The catalog names are configured in the Backup Set Catalog box so that all backup sets in a particular backup cycle branch from the master catalog. For detailed information on backup catalogs, read *The Backup Catalog* in Chapter 15.

TIP

If you want to restore the backup sets of an entire backup cycle, select the master catalog in the Backup Set Catalog box. Master catalogs always have the extension .CAT.

To choose a backup set to be restored:

▲ In the Restore window, click on the Backup Set Catalog scroll button to display a pulldown list of catalog names.

▲ Click on the desired catalog name. The catalog will now appear in the Backup Set Catalog box.

There may come a time when the catalog you're looking for is not displayed in the Backup Set Catalog box. In this case, you can retrieve it from the backup set itself, using the Catalog menu.

To retrieve a catalog from a backup diskette:

▲ Choose Catalog Retrieve. The Retrieve Catalog dialog box appears (see Figure 16.5).

▲ In the From box, click on the medium that contains the backup set catalog (for instance, drive A).

▲ Click the OK button.

▲ As indicated next on the screen, make sure that the *last* disk of the backup set is in the disk drive, then click the OK button twice.

▲ You are returned to the Restore window, where the retrieved catalog now shows in the Backup Set Catalog box.

▲ If you see a message asking you if it's okay to overwrite a catalog, click the OK button. (This means that Norton Backup knows where the catalog is on the hard disk, and that it will overwrite that file with the catalog on the floppy disk.)

▲ The catalog on the floppy disk is copied to the hard disk. You can now load it into the Restore window.

To load a catalog that is not listed in the Backup Set Catalog box:

Selecting the Files to Be Restored

▲ Choose Load from the Catalog menu in the Restore window. The Load Catalog dialog box appears.

▲ Double-click on the drive or directory in the Directories box if you are not currently in the correct path.

▲ Click on the name of the catalog you want in the Files box.

▲ Click the OK button. The catalog will now appear in the Backup Set Catalog box.

Selecting Drives to Be Restored

After you select a catalog, all the drives that were backed up and therefore listed in the backup catalog will be displayed in the Restore Files box. To restore all of the files on a drive, select that drive. If you want to restore only some of the files on a drive, follow the procedures in the next section.

To select all files on a drive to be restored:

▲ Double-click on the appropriate drive name in the Restore Files box, or click on the drive name with the right mouse button. A selection icon appears next to the drive, indicating that all the files in the drive have been selected for restoring.

To select multiple drives, repeat the above step. To deselect a drive, double-click on the drive again.

Selecting Only Certain Files to Be Restored

There may be times when you don't want to restore all of the files in a backup set. In such a situation, click on the Select Files button, then specify which files you want to restore. Follow the same procedures you used in Chapter 14 to select files for a backup. Make sure that the correct catalog is displayed in the Backup Set Catalog box before you click on the Select Files button.

To use the Select Restore Files window:

▲ In the Restore window, display the appropriate catalog in the Backup Set Catalog box.

▲ Click on the Select Files button. The Select Restore Files window appears, as shown in Figure 16.3.

▲ Select files following the same procedures discussed in Chapter 14 to select files in the Select Backup Files window.

▲ Click the OK button.

TIP

When restoring incremental backups while a master catalog is loaded, more than one version of a file may exist. If the Version button becomes active when you position the cursor over a file name, you'll know that the file has more than one version. Click on the Version button while it's active to get a list of the different file versions, then click on the version you want to restore.

▼ *Figure 16.3. Select Restore Files Window*

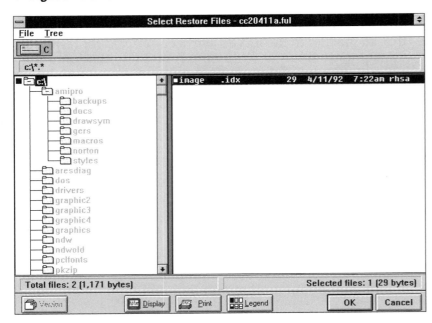

CHECK YOURSELF

Select all files specified in a backup set on drives C and D to be restored.

1. Double-click on the C: drive in the Restore Files box.

2. Double-click on the D: drive in the Restore Files box.

Where to Restore?

You'll probably restore backed-up files to the original drive and directory they were backed up from. However, if you've changed your directory structure or are restoring files to a different computer, you may need to specify a different drive and/or directory from the original, using the Restore To box. Here is a description of each of the alternative Restore To options:

▲ *Alternate Drives:* All files to be restored are placed on a drive other than the one from which the original files were backed up. A dialog box appears during the Restore asking you to enter the name of the new drive and, if applicable, a path name.

▲ *Alternate Directories:* Each directory to be restored is placed in a directory other than the one from which the original files were backed up. A dialog box appears during the compare, asking you to enter the name of the new directories.

▲ *Single Directory:* All files to be restored, regardless of their original drives and directory, are restored to a single directory. A dialog box appears during the compare asking you to enter the name of that new directory.

CHECK YOURSELF

Tell Restore to restore files from a backup set to a directory called RESTORED.

1. Click on Single Directory in the Restore To box.

2. In the box that appears, type **RESTORED**.

Performing the Restore

You can perform a Restore at any of the three program levels, though in this book we'll concentrate only on the Basic level. The only difference between the Basic and Advanced program level Restores is that you have more sophisticated options at the Advanced level than at the Basic level. When it comes to actually running a Restore, however, you will use the same procedures at both levels.

To perform a Restore:

▲ Have the backup set material (diskettes, tapes, and so on) on hand.

▲ Open the Backup window if it is not already open, then click on the Restore icon located at the top of the Backup window. Make sure the Restore window is set at the Basic level.

▲ Click on the Backup Set Catalog scroll button to display a pulldown list of available catalogs, then click on the backup set you wish to restore. If the catalog is not listed in the box, load the catalog from the backup set itself, following the directions given in *Selecting the Files to Be Compared.*

▲ Click on the Restore From scroll button, then click on the source that contains the backup set you wish to restore.

▲ To select all files (specified in the backup set) on a drive, in the Restore Files box, double-click on the drive(s) you want to restore from.

▲ If you want to select only some of the files in the backup set to be restored, click on the Select Files button, select the files in the Select Restore Files window, then click the OK button.

▲ If you are not restoring the backup set files to their original location, click on the Restore To scroll button to display a pulldown list of available items and then click on the location you wish to restore the files to.

▲ Click on the Start Restore button. The Restore process begins immediately and the Restore Progress window appears, as shown in Figure 16.4.

▼ *Figure 16.4. Restore Progress Window*

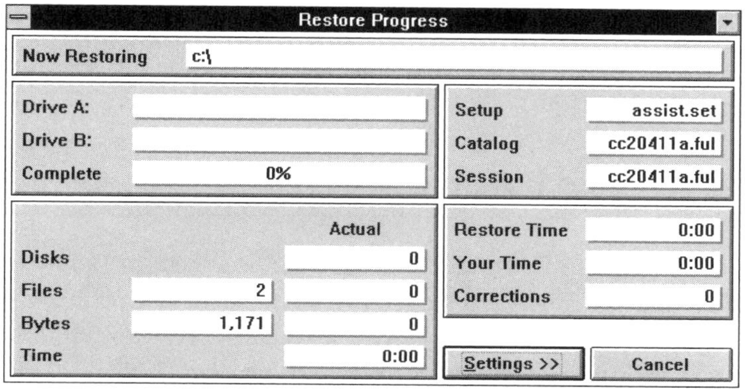

Restore Progress			
Now Restoring	c:\		
Drive A:		Setup	assist.set
Drive B:		Catalog	cc20411a.ful
Complete	0%	Session	cc20411a.ful
	Actual	Restore Time	0:00
Disks	0	Your Time	0:00
Files	2	0	Corrections	0
Bytes	1,171	0		
Time	0:00	Settings >>	Cancel

TIP

If the Start Restore button is dimmed, this means that no files have been selected. You must double-click on the drive to select all backup files to be restored or use the Select Restore Files window to select some of the backup set files to be restored.

The Restore Progress window looks and works similarly to the Backup Progress window. Pay attention to the information in the top left pane, which will tell you when to insert another diskette (if necessary). This area also continually displays the percentage of the Restore that is completed until the job is finished.

CHECK YOURSELF

At the Basic level, restore all files in a backup set called DD20413A.FUL, located on floppy drive A, to their original location on the D drive.

1. Insert the first backup set floppy diskette in drive A.

2. If you're not already at the Basic program level, click on the Configure icon and then on the appropriate level in the Program Level box. Then click on the Restore icon to return to the Restore window.

3. Click on catalog DD20413A.FUL in the Backup Set Catalog box.

4. Click on floppy drive A in the Restore From box.

5. In the Restore Files box, double-click on drive D.

6. Click on the Start Restore button.

After Restore Has Finished

At the end of the Restore process, a dialog box appears telling you how many files were selected for the Restore and how many files were actually restored. You can prevent this dialog box from appearing and automatically exit Norton Backup each time a Restore has been completed by choosing the Quit After Restore option in the Basic Disk Restore Options dialog box.

Canceling or Pausing a Restore in Progress

You can pause a Restore while it's running or cancel it altogether before it has finished. Use the Cancel button in the Restore Progress window (see Figure 16.4) to both pause and terminate a Restore.

To pause a Restore in progress:

▲ Click on the Cancel button in the Restore Progress window. An alert box appears asking you whether you're sure you want to cancel the Restore.

▲ Click on No to resume the Restore process.

To cancel a Restore in progress:

▲ Click on the Cancel button in the Restore Progress window. An alert box appears asking you whether you're sure you want to cancel the Restore.

▲ Click on Yes. The process will be canceled immediately, the Restore Progress window will close, and you'll be returned to the Restore window.

Recovering from a Hard Disk Failure

TIP

If various symptoms cause you to suspect that your hard disk may be failing, try using Norton Disk Doctor to diagnose and repair disk problems before you lose any data.

If you have a disk failure, you'll need to get it repaired or replaced before you can do *anything.* Then:

▲ If necessary, repartition your hard disk and then reformat it (if in doubt, consult expert advice for these important steps).

▲ Reinstall DOS, Microsoft Windows, and Norton Desktop for Windows in that order (see Appendix A, *Installing Norton Desktop for Windows* for help on installation procedures).

▲ Restore your programs, either from the original disks by reinstalling each program, or from backup sets created by Norton Backup. (The following section describes the details about restoring your *data.* You can use similar steps to re-store programs that have been backed up.)

▲ Restore your data files from the most recent backup set created with Norton Backup. The following section describes the details of this process.

Restoring your Data Files

For you to restore your data files, Norton Backup needs to know the catalog names of each backup set in the most recent backup cycle. For you to restore the most current version of each file, Norton Backup will use the catalog for the latest full backup as well as the catalogs from all incremental backups or the most recent differential backup. Norton Backup always stores the catalog file on the last diskette of a backup set. Thus, if you have used more than one floppy diskette for a backup *set* (not cycle), the last diskette used for that backup set will contain the catalog file. Insert this diskette in the appropriate drive when using the Catalog Retrieve menu command.

To retrieve backup catalogs from the last full and differential or last full and all incremental backup sets:

1. Have the backup set material for the last full backup (diskettes, tapes, and so on) on hand.

2. Open the Backup window if necessary, then click on the Restore icon located at the top of the Backup window. Make sure the Restore window is set at the Basic level.

3. Choose Catalog Retrieve. The Retrieve Catalog dialog box appears, as shown in Figure 16.5.

4. In the From box, click on the medium that contains the backup set catalog (for instance, drive A).

5. Click the OK button.

6. If you're retrieving from a diskette, place the *last* diskette of the full backup set in the appropriate drive, then click the OK button twice.

7. You are returned to the Restore window, where the retrieved catalog now shows in the Backup Set Catalog box.

8. Repeat Steps 3 through 7 for each incremental backup set or the latest differential backup.

▼ *Figure 16.5. Retrieve Catalog Dialog Box*

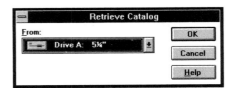

Restoring the Files

Now that the catalogs have been retrieved, you are ready to restore the data. You must follow a certain order when restoring files to a hard disk: Always restore the latest full backup set first, followed by either the incremental backup sets in the order they were created, or the most recent differential backup.

TIP

The Verify Restored Files option in the Basic Disk Restore Options dialog box should be turned on before restoring files.

To restore backup files to the hard disk:

▲ Make sure the catalog for the full backup set is showing in the Backup Set Catalog box of the Restore window. The catalog file has the extension .FUL.

▲ Click on the Restore From scroll button to display a pulldown list of available items, then click on the source that contains the backup set you wish to restore (for instance, drive B).

▲ In the Restore Files box, double-click on the drive(s) you want to restore from. This selects all files (specified in the backup set) on that drive.

▲ Select Original Locations in the Restore To box.

▲ Click on the Start Restore button. The Restore process begins immediately and the Restore Progress window appears.

▲ Repeat Steps 1 through 5 for each incremental (.INC) backup set (make sure to restore in order) or the latest differential (.DIF) backup set.

QUICK SUMMARY

Command	To Do This
Restore icon	Open the Restore window.
Catalog Load	Load a catalog that is not listed in the Backup Set Catalog box.

Command	To Do This
Options button	Select options for the Basic and Advanced Restore levels.
Start Restore button	Start the Restore process.
Select Files button	Select only certain files in a backup set to be restored.
Restore Progress: Cancel button	Pause or cancel a Restore in progress.
Catalog Retrieve	Retrieve backup catalogs, loading them into the Backup Set Catalog box in the Restore window (a necessary step when recovering from hard disk failure).

PRACTICE WHAT YOU'VE LEARNED

Your hard disk has failed. Restore it to the state it was in at the time of the last backup (which was a differential backup), using floppy drive B.

1. Have the backup set material for the last full backup (diskettes, tapes, and so on) on hand.

2. Open the Restore window and set it to the Advanced level.

3. Choose Catalog Retrieve. The Retrieve Catalog dialog box appears.

4. In the From box, click on drive B, then click the OK button.

5. Place the *last* diskette of the full backup set in drive B, then click the OK button twice.

6. The retrieved catalog appears in the Backup Set Catalog box.

7. Repeat Steps 3 through 6 for the latest differential backup.

8. Make sure the catalog for the full backup set (.FUL) is showing in the Backup Set Catalog box in the Restore window.

9. Click on drive B in the Restore From box.

10. In the Restore Files box, double-click on drive B.

11. Select Original Locations in the Restore To box.

12. Click on the Start Restore button.

13. Make sure the catalog for the differential backup set (.DIF) is showing in the Backup Set Catalog box.

14. Repeat steps 9 through 12.

Installing Norton Desktop for Windows

Fortunately, installing Norton Desktop for Windows is usually a simple process. If you plan to install the complete package, the Norton Desktop Install program will basically do all the work for you. On the other hand, you can also install only certain programs in Norton Desktop—for example, if you're running low on disk space or if you already have a virus checker program. Before you install Norton Desktop, you need to make sure that your computer has the capacity to run it properly. This appendix tells you what Norton Desktop's system requirements are and offers some valuable hints about various options you'll have to select during the installation.

System Requirements

To run Norton Desktop on your computer, your system must meet the requirements listed below. If you aren't sure about your hardware configuration, check the owner's manual. Likewise, if you can't remember what version of software your system is running, check the appropriate software manual.

▲ Windows 3.0 or higher

▲ DOS 3.1 or higher

▲ IBM AT, PS/2 or 100-percent compatible, or a 386 or 486 machine

▲ 2 megabytes of RAM (Random Access Memory)

▲ 9 megabytes of available disk space for a complete installation (less if you wish to install only parts of Norton Desktop)

▲ VGA, SVGA, EGA, or XGA video card

▲ Microsoft or 100-percent-compatible mouse (other types of mice *may* work)

The Installation Process

You can install Norton Desktop either from within Windows or from the DOS prompt. If you start from Windows, the installation process will begin more quickly.

To begin the installation process from Windows:

s Insert Program Disk #1 in the appropriate floppy drive.

▲ Choose Run from the Program Manager File menu.

▲ Type **A:INSTALL** or **B:INSTALL**, depending on which floppy drive you're using.

▲ Click the OK button. The install process begins.

To start the installation process from DOS:

▲ Insert Program Disk #1 in the appropriate floppy drive.

▲ At the DOS prompt (C:>), type **A:INSTALL** or **B:INSTALL**, depending on which floppy drive you're using. The install process begins.

The Install program now searches your system to see if a previous copy of Norton Desktop for Windows exists on your system.

The Installation Process

Assigning the Norton Desktop Directory

After the Install program searches for a previous Norton Desktop version, it displays the Install Norton Desktop Files To dialog box. If a previous version of Norton Desktop is found, its directory will be identified next to *Previous Version* in the dialog box. If this is the case, we suggest that you overwrite the files in that directory by having Install copy the new files to the same directory (usually \NDW), which automatically appears in the Install To box.

If no previous versions of Norton Desktop are found, Install places "NDW" in the Install To box, suggesting you use this as the directory name. If you don't want to use the NDW directory, type a different name in the Install To box.

Notice that the bars in the Target Drive Status area in the dialog box show how much disk space is presently occupied and how much will be used after installation. Also notice that a Help button is located in the dialog box. All installation dialog boxes provide Help buttons that you can click on if you are unsure about how to proceed.

If you want to install Norton Desktop in its entirety on your system, click the OK button now. Otherwise, if you want to install only certain parts of the entire package, skip to the section *Using Custom Install* later in this chapter.

Modifying Your CONFIG.SYS and AUTOEXEC.BAT Files

During installation, the program informs you that the line DEVICE=C:\NDW\NAV&.SYS /B needs to be added to your CONFIG.SYS file (unless you already have Norton AntiVirus running on your system). This new line will allow Norton AntiVirus to scan for viruses each time you start your computer. Unless you have a reason for doing otherwise, let the Install program add the new line to your CONFIG.SYS file.

Install also asks you if it's okay to insert a few new lines to your AUTOEXEC.BAT file. Again, unless you have reasons for doing otherwise (such as if you have multiple hard disks on your computer), you should simply let Install update your AUTOEXEC.BAT file for you. However, if you do have multiple hard disks, you'll need to edit the AUTOEXEC.BAT file yourself, as shown below, so that all the disks are automatically protected against accidental file deletions:

▲ Click on the Edit button.

▲ Locate the line that reads C:\NDW\IMAGE.

▲ Modify the line so that it includes the letters for all of your hard drives at the end of the line, such as: **C:\NDW\IMAGE C: D: F:**.

▲ Click the OK button.

Selecting the Default Text Editor

You can choose which text editor that you want to be the Windows default. When you choose File Edit in Norton Desktop, the default text editor program is launched. You can use this editor to modify various files, and you can choose which text editor you'd like to have as the default. Usually, the Windows Notepad is the default text editor. However, Norton's Desktop Editor offers more features than Notepad, including file search, compare, and word wrap. Thus, you may wish to make Norton's Desktop Editor the default Windows text editor.

If you wish to change the default text editor after you've completed the installation, you can do so easily using the Configure Default Editor menu command.

Automatic Backups

You can choose whether to have Norton Backup automatically perform daily backups at 4:00 p.m. We suggest you turn on this option during installation—even if you plan to perform backups at a different time. Accepting this option sets up a Scheduler event that performs automatic backups for you. If you decline this option, you'll have to create a backup schedule from scratch later. It's much easier to accept the option now and then go into the Scheduler later on and edit the Automatic Backup event to reflect a new time. For example, you could change 4:00 p.m. to 10:00 p.m. very simply. Refer to Chapter 9, *Using the Scheduler,* for details.

Assigning the Windows Shell

You can select which shell to use each time Windows starts up. *The Shell* is the desktop area that serves as the foundation for all of the work you do in Windows. More technically, it is the interface between you and Windows.

You are probably used to having the Windows Program Manager as your shell. You can continue to keep the Program Manager as your shell if you wish to, though we don't recommend it; having Norton Desktop as your shell will let you quickly access all of Norton Desktop's valuable features. Though it may be unfamiliar territory to you now, it won't take long for you to get used to the Norton Desktop. Taking a few hours now to familiarize yourself with the Norton Desktop shell will save countless hours wasted trying to use the various Norton Desktop features from the Program Manager later, should you hold on to the Program Manager shell. After all, you're installing Norton Desktop to make life easier for yourself, so take full advantage of the Desktop!

Completing the Installation Process

When you see the dialog box informing your that the installation is complete, make sure you reboot your computer so that Norton Desktop runs from a fresh start. Then refer to Chapter 1, *Using the Basic Features,* to start learning about Norton Desktop for Windows.

Using Custom Install

There may be situations in which you don't want to install all of Norton Desktop's programs (that is, features). For instance, perhaps you don't have quite enough disk space needed to install Norton Desktop in its entirety. Fortunately, you don't have to forgo the installation altogether; rather, you can simply deselect one or more Norton Desktop programs so that they won't be installed on your system. Another example would be if you already have a comparable program to one of Norton Desktop's and don't want to install the Desktop program that serves the same function as the existing one. For instance, you may already have a sophisticated screen saver or virus program, in which case you can choose not to install the corresponding Norton programs.

You can customize the installation by clicking on the Custom Install button in the Install Norton Desktop Files To dialog box (which appears near the beginning of the installation). By default, all applications are selected on this screen to be installed.

To deselect applications from the Install process:

▲ Click on the Custom Install button in the Install Norton Desktop Files To dialog box. The Application Selection dialog box appears.

▲ Deselect each application you do not wish to install on your system. (Keyboard users can press the **Spacebar** to deselect an application.)

▲ Click the OK button. The deselected applications will not be installed.

Index